REMAPPING BRAZILIAN FILM CULTURE IN THE TWENTY-FIRST CENTURY

Remapping Brazilian Film Culture in the Twenty-First Century makes a significant contribution not only to debates about Brazilian national cinema, but more generally about the development of world cinema in the twenty-first century.

This book charts the key features of Brazilian film culture of the first two decades of the twenty-first century, including: the latest cultural debates within Brazil on film funding and distribution practices; the impact of diversity politics on the Brazilian film industry; the reception and circulation of Brazilian films on the international film festival circuit; and the impact on cultural production of the sharp change in political direction at national level experienced post-2016. The principle of "remapping" here is based on a need to move on from potentially limiting concepts such as "the national", which can serve to unduly ghettoise a cinema, film industry and audience. The book argues that Brazilian film culture should be read as being part of a globally articulated film culture whose internal workings are necessarily distinctive and thus deserving of world cinema scholars' attention.

A blend of industry studies, audience reception and cultural studies, *Remapping Brazilian Film Culture in the Twenty-First Century* is a dynamic volume for students and researchers in film studies, particularly Brazilian, Latin American and world cinema.

Stephanie Dennison is Professor of Brazilian Studies and directs the Centre for World Cinemas at the University of Leeds. She has published widely on both world cinema and Brazilian film: she co-authored with Lisa Shaw *Popular Cinema in Brazil* (2004) and *Brazilian National Cinema* (2007).

REMAPPING WORLD CINEMA: REGIONAL TENSIONS AND GLOBAL TRANSFORMATIONS

Series Editors: *Rob Stone, Paul Cooke, Stephanie Dennison and Alex Marlow-Mann*

Remapping World Cinema: Regional Tensions and Global Transformations rewrites the territory of contemporary world cinema, revising outdated assumptions of national cinemas, challenging complacent views of hegemonic film cultures and questioning common ideas of production, distribution and reception. It will remap established territories such as American, European and Asian cinema and explore new territories that exist both within and beyond nation-states such as regional cinemas and online communities, while also demarcating important contexts for global cinema such as festival circuits and the discipline of film studies itself.

This book series is jointly coordinated by *B-Film: The Birmingham Centre for Film Studies* based at the University of Birmingham, the *Centre for World Cinemas and Digital Cultures* at the University of Leeds and the *Centre for Film and Media Research* at the University of Kent.

Middlebrow Cinema
Edited by Sally Faulkner

The Routledge Companion to World Cinema
Edited by Rob Stone, Paul Cooke, Stephanie Dennison and Alex Marlow-Mann

Cinema Against Doublethink
Ethical Encounters with the Lost Pasts of World History
David Martin-Jones

Remapping Brazilian Film Culture in the Twenty-First Century
Stephanie Dennison

For more information about this series, please visit: https://www.routledge.com/Remapping-World-Cinema/book-series/RWC

REMAPPING BRAZILIAN FILM CULTURE IN THE TWENTY-FIRST CENTURY

Stephanie Dennison

LONDON AND NEW YORK

First published 2020
by Routledge
2 Park Square, Milton Park, Abingdon, Oxon OX14 4RN

and by Routledge
52 Vanderbilt Avenue, New York, NY 10017

Routledge is an imprint of the Taylor & Francis Group, an informa business

© 2020 Stephanie Dennison

British Library Cataloguing-in-Publication Data
A catalogue record for this book is available from the British Library

Library of Congress Cataloging-in-Publication Data
A catalog record has been requested for this book

ISBN: 978-1-138-11983-3 (hbk)
ISBN: 978-1-138-11992-5 (pbk)
ISBN: 978-1-315-65203-0 (ebk)

Typeset in Bembo
by Newgen Publishing UK

For Anna, my favourite UK-Brazil co-production

CONTENTS

FIGURES

PREFACE

All translations into English are mine, unless otherwise stated. Films are cited first by their original title, and then where applicable in English (in italics where a film has been released in an English-speaking country). Thereafter, films are cited in their original title only, unless they are sufficiently well known in their English versions (e.g. *City of God*). The term favela is used instead of the now preferred *comunidade* (literally, community) for the sake of clarity.

ACKNOWLEDGEMENTS

I have had unfailing support from my institution, the University of Leeds, in the research and writing of this book, including two periods of funded research leave. I would like to thank my colleagues at Leeds, and especially my fellow attendees of the School of Languages, Cultures and Societies' structured writing sessions, who buoyed me up in the tough, final writing stages.

I spent three periods of extended fieldwork in Brazil, funded by the World Universities Network, the Leverhulme Trust and Mackpesquisa/Mackenzie Presbyterian University: I am especially grateful to Fernão Ramos and Jane de Almeida for hosting me at their institutions during those trips, and to staff and students at the Instituto de Artes, UNICAMP, and Labcine at the Universidade Presbiteriana Mackenzie for their enthusiasm and friendship. Thanks also to Jayme Liande, Rui Silva, Larissa Carpintero and Nelson Felice for making those trips so memorable for me and my daughter Anna.

I have benefitted from insights from the following scholars, who generously read and commented on draft chapters of the book: Alfredo Suppia, Deborah Shaw, Laura Cánepa, Thea Pitman, Rebecca Jarman, Joey Whitfield, Tori Holmes, Lisa Shaw, Claire Williams, Paul Cooke, Belisa Figueiró, Tatiana Heise, Gilberto Sobrinho, Roberta Gregoli and Cacilda Rego. I'm incredibly grateful for their input.

I had the opportunity to learn directly from a number of filmmakers and film industry "players" during the course of my research: Lúcia Murat, Deborah Ivanov, Day Rodrigues, Steve Solot, staff at BRAVI, Spcine, Mostra Internacional de São Paulo, Gustavo Rolla and Viviane Ferreira. I am particularly grateful to Maria Augusta Ramos and Kleber Mendonça Filho for coming to Leeds and sharing their wonderful work with my colleagues and students. I would add that the courage demonstrated by filmmakers such as Maria Augusta and Kleber gives me hope and a real sense of purpose in what must, for many Brazilians and Brazilianists, otherwise feel like pretty dark days.

Thanks also to the following people for helping with the book in all sorts of ways: Ivonete Pinto, Dai Dantas, Rafael de Luna Freire, Tunico Amâncio, Alessandra Meleiro, Marcelo Ikeda, Sara Brandellero, Maite Conde, Alessandra Brites, my mother, Rhona, the Caldeira Barbosas, Lúcia Nagib, Alvaro Zeini Cruz and Mary Freedman. Thanks to my fellow series editors, and Jennifer Vennall and Natalie Foster at Routledge for helping to bring this book to fruition with patience and optimism.

Finally, thanks to Andrew, who has accompanied me throughout this journey and hopefully learnt a thing or two about Brazilian cinema along the way. "You'll do".

This book is dedicated to the memory of my dad, Roy, and of Sorrell Leczkowski.

INTRODUCTION

The inspiration for writing this book comes in large part from a curiosity regarding the impact of the PT (Workers Party) government (2003–2016) on cultural policy and production in Brazil. When I first pitched the idea for the book to Routledge in 2014, I noted that much had changed over the course of the twenty-first century in relation to film culture in the country. This claim still holds true, but in ways that I could not have imagined at the time, given the deep economic crisis into which Brazil has been plunged, and the abrupt end to Workers Party rule. As originally planned, this book seeks to chart the key changes of the first two decades of the twenty-first century, including: the latest cultural debates within Brazil on film funding and distribution practices; the impact of diversity politics on the Brazilian film industry; the reception and circulation of Brazilian films on the international film festival circuit; the impact of new modes of exhibition on viewing practices; the representation of Brazil by foreign film-makers; and the role of the mighty Globo media corporation in the latest boom in production. But it will also examine the impact on cultural production of the sharp change in political direction at national level experienced post-2016 and the parliamentary coup that brought about the impeachment of president Dilma Rousseff.

The rise of the Workers Party to power in Brazil roughly coincides with the end of what is referred to as the *retomada* or renaissance of Brazilian filmmaking, after the "obscurantist disaster" (Nagib 2003: xvii) of Fernando Collor de Melo's short-lived government (1990–1992), and the beginning of a new phase in filmmaking and support for the film industry. My focus, then, is the path carved by Brazilian cinema in the cultural landscape post-2002 and the release of the iconic *Cidade de Deus* (*City of God*, Fernando Meirelles and Kátia Lund).[1] While my end point is 2018, I do provide some reflection in an epilogue on the likely impact on film culture of Jair Bolsonaro's presidency from 1st January 2019 onwards.

Film culture

My interpretation of Film Culture draws on the work of Janet Harbord (2002), Graeme Turner (2002) and Brazil's foremost film critic and cinephile, Paulo Emílio Salles Gomes (Conde and Dennison 2018).[2] In brief, it consists of the analysis of "the practices that shape the flow of film" (Harbord 2002: 5), including "production strategies, marketing, film festivals, reviewing, distribution channels and sites of exhibition" (5). The focus, then, is the cultural, social and economic imperatives that drive the industry, the context of promotion of film culture; and the reception and consumption of films by film audiences: "the spaces between production and consumption […] which open out into a spectacular array of circuits, networks and pathways" (Harbord 2002: 2).

The advantage to taking such a holistic approach to understanding contemporary Brazilian cinema is that it is not restricted to straightforward (if undoubtedly useful) close readings of films in isolation from the forces that drive film production both nationally and internationally, and at the same time it provides illustrations and discussions that go beyond a general overview of the workings of the film industry and that situate film within broader discussions of cultural production. The principle of "remapping" here reflects the precepts of the *Remapping World Cinema* book series in that it is based on a need to move on from potentially limiting concepts such as "the national" (Higson 1989), which can serve to unduly ghettoise a cinema, film industry and audience. Brazilian film culture consists of much more than on the one hand commercially driven mimicry of Hollywood and on the other challenges to Hollywood domination via its art house film scene, an outmoded but still common approach to reading film cultures beyond Hollywood and Bollywood. In terms of storytelling, use made of local and international sources of funding, viewing practices and relationship with new technologies, for example, Brazilian film culture should be read as being part of a globally articulated film culture whose internal workings are necessarily distinctive and thus deserving of World Cinema scholars' attention.

Film culture embraces the full range of films with which an audience engages, from Hollywood blockbusters viewed at the local multiplex to hastily produced short political "documentaries" uploaded onto YouTube. Thus, while my focus is domestically produced films with theatrical releases in Brazil,[3] I do engage with "other" film viewing and filmmaking practices that might inform the public's relation with Brazilian film production. Such an examination of film culture means that I avoid the trap of assuming that: a) the only films being viewed or discussed by the Brazilian public are blockbusters and b) these blockbusters lend little to our understanding of Brazilian culture. The tastes of the *grande público* or public at large continue to be dismissed by many cultural commentators, reinforcing an age-old view of a division between those capable of greater intellectual engagement who support an art-house production (including international audiences) and those who are limited in their tastes and stick with films that provide tropes, style and a cast recognisable from TV viewing.

Film and the cinema frequently take a back seat in discussions about media and its influence in Brazil, which tend to focus on *telenovelas* (TV soaps) and social media. By way of example, the latest high-profile debate regarding the representation of race emerged from a *telenovela*, *Segundo Sol* (Second Sun), whereby the population of Brazil's most Afro-Brazilian of cities (Salvador) was represented on the small screen by a predominantly white cast (Catraca Livre 2018). And *telenovelas* have throughout this century functioned as barometers for the acceptance or otherwise of same-sex relationships and demonstrations of affection on screen. With regard to social media, consider, for example, its influence on the *jornadas de junho* or June 2013 protests that arguably triggered a process that led to both the impeachment of Dilma Rousseff in 2016 and the victory of the far-right Jair Bolsonaro in the presidential elections of 2018. Consider also the controversy surrounding the widespread use of WhatsApp for spreading fake news during the 2018 elections (Phillips 2018). Given its importance in contemporary social life in Brazil, it is no coincidence that I discuss a number of film-related polemics that either began or were played out on social media.

I am interested, therefore, in examining where cinema sits in the cultural and socio-political landscape, without necessarily inflating its importance. Brazil's film industry is the tenth largest in the world, but a large part of the Brazilian population does not have access to a cinema. Yet as Harbord (2002: 1) argues, there are many different ways that "film enters our lives". Thus, a film such as Kleber Mendonça Filho's *Aquarius* (2016), the focus of Chapter 10 of this monograph, has arguably contributed more to debates on the role of filmmakers in Brazilian society, State funding of the Arts, censorship and the image of Brazil abroad, than it has on the socio-political issues that might be raised from a viewing of the film itself. *Aquarius* fared relatively well at the box-office and is available to view on Netflix, but it will still have been viewed by a negligible proportion of the population, Brazilian or otherwise.

If there is still a strong tradition of cinephilia in Brazil in certain circles, Paulo Emílio Salles Gomes has a great deal to do with it.[4] By engaging with the broader picture of film and filmmaking, and films' relationship with the socio-political context in which they are produced, Salles Gomes was instrumental in creating a central place for film in twentieth-century cultural history, or what Harbord refers to as "a discursive space for film within an intellectual environment" (2002: 100). It is perhaps no exaggeration to claim that it was thanks to Salles Gomes and his trailblazing work on film culture that filmmakers, curators and critics are afforded a privileged position within cultural debates in Brazil to this day. This monograph, then, seeks to capture the impact of filmmakers as opinion-formers within some of those key debates.

At the turn of the twenty-first century Graeme Turner wrote of a new agenda for film studies. "Prominent in this agenda […] is research into the cultural function of popular cinema genres, into audience reception and consumption of the movies, and into a version of film history that is more interested in industry economics than the formation of a canon" (2002: 7). In this context it is interesting to note that as early as 1957 Paulo Emílio Salles Gomes had argued that it was critics' responsibility to familiarise themselves with the economic and legislative problems associated with Brazilian film culture, and to join the effort to resolve them (Conde and Dennison 2018).

Structure of the book

The book is structured into two sections: Section One discusses the context of film culture in Brazil in the twenty-first century, while Section Two includes close readings of four films that provide illustrations for the key issues raised in Section One. In Chapter 1 "Making films in twenty-first-century Brazil" I set the scene for twenty-first-century filmmaking by discussing film policy in Brazil, with a focus on how films are funded, distributed and exhibited. I include discussions of a number of polemics arising from film funding, driven both by the public and members of the filmmaking community, such as claims that filmmakers abuse State resources to promote a leftist agenda, and that the State favours the US Majors in detriment to local producers. I also chart the development of film exhibition (multiplexes, art-house chains, film festivals, television) and discuss examples of alternative film exhibition and distribution practices.

Chapter 2, "Engaging with audiences at home and abroad", is divided into two parts. The first discusses film phenomena associated with domestic box-office success: the films produced by the Universal Church of the Kingdom of God and other religious groups, and the so-called *globochanchadas* or comedies with input from Globo Filmes. Rather than argue for such films' inclusion in a film canon as it is traditionally understood, my reason for including these discussions is that such films are responsible in large part for the boom in audiences for domestic films in the twenty-first century, and a contributing factor in the subsequent reinvigoration of audio-visual culture in Brazil, at a time when state-funded support for the Arts is under considerable scrutiny from lawmakers and the public alike. Part two discusses the trajectory of twenty-first-century Brazilian films, filmmakers and producers on the global stage, looking at, for example, the symbiotic relationship (Toribio 2013: 100) between film directors and European and US film festivals such as Berlin and Sundance and how the State facilitates such interactions. Both sections, then, speak to the two main concerns of current film policy: to improve the economic viability of the domestic film industry and to increase the visibility of film and other audio-visual products abroad.

In response to the shift in focus of cultural policy in Brazil post 2002 towards inclusion and diversity, the next chapters examine film culture in relation to women, LGBTQ communities, Afro-Brazilians and indigenous groups respectively. Chapter 3, "Women and film culture in Brazil" focuses on the years 2014–2018 by way of providing a snapshot of the conditions in which women make films in Brazil. Chapter 4 "Brazil's LGBTQ communities and film culture" reflects upon the inter-action between film culture and both the LGBTQ communities and society at large in the twenty-first century, with greater emphasis here being afforded to the notable shifts in representation of LGBTQ communities and exhibition of LGBTQ films. Chapter 5 "Afro-Brazilian filmmaking in the twenty-first century" focuses on black filmmakers and their films, discussed in the context of racial politics under Workers Party rule. Chapter 6, "Screening the indigenous experience in Brazil" combines an analysis of the representation of indigenous peoples on the big screen with an exposition of the use made of the medium of film by indigenous groups for community-building, self-protection and to denounce injustices.

There then follow four discrete chapters examining in closer detail five key films made between 2006 and 2016. All five films touch upon themes that are particularly significant in twenty-first-century Brazilian culture. José Padilha's *Tropa de elite* (2007) and its sequel (2011), analysed in Chapter 7 ("Cinema and public security: the *Elite Squad* phenomenon"), have been instrumental, I argue, in informing debates regarding the spiralling crisis in public security and the role of the security forces in contemporary Brazilian society. They also provide fascinating examples of how films can "slip into various practices and texts of everyday life" (Harbord 2002: 3), from the seemingly innocuous quoting of lines from the film, to the co-opting of the films' hero, Captain Nascimento, by those promoting the belief in the need for a (heavily armed) saviour to rid the country of crime and corruption in the twenty-first century.

Chapter 8 "Lúcia Murat's *Olhar Estrangeiro* (2005) and the representation of Brazil on foreign screens" turns its attention to the crisis of representation of Brazil abroad, a representation that in cinematic terms has arguably always been problematic, and has tended to overemphasise supposedly exotic and hypersexual national characteristics. Lúcia Murat's documentary *Olhar estrangeiro* (*Foreign View*) provides an illustration both of foreign filmmakers' at once ham-fisted and insensitive portrayals of Brazil and Brazilians, and of the trend in Brazilian cinema for research-based documentaries that make timely interventions on contemporary issues of concern.

In Chapter 9 "Hope springs from rubbish: *Trash* (2014) and the garbage aesthetic" I analyse Stephen Daldry and Christian Duurvoort's *Trash: a esperança vem do lixo* (*Trash*, 2014), an international co-production, a financing and production method that has gained considerable traction in the filmmaking landscape in contemporary Brazil. The film also highlights the importance of the motif of trash in Brazilian cultural production, as well as returning to the familiar theme of children, favelas and extreme poverty in Brazilian cities.

In Chapter 10 "A cordial view from Brazil's north-east: Kleber Mendonça Filho's *Aquarius* (2016)", I read Mendonça Filho's film as contributing to contemporary debates on deeply entrenched uneven social relations as characterised, for example, by the working conditions of domestic maids in middle-class homes. As well as being an example of a film produced in a context that is removed from the axis of Rio and São Paulo (in this case, the northeastern city of Recife), *Aquarius* also provides a useful illustration of "the meaning that accrues to a film, independent of what the film is in itself, when it travels a festival circuit" (Harbord 2002: 2).

Notes

1 There is an ever-growing body of work that analyses both the *retomada* and *City of God*'s contribution to film culture. See, for example, Nagib (2002; 2003) and Ramos (2018) on the *retomada* and Vieira (2005) and McClennan (2011) on *City of God*.
2 Further inspiration was drawn from the approach to reading films adopted by Nuria Triana Toribio (2016), Randal Johnson (2005) and Deborah Shaw (2003; 2013).
3 Here I follow Marcelo Ikeda's lead in an interpretation of the term cinema: Ikeda (2018: 468) defines this as films that ideally seek exhibition first and foremost in a film theatre.
4 Best known outside Brazil for his work on French cinema, notably his definitive study of the eponymous *Jean Vigo* (1957), Paulo Emílio Salles Gomes (1916–1977) is revered within Brazil as one of the country's founding fathers of film criticism and film studies, both through the large volume of essays he published throughout his life (some 400) and latterly through his teaching at a number of important film schools; as an instrumental figure in the development of film archiving, both in Europe and in Brazil; and as the first ardent defender and promoter of Brazilian cinema.

References

Catraca Livre. 2018. "*Segundo Sol* é criticada por mostrar uma 'Bahia branca demais'". 24 April. https://catracalivre.com.br/cidadania/segundo-sol-bahia-branca/.

Conde, M. and Dennison, S. (ed). 2018. *Paulo Emílio Salles Gomes: On Brazil and Global Cinema*. Cardiff: University of Wales Press.

Higson, A. 1989. "The Concept of National Cinema". *Screen* 30: 4, pp. 36–46.

Harbord, J. 2002. *Film Cultures*. London: Sage.

Ikeda, M. 2018. "O 'cinema de garagem', provisoriamente: notas sobre o contexto de renovação do cinema brasileiro a partir da virada do século". *Revista Aniki* 5: 2, pp. 457–479.

Johnson, R. 2005. "TV Globo, the MPA and Contemporary Brazilian Cinema". In Shaw, L. and Dennison, S. (eds) *Latin American Cinema: Essays on Modernity, Gender and National Identity*. Jefferson NC: McFarland, pp. 11–38.

McClennan, S. 2011. "From the Aesthetics of Hunger to the Cosmetics of Hunger in Brazilian Cinema: Meirelles' *City of God*". *Symploke* 19: 1–2, pp. 95–106.

Nagib, L. 2002. *O cinema da retomada: depoimentos de 90 cineastas dos anos 90*. São Paulo: Editora 34.

Nagib, L. 2003. "Introduction". In Nagib, L. (ed), *The New Brazilian Cinema*. London and New York: IB Tauris, pp. xvii–xxvi.

Nagib, L. (ed) 2003. *The New Brazilian Cinema*. London and New York: IB Tauris.

Phillips, D. 2018. "Brazil battles fake news 'tsunami' amid polarized presidential election". *Guardian*, 10 October www.theguardian.com/world/2018/oct/10/brazil-fake-news-presidential-election-whatsapp-facebook.

Ramos, F. P. 2018. "A retomada: nação inviável, narcisismo às avessas e má consciência". In Ramos, F. P. and Schvarzman, S. (eds) *Nova história do cinema brasileiro* Vol 2. São Paulo: SESC, pp. 410–471.

Shaw, D. 2003 *Contemporary Latin American Cinema: Ten Key Films*. London: Continuum.

Shaw, D. 2013. "Deconstructing and Reconstructing Transnational Cinema". In S. Dennison (ed.), *Contemporary Hispanic Cinema: Interrogating the Transnational in Spanish and Latin American Film*. London: Tamesis, pp. 47–65.

Toribio, N. T. 2013. "Building Latin American Cinema in Europe: Cine en Construcción/ Cinéma en construction". In Dennison, S. (ed) *Contemporary Hispanic Cinema: Interrogating the Transnational in Spanish and Latin American Film.* London: Tamesis, pp. 89–112.

Toribio, N. T. 2016. *Spanish Film Cultures: The Making and Unmaking of Spanish Cinema.* Palgrave: British Film Institute.

Turner, G. 2002. "Editor's Introduction". In Turner, G. (ed), *The Film Cultures Reader.* London and New York: Routledge, pp. 1–10.

Vieira, E. (ed) 2005. *City of God in Several Voices: Brazilian Social Cinema as Action.* Nottingham: CCC Press.

PART I

1

MAKING FILMS IN TWENTY-FIRST-CENTURY BRAZIL

Brazil is configured along the lines of most world cinema cultures in that its film industry is "shaped by multiple economic, ideological, social and cultural exigencies that are compounded by US domination of the local film market and the consequent need for diverse forms of state support" (Johnson 2005: 14). It has likewise experienced the peaks and troughs in cinema-going tied to both fluctuations in ticket prices/public spending power and access to cinemas that mirror many of the world's film cultures, and particularly those found in so-called emerging economies. With exhibition that dates from as early as 1896 and production from 1897, Brazil has experienced cycles of intense production and state funding, predicated on the twin pillars of belief in the significant contribution film makes to national identity, and its potential for contributing financially to state coffers.[1] While many observers argue that film production in Brazil has never constituted an industry *per se*, the country is much better placed than most of its neighbours in South America to claim the existence of what was once unproblematically referred to as a "national cinema" (Shaw and Dennison 2007: 1–5). Brazilians in their millions flocked to watch the home-grown chanchadas or comedies of the 1940s and 50s, and by the mid-1970s Brazilian films had reached a very respectable 30% participation in the market (Ikeda 2015: 79), thanks in large part to generous state support for production and distribution. As explored in Chapter 2, Brazilian films have been a constant presence in the major European film festivals, with the avant-garde *Cinema Novo* movement of the 1960s cementing the country's fame for producing exportable films that are both aesthetically innovative and that contribute to debates on the social issues of the day. In the second decade of the twenty-first century the broad view of Brazilian cinema is that it is currently riding high: Brazil constitutes the world's eighth largest audience (Rufino 2018); Brazilians view films on a record number of cinema screens (Moraes 2018); the audio-visual industry generates billions of reals annually (Festival de Gramado 2018); and as I will discuss in more detail in Chapter 2, domestic films are breaking box-office records.

The troughs experienced by film production in Brazil include the bankruptcy of the ambitious Vera Cruz studio complex in São Paulo in 1954 in what amounted to a failed attempt to create a film industry modelled on the US studio system, and the migration in the 1980s of film audiences to home video and the domination of the market by hard-core pornography. Neither of these, however, had the impact of killing off film production: that honour was held by Fernando Collor de Melo, Brazil's first president, elected by universal suffrage after the period of dictatorship that ran from 1964 to 1984.

The development of film policy in twenty-first-century Brazil

In 1990, as a result of the election in 1989 of neo-liberal Collor de Melo and the hasty introduction of a "scorched-earth policy" (Johnson 2005:14) in the spirit of the promotion of free trade, 11 state enterprises and 13 other agencies were closed down (Ikeda 2015: 19). With one decree the principle institutions supporting the film industry were disbanded (Ikeda 2018: 458), effectively forcing Brazilian cinema into an "induced coma" (459). The National Film Council (Conselho Nacional de Cinema or CONCINE), the Fundação do Cinema Brasileiro (Brazilian Film Foundation), Embrafilme, the state film production and distribution company, and the Lei Sarney or Sarney Law of 1986 which was responsible for funding films, were all abolished, and the Ministry of Culture was reduced to a Secretariat.

Only three films were released in 1992. This halt to Brazilian film production was in fact very short-lived (two years) but much has been made of it, not least as it provides clear evidence of what can happen to an otherwise healthy film industry if sources of support are removed, even briefly. The Sarney Law of 1986 was temporarily replaced with the Prêmio Resgate, or Brazilian cinema rescue award, which was awarded to 90 projects in 1993 and 1994 and credited by Cacilda Rêgo (2011: 37) as the spark that gave life to a cinema reborn. However, still under Collor, the Culture Secretary Sérgio Paulo Rouanet introduced, in December 1991, what is referred to as the Lei Rouanet or Rouanet Law, an arts-related law which remains in force and has had a long-term impact on film culture. The Rouanet Law introduced the Fundo Nacional de Cultura (FNC), a federal government fund, partly supported by the National Lottery, which provided direct financial support for cultural production in Brazil. The law also established a mechanism, known as the Incentivo Fiscal, to provide for *mecenato* (patronage for the arts): businesses or individuals could invest part of their income tax into cultural activities that had been approved by the Ministry of Culture (not exclusively film or audio-visual related). Based on arts support schemes in place elsewhere, such as in France, over one billion reals were invested in the arts via the Lei Rouanet's fiscal incentive mechanism in 2017 alone.

In December 1992 President Collor resigned amid accusations of corruption and an impending impeachment vote. Under his vice-president Itamar Franco the

Ministry of Culture was reinstated. In 1993 the Lei do Audiovisual, or Audio-visual Law, was introduced, also based on fiscal incentives. After the Rouanet Law, it was the second most important piece of legislation in support of the gradually revitalising film industry. Ikeda (2015: 29) highlights the political influence of audio-visual culture in Brazil demonstrated by the introduction of this law: it was the only part of the cultural industries to have its own dedicated incentive scheme. The audio-visual law was responsible for the so-called *retomada*, or rebirth, of Brazilian cinema from 1995 (Shaw and Dennison 2007: 37). This positive scenario was completed by the creation in 1992 of RioFilme (a film distribution and promotion company attached to the municipal government of Rio de Janeiro) and a number of *polos regionais* or regionally supported filmmaking production centres (Ikeda 2015: 21). Ikeda also cites two filmic success stories released in 1995: Carla Camurati's *Carlota Joaquina: princesa do Brazil* (*Carlota Joaquina*), which drew an impressive 1.5 million viewers to film theatres, even though the film had no distributor, and Fábio Barreto's *O quatrilho*, which made the shortlist for the Oscar for best foreign film (33).[2]

According to Ikeda (2015: 14), it was under the two presidential terms of Fernando Henrique Cardoso (1995–2002) that film policy based on fiscal incentives was consolidated. The Brazilian state continued to be the "conduit" for film production, but now market agents were introduced as an intrinsic part of the model (Ikeda 2015: 15), following a logic of sharing of responsibilities between the state and the market in the production of works of culture (26). During Cardoso's presidency Ancine was set up (in 2001), the national film agency that has been instrumental in regulating audio-visual production in Brazil throughout this century. In 2006 the agency became responsible for the administration of direct forms of support for film production via national funding calls (*editais*), as well as the increasingly significant Fundo Setorial do Audiovisual (FSA) – the Audio-visual Sector Fund, part of the previously mentioned Fundo Nacional da Cultura, which supports independently produced feature-length films and their distribution in Brazil. As explored in the following chapters, for two decades funding calls have reflected the shift towards a more inclusive and diversity-led cultural agenda.

The FSA makes an important contribution to addressing long-standing concerns within the film industry in Brazil, incorporating the various segments of the production chain: from funding film production to distribution and exhibition. It also provides for a degree of state financial return on investment in films. Likewise, since 2012 the Ancine-administered programme Cinema Perto de Você (A Cinema Near You) has made funding available for the construction of new theatres, thus going some way to meeting the demand for investment in exhibition and audience-generation initiatives. And to address, at least on paper,[3] the frequently aired concern that film producers are given no incentive to make films that engage with audiences, the Prêmio Adicional de Renda (the Additional Income Prize) was introduced in 2005 to reward independent filmmakers for box-office success.

This national funding scenario is supplemented by a number of regional and transnational initiatives. One of the most striking of these, in terms of the films it has supported, is Funcultura – funding for cultural activities administered by the state of Pernambuco, in Brazil's north-east.[4] In the 2018 funding call priority was given to cultural activities conducted by women, Afro-descendants, indigenous populations, those from the interior and public school attendees (Barros 2017), thus reflecting a broad diversity agenda that has attracted much direct funding to the arts over the course of this century (see Chapter 5). The main source of transnational funding, and one increasingly sought with the growth of interest in making inter-national co-productions (see Chapter 2), is Ibermedia. The Programa Ibermedia is a film-financing pool set up in 1998. Spain, Portugal and Italy contribute to it, along with 18 Latin American countries – including Brazil via Ancine. It is modelled on Europe's Eurimages and Media Plus programmes (Falicov 2013: 68). A notable recipient of Ibermedia funding (both for script development and co-production) is Brazilian filmmaker Beatriz Seigner, for the critically acclaimed *Los silencios* (2018), a Colombian/Brazilian/French co-production which premiered at the Directors' Fortnight at Cannes and went on to win awards at the Brasilia Film Festival in 2018.

Such initiatives tend to be accessed by producers, where permissible, as supple-mentary to the more substantial national funds discussed above. As discussed in Chapter 2, further funds, such as those to cover pre- and post-production costs, are open to Brazilian filmmakers via film festivals such as Sundance, Rotterdam, Berlin and San Sebastian. Also, Brazilian producers are increasingly working with TV channels, for example the Globo-owned Canal Brasil (Brazil) and RAI (Italy), and the US majors (for distribution), completing a diverse picture of domestic funding for feature-length films.

Criticism of film funding schemes

Two of the first films to benefit from fiscal incentive funds (introduced post-1990) have proved controversial and have arguably set the tone for how film funding is broadly perceived by a large part of the Brazilian public. Norma Bengell's big-budget *O guarani* (1996), based on the nineteenth-century foundational novel of the same name by José de Alencar, was the first in a steady line of films to be singled out for public opprobrium after the Ministry of Culture rejected the accounts presented by the film's producers. As a result, until her death in 2013 Bengell was under investigation for fraud. Moreover, according to Ikeda (2015: 34), many businesses sought to distance themselves from Brazilian cinema. Furthermore, *O guarani* was a critical and commercial flop, which exacerbated debate about the wastefulness of investing in costly art forms such as feature-length films.

Around the same time, inexperienced filmmaker Guilherme Fontes raised eyebrows when he was awarded 8.6 million reals, through the Rouanet scheme, to make a film based on the life of controversial communications magnate Assis Chateaubriand, *Chatô, o rei do Brasil* (*Chatô, King of Brazil*). Fontes continued to make headlines and provoke discontent with the Rouanet Law, by delaying the release of the film by two years, then shelving the production altogether while he was investigated for fraud, and then finally releasing the film 20 years later, in 2015, while still under investigation.

FIGURE 1.1 Assis Chateaubriand introduces television to Brazil. Still from trailer for *Chatô, o rei do Brasil*

(*Chatô, King of Brazil*, Guilherme Fontes, 2015)

As part of a very broad programme of working to uncover fraud within state enterprises in Brazil, since 2014 the Federal Police-led Operação Boca Livre (Free Lunch Operation) has been investigating million-dollar corruption within the Lei Rouanet fiscal incentive mechanism, uncovering cases of funds being used to pay for luxury weddings, for example (Alessi and Moraes 2016). Inevitably, such juicy stories provide more appealing clickbait on social media than reports on the effective use of Rouanet funds to run internationally recognised film festivals, to maintain national museums, to support emerging artists trying to break into international markets, and so on.

The name given by the Federal Police to the investigation (Boca Livre) is revealing of how artists and cultural producers are (mis)understood, particularly at a time of economic crisis, when it is not unusual for demands to be made for funding for the arts to cease, and investment made instead in health and education. In some cases public indignation seems justified: in 2006 the world-famous Cirque de Soleil received 9.4 million reals for a tour of Brazil where tickets cost up to 370 reals (Moraes 2016). Those working in the arts, as well as being invariably painted as leftist, are perceived by those on the right to be *vagabundos* (workshy) who, to repeat a frequently used phrase, "suckle on the teats of the state" (*mamam nas tetas do estado*). Artists, including high-profile actors and recording artists who were openly critical of the impeachment of Dilma Rousseff and the presidential election campaign of Jair Bolsonaro, for example, were frequently accused on social media of "living off the Rouanet Law". After ex-Pink Floyd bass player Roger Waters pilloried Bolsonaro in a series of large-scale gigs in Brazil in late 2018, the Ministry of Culture was compelled to post a press release denying claims that Waters had made use of the Rouanet Law to finance his shows in Brazil (Peron and Martins 2018).

A very telling example of such prejudice against state-funded arts production, but specifically in relation to film, unfolded at the 2016 Cannes film festival. For the first time in many years a Brazilian film, *Aquarius* (Kleber Mendonça Filho, 2016), was selected for the official competition.[5] At Cannes there was some discussion of the film itself, which received rave reviews, but what ultimately made the headlines was the opportunity that the film's cast and crew took on the red carpet to protest the perceived undermining of democracy taking place in Brazil with the impeachment process. The backlash at home from supporters of impeachment was severe, and centred on the extent to which the film production and the cast and crew's attendance at Cannes were funded by public money. As we will see in Chapter 10, Mendonça Filho paid a high price for this protest: despite being regarded as a front-runner, *Aquarius* was not selected to represent Brazil at the Oscars in the foreign film category.

With the increase in alternative and dedicated sources of funding, fewer domestic film producers now turn to the Rouanet Law as a source of financial support for their productions. This fact bears little weight with those who seek to undermine the importance and relevance of domestic film production. For a start, all state funding for the arts in Brazil is quite regularly conflated into the fiscal incentive mechanism (*mecenato*) within the Rouanet Law for the sake of discussions on social media, and electioneering, for example. The impact of such misinformation on funding was demonstrated by the fact that the Ministry of Culture was obliged to introduce a section to their website outlining and correcting the myths about the Rouanet Law.[6]

Many working within the cultural industries are also critical of the Rouanet Law, albeit not to the extent that they argue for removing it altogether. The fiscal incentive mechanism within the Rouanet Law states that the Ministry of Culture does not make subjective judgements on projects, but that rather, it rubber-stamps those that adhere to all the administrative and viability requirements of submission to the scheme. What is implicit, then, is that subjective judgement on the quality of artistic production passes to the businesses and individuals who wish to invest. This has been a bone of contention, with complaints about the involvement of marketing departments in making crucial decisions on what cultural activities get funded. Marketing departments are less likely to support unknown and/or emerging artists. And as critic Jean-Claude Bernardet has argued, no filmmaker would make a film about the extent to which the state oil company Petrobras pollutes the environment, given that Petrobras is one of Brazilian cinema's main funders (in Marcolin 2014). One imagines that a film dealing with Petrobras's involvement in the Lava-Jato or Car-wash grafting scandal will not find support from the company via *mecenato* funding schemes either.[7]

With regard to the Audio-visual Law, criticism from within the filmmaking community has tended to focus on Article 3 of the law, and particularly its iteration post-2002. The article enables foreign film distributors (essentially the Majors) to access tax rebates for co-producing Brazilian films.[8] These tend to be the most commercially driven films (Schvarzman 2018: 524): for Ikeda (2012) Article 3 served as a springboard for the production of domestic blockbusters. *Dois filhos de Francisco* (*Two Sons of Francisco*, Breno Silveira, 2005) is often cited as an example of this co-production model, given the film's success (5,319,677 viewers: Schvarzman 2018: 537), and the extent to which Columbia reportedly controlled the project, from script development, to the choice of co-producer (Conspiração Filmes), through to the completed film (Schvarzman 2018: 524; Meleiro 2013: 188). The rapid domination of the box office for domestic production by the Majors is described by Alessandra Meleiro (2013: 203) as tantamount to the denationalisation of control over the economics of national film. The opportunities afforded independent (local) distributors (such as Downtown and Paris Filmes) via the FSA has gone some way to tackling this monopoly on distribution, even if the blockbusters being produced, as explored in Chapter 2, have changed little.[9]

Issues in National Film Exhibition

Ahead of the 2018 Brasília Film Festival film critic for the *Folha de S. Paulo* Inácio Araújo (2018), rather than focusing on the good-news story of women's and Afro-Brazilians' participation in the festival as highlighted in Chapters Three and Four of this monograph, headlined his featurette with "Brasilia Film Festival Kicks off Amid Public Disinterest in Brazilian Cinema", seemingly reducing in one fell swoop the efforts of all filmmakers involved in the festival to complete irrelevance. The focus of the feature was in fact festival curator Eduardo Valente's take on the state of the film industry, and in particular his raising of the issues of lack of distribution opportunities for Brazilian cinema and the domination of Hollywood. In this he drew attention to the difference in exhibition experiences of commercial and what are perceived to be more "art house" films, of the kind likely to be screened at the Brasilia Film festival.

According to the official reports of the National Cinema Agency (Ancine 2018a), 142 Brazilian films were released in cinemas in 2016. If the number of films released is expressive, the data masks another reality. While six films surpassed the one million spectator mark, the vast majority of Brazilian films remain virtually unseen. Among the 142 films, 94 (66.2%) did not reach 10,000 viewers and 43 films (or 30.3%), less than 1,000 viewers.[10] That is, two out of three Brazilian films released did not reach a public of 10,000 viewers in theatres. In 2017 a record 160 films were released (Ancine 2018b), yet domestic production had its lowest market participation in ten years, with just 9.6% of cinema ticket sales (Pinheiro 2018: 35–36).

Sérgio Sá Leitão, the last Minister of Culture before the Ministry was disbanded by newly elected president Jair Bolsonaro in January 2019, in a presentation in 2017 on national cinema drew attention to the fact that 49% of films produced in Brazil between 2012 and 2017 (438 out of 881 productions) sold less than 3,650 tickets in cinemas (Engler 2017). Sá Leitão then ironically quipped that he had more than 3,650 friends on Facebook (Engler 2017), causing consternation among the audience. While he did go on in his presentation to contextualise this figure by arguing that not all films are made, or should be made, with theatrical release in mind, with a number going on to fare well on TV and VOD, it was the aforementioned critical soundbite that went viral.

Marcelo Ikeda (2015: 34) recalls a sensationalist article published in *Veja* magazine in 1999 entitled "Expensive, Bad and You're Paying", which ultimately condemned Brazilian film production as being too costly an art form to be supported by the state, particularly given the low numbers of viewers for domestic production. While the domestic box office has improved exponentially since 1999, and while the audio-visual sector as a whole regularly boasts of contributing more to Brazil's GDP (0.46% in 2017: Festival de Gramado 2018) than many other significant industries such as pharmaceuticals,[11] these three examples of criticism of box-office returns illustrate clearly the varying degrees of naysaying to which the industry has had to respond, from the cinephile festival curator frustrated at spectator apathy (Valente), to the neoliberal fan of commercial Brazilian cinema (Sá Leitão) and finally to the influential tabloid news headline seeker who criticises all state funding for Arts and culture (*Veja*).

The film theatre circuit and quotas for Brazilian films

As early as 1920 Brazil already had 700 cinemas (Heffner 2000: 81), and exhibition was controlled almost exclusively up until at least the 1950s by two men: Luiz Severiano Ribeiro and the Spanish-born Francisco Serrador, and the companies they started (Trindade 2014). Competition from television, followed by home video and DVD was felt from the 1960s onwards, with many *cinemas de rua* or cinemas in downtown areas turning to screening hardcore pornography in order to survive (Shaw and Dennison 2007: 99), and with others being converted into supermarkets and evangelical churches, for example. With the opening up of the economy to foreign investment post-dictatorship, foreign exhibitors, such as the US-based Cineplex and UCI, and the Mexican Cinépolis quickly took over the exhibition market, bringing with them the multiplex model that now dominates the sector. Only the national Severiano Ribeiro Group proved agile enough to survive the competition from television and the shifts to multiplex and digital screens.

The growth of the multiplex phenomenon in Brazil moves hand-in-hand with the increase in number of shopping centres, itself a reflection of the increased spending power of a sizeable part of the population (at least until 2014). In 2016 2,367 of Brazil's 3,118 screens were in multiplexes, most of which are located in shopping centres, which in turn are located in larger towns and cities. Thus, despite the huge growth in screens (3,279 in 2018, the highest number of all time: Moraes 2018), fewer than 7% of municipalities in 2016 possessed a cinema (*Filme B* 2018), which demonstrates how challenging the task is of democratising access to cinemas, even with the vital support of the Cinema Perto de Você (A Cinema Near You) initiative. The overall numbers, while at record levels for Brazil, are still very poor when converted into a ratio of number of inhabitants per cinema (70,000:1). (Christian De Castro, quoted in Sousa 2018: 32). The equivalent figures for Argentina and Mexico respectively are 30,000:1 and 25:000:1 (32).

The other significant player in the film theatre market is Adhemar Oliveira who from running *cineclubes* (film clubs) in the 1980s progressed to establishing an arthouse cinema chain, first in Rio de Janeiro (the Cineclube Estação Botafogo, established in 1985) and then expanding into São Paulo with the support of corporate sponsorship (the Espaço Unibanco de Cinema from 1993). The Espaço de Cinema group in 2012 boasted a total of 120 screens in 25 complexes, mostly (but not exclusively) in the states of Rio de Janeiro and São Paulo. The group's current screening strategy is unique in that it includes a mix of global commercial hits and art house productions.

Screen quotas (*cotas de tela*) for feature films have existed in Brazil since 1932 and the nationalist government of Getúlio Vargas, and as in most world cinema cultures they are regarded as essential for the dissemination of domestic film production, particularly in the light of the dominance of Hollywood product and the power of the Majors in Brazilian film culture. Quotas for domestic films were gradually increased from 42 days per year in the late 1950s, to 56 days in 1963, and then to a remarkable 112 days in 1975, the height of the domestic box office boom. The current (2018) quota figures stand at 28 days per year for single-screen theatres, increasing to 280 for five-screen multiplexes. Attempts to limit the ability of multiplexes to exhibit the same film on more than one screen (invariably a Hollywood blockbuster: *Fast and Furious 8* simultaneously occupied 1,544 screens in 2017 [Ikeda 2018: 473]), and thus limit spectator choice, failed when one of the big multiplex chains that is active in Brazil, the Mexican Cinépolis, broke a "gentleman's agreement" set up by Ancine, forcing the other exhibitors (such as UCI and Cinemark) to follow suit (Schvarzman 2018: 525).

A further boost to cinema ticket sales was generated by the passing of a federal law obliging cinemas to offer a half-price ticket (*meia-entrada*) for minors, students, and so on, whereby comparatively costly cinema ticket prices are made more accessible for a large part of the population. It is perhaps needless to say that the system is very open to abuse, and is viewed as very controversial by the exhibition sector.

By far the most impactful quotas to be introduced in the twenty-first century are those pertaining to the Lei da TV Paga (Subscription TV Law), introduced in 2011 with the express purpose of augmenting the volume of Brazilian content on Brazil's subscription TV channels. With the exception of those that exclusively screen news and sport such as ESPN, subscription channels are obliged by law to screen 3.5 hours of Brazilian content in primetime slots, with 50% of this being made by independent producers (Ancine website). As well as fostering a growth in independent A-V production companies, the law has revolutionised the relationship between cinema and television even more than the advent of Globo Filmes. No quota system has ever existed for terrestrial TV channels, which while they have supported national TV series (and specifically their own in-house *telenovelas*), they have barely acknowledged the existence of national film production. Together with the FSA, the Subscription TV Law is described by Ancine as the third wave of Audio-visual policy, a policy celebrated by the agency for increasing viewing figures for Brazilian film to match those of the high point of the mid-1970s (Rufino 2018).

VOD and online viewing

Thus far (end of 2018) the Video on Demand (VOD) sector has escaped regulation with regard to screening domestic production, but the issue is the focus of intense debate within the audio-visual industry in Brazil, particularly around the need for quotas for domestic product and a tax on revenue. Brazil is the eighth largest market for VOD, and SVOD (Subscription Video on Demand) platforms such as Netflix are increasingly popular. Brazil was Netflix's first international market (from 2011) and subscriptions have grown in particular since 2014 with improvements both in broadband availability and in the quality of locally focused content. Amazon Prime and HBO Go have both been present in Brazil since 2016 and Globo's Globosat Play has 2.6 million subscribers and over 60 million hours of material viewed (Figueiró 2018b: 26).

Brazil is Netflix's third largest market after the US and UK, with over 7.5 million subscribers. In late 2018 the platform was screening six Brazilian-made and Portuguese-language series, the most of any language other than English, as well as the hugely successful English/Spanish-language series *Narcos* created by Brazilian filmmaker José Padilha. It also regularly features Brazilian films, from box office hits such as the evangelical *Nada a perder* (*Nothing to Lose,* 2018), discussed in Chapter 2, to romantic comedies such as *Entre idas e vindas* (*Back and Forth*, 2016) to "festival films" such as *Aquarius* (discussed in Chapter 10). Telecine Play has more than 1800 films available for streaming, many of which are Brazilian, but viewers must be cable subscribers to be able to access the platform.

Online video in Brazil is phenomenally popular: the country is now YouTube's fourth largest market globally, with the site obtaining almost 39 million unique viewers in 2012 alone. Brazil holds a number of records in relation to content on YouTube, including both the speed and number of subscriptions to YouTube channels and number of visualisations of music videos, and so on.[12] One of YouTube's first viral stars, Mystery Guitar Man (aka Joe Penna) is Brazilian. In 2018 he directed a feature film which premiered at Cannes: *Arctic* (2018).

According to Ikeda (2018: 473), "The potential of the Internet, as well as VOD channels, content for mobile phones and other portable devices, is underused by the audio-visual industry in Brazil". For a start, the two platforms for streaming Brazilian films, Cinebrasil Já and Spcine Play,[13] are at a very early stage in their development (Figueiró 2018b: 26). As Cesar Migliorin (2011) has observed, "the focus on the commercial trajectory of films disregards new forms of access, as if they were merely peripheral or residual". It is worth bearing in mind, however, that in Brazil just over 30% of households with a TV set have cable, meaning that a large proportion of the population continues to rely on the main terrestrial channels to watch films, and Brazilian films still very rarely screen on terrestrial TV. While much has been made of the growth of the middle class in Brazil in the first decade of the twenty-first century and its attendant spending power, the number of subscribers to cable has in fact been falling steadily since mid-2013, as a result of the extreme economic recession that has hit Brazil. One million households reportedly unsubscribed from cable in 2017 (*Brasil econômico* 2018). The number of Brazilians with access to the internet continues to grow regardless of recession, and the device of choice for accessing the internet is the smart phone (rather than via computers, tablets or smart TVs, for example).

With regard to the issue of downloading, Brazil is currently the fourth largest producer of pirated films:

> There are over 400 audio-visual piracy websites aimed at the Brazilian market, among which 57 receive more than one million visits per month, offering more than 13,000 domestic and foreign titles. These websites, for the most part, are hosted on servers located abroad, which imposes additional challenges to combat online piracy.
>
> *(Tendências 2016)*

The extent of the problem of piracy was best illustrated by the film *Tropa de Elite* (*Elite Squad*, José Padilha, 2007): the film was stolen while in post-production, and subsequently millions of viewers viewed pirated copies, impacting considerably on how it fared at the box office. What is more, savvy film pirates cobbled together footage of Brazilian police operations and sold DVDs shortly after the film's release as a sequel. The market for pirate DVDs continues to thrive in Brazil, with consumers showing scant concern for the quality of the films they view (Schvarzman 2018: 521).

Film festivals

In the *retomada* and post-*retomada* cinematic landscape Brazilian film festivals served to "safeguard domestic production [...] it was necessary to demonstrate to society [post-Collor] that Brazilian cinema needed to continue to exist, as a sign of affirmation of national identity and the wealth of Brazilian cultural production" (Ikeda 2018: 462). As well as serving as a window onto "quality" Brazilian filmmaking, the 200 or so annual festivals serve as an alternative form of exhibition, given that a number of them take place in parts of the country with no cinemas (Ballerini 2012: 189). A number of films of varying length are screened in a succession of festivals before being picked up by TV or VOD platforms, thereby bypassing altogether the traditional theatrical release.

The Festival de Brasília is the longest running festival in Brazil and is a key event in the calendar (September) for Brazilian filmmakers, given that it screens exclusively Brazilian films. Set up in 1965 by Paulo Emílio Salles Gomes, it has maintained throughout its 50-plus years its reputation for being the most politically inflected of the big festivals. The Festival de Gramado (August) in Brazil's southern-most state (Rio Grande do Sul) has been running since 1973 and is perhaps the country's most glamorous (and most televised), with a strong tradition of screening South American arthouse features. Other important festivals run annually in large cities, such as São Paulo (Mostra Internacional de Cinema de São

Paulo in October/November), Rio (Festival do Rio in September/October) and Recife (Cine PE in May and Janela Internacional in November), as well as smaller towns such as Tiradentes (January), a historical town in the state of Minas Gerais whose festival kicks off the festival year. The festival has contributed significantly to increasing tourism to the region and has been notably embraced by filmmakers who have emerged in the twenty-first century (Figueiroa 2014).

The international documentary festival É Tudo Verdade takes its name from Orson Welles' ill-fated and unfinished Brazil-set film *It's All True* of 1942, and it claims to be the largest documentary film festival in South America. Starting in 1996 with a programme of 40 films, by 2010 450 films were being screened during the festival (Ballerini 2012: 255), which in part reflects the huge increase in documentary filmmaking in Brazil in the twenty-first century, and economic growth in the first decade of the century. In 2016 85 films were screened (22 premieres) including a very rich vein of short films which gain much-sought-after Oscar accreditation. Twelve features/medium-length films and eight short films made up the competition list. The São Paulo-based festival was founded and is curated by Amir Labaki, a journalist, film critic and graduate of the University of São Paulo film school. The festival is now held simultaneously in the cities of São Paulo and Rio, with an "itinerant festival" screening the winning films in cities such as Santos, Recife, Belo Horizonte and Brasilia.[14]

There is also a growing number of recurring specialist festivals such as the LGBTQ-focused Mix Brazil, discussed in Chapter 4, which serve not only as a key exhibition space, but also as a mechanism for audience generation and, increasingly, as a site of resistance for filmmakers and cinema-goers alike. The Amazonas Film Festival, which ran in the Amazonian capital of Manaus from 2004 to 2013, played the dual role of providing much needed exhibition space for local filmmakers and viewing opportunities for film fans, and of focusing on films that deal with issues relating to the vast Amazonian region and its peoples. After 2013, as a result of economic crisis, the state governor's office withdrew support for the festival. It was replaced with the lower-key Mostra de Cinema Amazonense in 2015, which focuses on locally produced films.

The economic crisis has hit festivals across the board, a situation exacerbated by the corruption scandal facing Petrobras, one of the domestic circuit's biggest sponsors. For example in 2018 the festivals Janela (Recife) and É Tudo Verdade (São Paulo) were pared back affairs, with shorter schedules and a smaller number of films being screened. The 2018 Rio Film Festival was also hit by sponsorship issues, having to push back its launch date while it worked to secure funding. The Festival Paulínia de Cinema, which began in 2008 and was beginning to garner a reputation as a serious player on the domestic festival circuit, had its municipal funding cut with a change of local government and thus ceased to exist in 2011. And with the continued difficulties of the local government (hit by corruption charges) the multi-million investment in a film studio complex in Paulínia, which functioned between 2007 and 2015 and provided location shooting for films such as *Blindness*

(Fernando Meirelles, 2008) and *De pernas pro ar* (*Head Over Heels*, Roberto Santucci, 2010, discussed in Chapter 2) has been abandoned.

Tensions occasionally arise between festival directors and filmmakers, and/or between festivals and audiences, and these are most commonly predicated on divergences of political opinion. The most high-profile of recent tensions played out at the Cine PE in Recife in 2017, when eight directors withdrew their films from the festival in protest over the selection of films that were claimed to be indicative of the festival directors' support for Michel Temer's right-wing political agenda and therefore of what they understood to be the coup that ousted Dilma Rousseff from power in 2016. The main focus of the protest was *O jardim das aflições* (*The Garden of Afflictions*, Josias Teófilo, 2017) a feature-length film based on the book of the same name by controversial Brazilian philosopher Olavo de Carvalho, considered the guru of the far right in contemporary Brazil. Suspicion of the direction the festival was perceived to be taking was compounded by the fact that Alfredo Bertini, festival founder and husband of the director Sandra Bertini, had accepted the role of Audio-visual Secretary in Michel Temer's government shortly after Rousseff was removed from power. The boycott obliged director Bertini to postpone the festival until the programme could be rearranged (JC Online 2017).

There had already been protests at Cine PE in 2011 when the festival closing ceremony was invaded by protestors demanding "menos glamour, mais cinema" (less glamour, more cinema), in reaction to the perceived growing focus of the festival on breaking audience records. According to Alexandre Figueiroa (2014), as well as seeking the spotlight and attention from the centre-south region (Rio and São Paulo in essence) to the detriment of thoughtful programming, Cine PE struggled to compete with the newer and much "cooler" Janela festival, directed by Kleber Mendonça Filho's Cinemascópio production company since 2008.

With regard to the 2017 controversy, film critic Sérgio Alpendre described the episode as "pathetic" and asked why, if the political persuasion of the festival organisers was no secret, filmmakers signed up to take part in the first place (in Domingos de Lima 2017). "They complained about the political decision not to nominate *Aquarius* for the Oscar and then they carry out an act of veiled censorship like this? This is all really deplorable". Fellow film critic José Geraldo Couto saw the episode as the apex of a process of polarisation and a continuation of the *Aquarius* Oscar dispute, in which the cohesive position of a large part of the filmmaking community was pitched against the power-holders, their representatives and allies (Domingos de Lima 2017).

Cinema ambulante

A number of initiatives have emerged that complement the role of festivals in bringing films to communities that might otherwise struggle to have access to Brazilian films. Filmmakers Lais Bodansky and Luiz Bolognesi are separately behind two of the most interesting films of 2017 and 2018: *Como nossos pais* (*Just Like Our Parents*) and *Ex-pajé* (*Ex-Shaman*) respectively. Together they run Buriti Films and the social and educational project Cine Tela Brasil, one of the most striking of a variety of outreach projects that build on the long-standing tradition of *cinema ambulante* or travelling cinema which for generations of Brazilians in remote areas provided their only contact with moving images. Between 1996 and 2016 Cine Tela Brasil organised free screenings of Brazilian films and ran workshops in the more remote areas of the states of Rio de Janeiro, São Paulo and Paraná. The project garnered an audience of one million, including many people who viewed a film on a big screen for the first time. Bodansky documented her experiences with the travelling cinema project in the documentary *Cine mambembe, o cinema descobre o Brasil* (Travelling Films: Cinema Discovers Brazil, 2014) and published a book *Cine Tela Brasil e Oficinas Tela Brasil: 10 anos levando cinema a escolas públicas e comunidades de baixa renda* (2014).

One of the most interesting aspects of the project was the choice of films and the downloadable school material produced to accompany the screenings, including sections on *reflexão e cidadania* (reflection and citizenship). Thus, the screening of a popular film such as *Se eu fosse você 2* (*If I Were You 2*, Daniel Filho, 2009), a blockbuster comedy produced by Globo Filmes with a male/female body swap storyline, was accompanied by material including discussions of gender. With the introduction of a Federal Law in 2014 obliging schools to screen two hours of Brazilian films per month (Schvarzman 2018: 520) the production and dissemination of such material to accompany domestic films has become all the more useful.

Democratising production

Consecrated (white male) filmmakers such as Carlos Diegues and Bruno Barreto, who have been making films since the 1960s and 1970s respectively, continue to make feature-length films well into the second decade of the twenty-first century. In the realm of documentary, Eduardo Coutinho, who made *Cabra marcado para morrer* (*Twenty Years Later*) in 1984, a documentary that regularly tops the list of greatest Brazilian films, continued to make impactful documentaries such as *Edifício Master* (2002), *Jogo de cena* (*Playing*, 2007) and the posthumous *Últimas conversas* (*Last Conversations*, 2016), until his tragic death in 2014. The bulk of filmmakers currently making films, however, either emerged during the *retomada* years, or after.

These include an increasing number of producers, directors, editors, technicians and actors who straddle the related areas of television and publicity, such as Alexandre Avancini, the Globo TV-trained director responsible for the box office record-breaking *Nada a perder*, discussed in Chapter 2, and Fernando Meirelles, co-director of *City of God* and responsible for some of Nike's most iconic TV adverts. Many are film-school-trained directors, such as Anna Muylaert, Beto Brant, Laiz Bodansky and Jefferson De, graduates of the University of São Paulo's prestigious School of Communication and Arts who have made a number of bigger-budget feature films, as well as current students and recent graduates who take advantage of the raft of *editais* (funding calls) from a variety of sources to make smaller-budget documentary shorts, for example. Despite the opening-up of higher education to underrepresented groups in the twenty-first century as a result of affirmative action initiatives, filmmakers emerging through the film school route (as well as those trained in TV and publicity) continue to be predominantly white and middle-class, and still mostly males.

Thus, while the *retomada* undoubtedly ushered in a period of renewal in the Brazilian film industry, we have to look elsewhere to find widening participation projects that shifted the demographics towards something more representative of the Brazilian population. I discuss progress made towards increasing the participation of women, Afro-Brazilians and indigenous populations in proceeding chapters in this monograph. In Chapter 6 I consider, for example, films produced by the high-profile widening participation initiative Vídeo nas Aldeias (Video in the Villages), which since 1986 has been training indigenous peoples to use film to document their history, daily lives and tribulations. There is little doubt that both Vídeo nas Aldeias and the favela-based Cinema Nosso organisation, discussed in Chapter 5, have been very influential in the approach adopted to widening access to filmmaking, facilitated in the twenty-first century with the gradual ease of access to cheaper, lightweight and easy-to-use digital filming and editing equipment. New technologies, and in particular an openness to exploring the potential of smart phones and cheaper cameras to make films has led to many NGOS and social organisations encouraging engagement and consciousness-raising via competitions, "one-minute film festivals" and short workshops on the basics of filmmaking and editing. Millions of videos have been uploaded to sites such as YouTube by Brazilians in the twenty-first century, including those that seek to denounce crime, injustice or simply sound off about corruption and the political direction the country is taking.[15]

Alternative filmmaking and distribution initiatives: Cinema de Garagem and Cinema de Bordas

Around 2005 onwards a very low-budget alternative filmmaking practice was identified as emerging in different regions of the country and given a moniker by an academic researcher (Marcelo Ikeda of the Federal University of Ceará), who dubbed the films *Cinema de Garagem*, or Garage Cinema.[16] According to Ikeda (2018: 460), Garage Cinema emerged precisely because of, on the one hand, the difficulty for a budding filmmaker to fund feature-length films, and on the other the greater ease of purchasing and using digital technology from mid-1990s onwards. The alternative circuits for screening the Garage films emerged because while nowadays 100% of film theatres are equipped to screen in digital format, it was until very recently difficult to screen anything other than 35 mm in film theatres in Brazil.[17] Garage Cinema, like the phenomenon of the garage band after which it is named, implies a very low-budget co-operative approach to filmmaking and viewing among friends (almost always male) with dreams of success and recognition for their work. Ikeda cites Alumbramento (Ceará), Símio filmes (Pernambuco) and Filmes de Plástico (Minas Gerais) as important co-operatives working within

FIGURE 1.2 The four actor-directors in a still from the trailer for *Estrada para Ythaca*

(*Road to Ythaca*, Guto Parente, Ricardo Pretti, Pedro Diógenes, Luiz Pretti, 2010)

the Cinema de Garagem dynamic. Alumbramento were responsible for *Estrada para Ythaca* (*Road to Ythaca*, 2010),[18] the most commercially successful and the most discussed of the Garage films to date. As well as winning awards at the Tiradentes Film Festival, and screening in festivals in Buenos Aires and Vienna, it gained a limited theatrical release at home, as well as attention from critics and scholars.[19] The Filmes de Plástico co-operative took part in the 2018 edition of the Boutique Cinema do Brasil (see Chapter 2). The feature films of co-operative member André Novais Oliveira, *Ela volta na quinta* (*She Comes Back on Thursday*, 2015) and *Temporada* (*Long Way Home*, 2018) have consolidated his reputation as one of the most important directors of *cinema negro* (see Chapter 5), while Gabriel Martins and Murilo Martins's *No coração do mundo* (*In the Heart of the World*) has been selected for the Bright Future strand of the 2019 Rotterdam Film Festival.

Ikeda (2018: 469) draws a distinction between the Cinema de Garagem and the so-called Cinema de Bordas, which he dismisses as "amateur" and lacking the aesthetic, ethical and political concerns of the former. Cinema de Bordas, which roughly translates as Border Cinema, is the name given to an *artisanal* or "home-made" filmmaking style involving filmmakers far removed from the centres of film production in terms of their origins, tastes and resources, which emerged in the late 1990s and found an audience beyond the traditional exhibition landscape of the multiplex, arthouse cinema and festivals, proving to be particularly popular in the home towns of the filmmakers (Lyra 2013: 31; Cánepa 2018)

The phenomenon was introduced to a wider public by researchers at the Anhembi Morumbi university in São Paulo, and in particular by Bernadette Lyra and Gelson Santana. According to Laura Cánepa (2018), after publishing two volumes of essays on the films which they dubbed *Cinema de Bordas*, and after a successful screening of a number of the films at Anhembi Morumbi, the influential Itaú Cultural Institute in São Paulo took interest, and hosted six mini-festivals between 2009 and 2015. Running over the course of five days, the mini-festivals attracted an impressive average audience of 800 viewers. Further screenings under the Cinema de Bordas rubric took place during this period in the cities of Vitória, Belo Horizonte and Juiz de Fora. The best-known filmmaker of the Cinema de Bordas group is the late Simião Martiniano, the self-styled *cineasta-camelô* (cineaste-street vendor) from the north-eastern state of Alagoas but based most of this working life in Recife, the capital of Pernambuco. His life and filmmaking is the subject of a documentary by Hilton Lacerda and Clara Angélica: *Simião Martiniano: O camelô do cinema* (Simião Martiniano: Cinema's Street-trader, 1998). He is often characterised as the Ed Wood of the north-east, given the large number of films he made (an impressive nine feature films) on Super 8, VHS and most recently on digital cameras, and their questionable quality. It is one of his older films, *O vagabundo faixa-preta* (The Black Belt Vagabond) of 1992 that is his best-known: it screened at Itaú Cultural as part of one of the *Cinema de Bordas* retrospectives.

Cinema de Bordas is an interesting case of films made in relative isolation and then grouped together and marketed by academics in the first instance. It points to the good working relationships that film studies scholars have built up with both private and public cultural institutes in Brazil such as Itaú Cultural, to the point of being able to contribute to audience-formation, on a small but still significant scale. Cánepa (2018) defines the *Cinema de Bordas* moment as being a typical Lula-era phenomenon, in the sense that it was an expression of the principles of inclusion driving cultural policy at the time. Not only were the filmmakers predominantly self-taught and from beyond the principal centres of cultural production such as Rio de Janeiro, São Paulo and other state capitals, but the festivals themselves were accompanied by "zero resource" filmmaking workshops.[20] It also reflected a renewed interest both in cult cinema and in ironic viewing practices (the poor quality of the films is frequently celebrated by viewers).

What might also explain the success of *Cinema de Bordas*, and its corporate sponsorship, is the extent to which it could be seen to represent a palatable expression of "the popular" within the filmmaking landscape. Even if the films were dismissed as poor-quality, and even if they frequently displayed ideologically suspect representations of gender, they were infinitely more digestible for the middle-class, educated audiences that would have attended screenings at the Itaú Cultural Institute than the popular (as in commercially successful) *globochanchadas* discussed in Chapter 2.

Notes

1 For more information on these cycles, see Shaw and Dennison (2007).
2 Further Oscar nominations were secured by Bruno Barreto's *O que e isso companheiro?* (*Four Days in September*, 1996), Walter Salles's *Central do Brasil* (*Central Station*, 1998) and Fernando Meirelles and Kátia Lund's *Cidade de Deus* (*City of God*). See Figueiró (2018a).

3　Marcelo Ikeda (2015: 227) describes the value of the award as negligible.

4　It is worth noting that most of the funding available for audio-visual projects supported by Funcultura (and other similar regional initiatives) comes from the FSA.

5　The last Brazilian film to make the official selection was Walter Salles's *Linha de Passe* (2008), while two co-productions made with minority Brazilian funding but directed by Brazilians, Fernando Meirelles's *Blindness* (2008) and Walter Salles's *On The Road* (2012) also premiered at Cannes in the years of their release. As we go to press (April 2019) Kleber Mendonça Filho's *Bacurau* has been selected for this year's official competition.

6　As we go to press (April 2019) the Rouanet Law has been tellingly rebranded the Law of Cultural Incentive.

7　Ironically, the right-wing sensationalist columnist Reinaldo de Azevedo, writing in 2007, referred to typically left-wing Brazilian films as conforming to a "Petrobras aesthetic".

8　Ikeda (2012) highlights that Article 3 is modelled on a mechanism that existed in Brazil in the 1960s and produced such memorable films as Joaquim Pedro de Andrade's late *cinema novo* film *Macunaíma* (1969).

9　For more detailed explorations of funding and its attendant polemics, see Ikeda (2015), Johnson (2005) and Trindade (2014).

10　*Ao sul de setembro*, directed by Amauri Tangará sold 59 tickets in cinemas in 2005 (Ballerini 2012: 239).

11　The audio-visual industry employs a workforce of 98,000, generating 25 billion reals (Festival de Gramado 2018).

12　A number of records have been broken by Felipe Neto, a Youtuber with 29 million subscribers.

13　CineBrasil Já is a platform set up by the cable TV channel CineBrasilTV, which repeats some TV content and brings some films and exclusive series to VOD. Spcine Play is a platform that is completely VOD, linked to a public institution (Spcine) and which only streams Brazilian films (Figueiró 2018c).

14　For more information see Dennison (2016).

15　These include, of course, films that unashamedly distort facts or simply present fake news with a view to manipulating unsuspecting viewers. Much has been made, for example, of the dissemination of fake news stories via social media on the run-up to the presidential elections of 2018. The production, funding and impact of such material merits a detailed study in the context of film culture, given that these are arguably the most viewed moving images of the contemporary period in Brazil.

16　Cezar Migliorin (2011) has referred to these films as *cinema pós-industrial* (Post-industrial cinema).

17　Ikeda (2018: 463) argues that at this time Garage cinema helped breathe new life into Brazil's *cineclube* or film club scene.

18　Alumbramento is a collective made up of cousins Pedro Diogenes and Guto Parente, and brothers Luiz and Ricardo Pretti, all of whom directed, wrote and starred in the film.

19　As well as Ikeda's work, see Lopes Silva (2013).

20　These were delivered by Recurso Zero Produções, a zero-resource production company run by Mariana Zani and Joel Caetano. Caetano's own films regularly featured in the *Cinema de Bordas* festivals.

References

Alessi, G., and Moraes, C. 2016. "Casamento de luxo pago via Lei Rouanet coloca legislação de novo na berlinda". *El país Brasil*. 28 June. https://brasil.elpais.com/brasil/2016/06/28/politica/1467133151_422166.html.

Ancine. 2018a. "Ancine apresenta estudo sobre diversidade de gênero e raça no mercado audiovisual". Ancine website. 25 January. www.ancine.gov.br/pt-br/sala-imprensa/noticias/ancine-apresenta-estudo-sobre-diversidade-de-g-nero-e-ra-no-mercado.

Ancine. 2018b. *Anuário estatístico do cinema brasileiro 2017* https://oca.ancine.gov.br/sites/default/files/repositorio/pdf/anuario_2017.pdf.

Araújo, I. 2018. "Festival de Brasília começa em meio a desinteresse do público por cinema nacional". *Folha de S. Paulo*. 13 September. www1.folha.uol.com.br/ilustrada/2018/09/festival-de-brasilia-comeca-em-meio-ao-desinteresse-do-publico-por-cinema-nacional.shtml.

Azevedo, R. 2007. "As bobagens de um dos roteiristas de *Tropa de Elite* e a Estética da Petrobras". *Veja*. 20 October. https://veja.abril.com.br/blog/reinaldo/as-bobagens-de-um-dos-roteiristas-de-tropa-de-elite-e-a-estetica-da-petrobras/.

Balleirini, F. 2012. *Cinema brasileiro no seculo 21*. São Paulo: Summus Editorial.

Barros, I. 2017. "Audiovisual puxa aumento no valor do Funcultura, que terá R$ 47 milhões em 2017/2018", *Diário de Pernambuco*. 29 December. www.diariodepernambuco.com.br/app/noticia/viver/2017/12/29/internas_viver,736348/audiovisual-puxa-aumento-no-valor-do-funcultura-que-tera-r-47-milhoe.shtml.

Brasil Econômico. 2018. "69% dos brasileiros já têm acesso à internet pelo celular, afirma IBGE" *IG*. 27 April. https://tecnologia.ig.com.br/2018-04-27/acesso-a-internet.html.

Cánepa, L. 2018. Email interview with the author. October.

Conde, M. and Dennison, S. (eds) 2018. *Paulo Emílio Salles Gomes: On Brazil and Global Cinema*. Cardiff: University of Wales Press.

Da Paz, J. 2018. "Com 7,5 milhões de assinantes, Brasil é campeão de séries não-inglesas na Netflix". *Notícias da TV*. 30 May. https://noticiasdatv.uol.com.br/noticia/series/com-75-milhoes-de-assinantes-brasil-e-campeao-de-series-nao-inglesas-na-netflix-20698?cpid=txt.

Dennison, S. 2016. "Latin America's Foremost Documentary Film Festival: É Tudo Verdade (It's All True)". *Mediatico*. 13 June. http://reframe.sussex.ac.uk/mediatico/2016/06/13/latin-americas-foremost-documentary-film-festival-e-tudo-verdade-its-all-true-by-stephanie-dennison/.

Domingos de Lima, J. 2017. "O que a retirada de filmes do Cine PE diz sobre cinema e política no Brasil de hoje". *Nexo Jornal*. 13 May. www.nexojornal.com.br/expresso/2017/05/13/O-que-a-retirada-de-filmes-do-Cine-PE-diz-sobre-cinema-e-pol%C3%ADtica-no-Brasil-de-hoje.

Engler, N. 2017. "Filme que vende 4.000 ingressos? O buraco do cinema nacional é mais embaixo". *Bol Noticias*. 27 October. http://noticias.bol.uol.com.br/ultimas-noticias/entretenimento/2017/10/27/filme-de-4000-ingressos-o-buraco-do-cinema-nacional-e-mais-embaixo.htm.

Falicov, T. 2013. "Ibero-Latin American Co-productions: Transnational Cinema, Spain's Public Relations Venture or Both?" in Dennison, S. (ed), *Contemporary Hispanic Cinema: Interrogating the Transnational in Spanish and Latin American Film*. Woodbridge: Tamesis, pp. 67–88.

Festival de Gramado. 2018. "PIB do audio-visual supera o da indústria farmacéutica no Brasil". Festival Website. www.festivaldegramado.net/pib-do-audiovisual-supera-o-da-industria-farmaceutica-no-brasil/.

Figueiró, B. 2018a. *Coprodução de cinema com a França: mercado e internacionalização*. São Paulo: Editora Senac.

Figueiró, B. 2018b. "Os entraves do VOD no Brasil". *Revista de cinema* 134 (April).

Figueiró, B. 2018c. Email interview with the author. December.

Figueiroa, A. 2014. "Cine PE mudou, mas continuou o mesmo", *Revista OGrito!* 29 April. http://revistaogrito.com/artigo-cine-pe-mudou-mas-continuou-o-mesmo/.

Filme B. 2018. "Estatísticas" www.filmeb.com.br/estatisticas.

Globo.2016."MarceloCalerocriticaprotestodeartistasemCannes".*Oglobo*,6June.http://oglobo. globo.com/cultura/marcelo-calero-critica-protesto-de-artistas-em-cannes-19447318

Harbord, J. 2002. *Film Cultures*. London: Sage.

Heffner, H. 2000. "Salas de cinema". In Ramos F. and Miranda L. F. (eds) *Enciclopédia do cinema brasileiro*. São Paulo: Senac, pp. 480–488.

Ikeda, M. 2012. "O art. 3° da lei do audiovisual e as políticas públicas para o setor audiovisual na 'retomada'". Anais do I Encontro Internacional de Direitos Culturais – I EIDC (Fortaleza/Unifor). September. www.direitosculturais.com.br/ojs/index.php/articles/article/view/31/89.

Ikeda, M. 2015. *Cinema brasileiro a partir da retomada: aspectos econômcios e politicos*. São Paulo: Summus Editorial.

Ikeda, M. 2018. "O 'cinema de garagem', provisoriamente: notas sobre o contexto de renovação do cinema brasileiro a partir da virada do século". *Revista Aniki* 5:2, pp. 457–479.

JC Online. 2017. "Cine PE é suspensa após polêmica". *Jornal do Comércio*. 11 May. https://jconline.ne10.uol.com.br/canal/cultura/cinema/noticia/2017/05/11/cine-pe-e-suspenso-apos-polemica-282988.php

Johnson, R. 2005. "TV Globo, the MPA and Contemporary Brazilian Cinema". In Shaw, L. and Dennison, S. (eds), *Latin American Cinema: Essays on Modernity, Gender and National Identity*. Jefferson (NC): MacFarland, pp. 11–38.

Lopes Silva, D. 2013. "O Alumbramento e o fracasso: uma leitura de Estrada para Ythaca" *Revista Galáxia* no. 26, pp. 72–83. https://revistas.pucsp.br/index.php/galaxia/article/view/12525.

Lyra, B. 2013. "Cultural Crossover: Cinema de Bordas in Brazil". In Pinazza, N. And Bayman, L. (eds), *Directory of World Cinema: Brazil*. Bristol: Intellect, pp. 29–31. Trans. Natália Pinazza.

Marcolin N. 2014. "Jean-Claude Bernardet: um critico contra a estética da miséria". *Revista pesquisa*. October. http://revistapesquisa.fapesp.br/2014/10/09/jean-claude- bernardet-um-critico-contra-estetica-da-miseria/.

Meleiro, A. 2013. "Finance and Co-productions in Brazil". In Dennison, S. (ed), Contemporary Hispanic Cienma: Interrogating the Transnational in Spanish and Latin American Film Woodbrige: Tamesis, pp. 181–204.

Migliorin, C. 2011. "Por um cinema pós-industrial: notas para um debate". *Revista Cinética*. February. www.revistacinetica.com.br/cinemaposindustrial.htm.

Moraes, C. 2016. Lei Rouanet explicada: como funciona, quais as vantagens e quais as críticas" *El país Brasil*. 29 June. https://brasil.elpais.com/brasil/2016/06/29/cultura/1467151863_473583.html.

Moraes, F. 2018. "Em 2018, Brasil tem número recorde de salas de cinema em funcionamento". *Metropoles*. 14 May. www.metropoles.com/entretenimento/cinema/em-2018-brasil-tem-numero-recorde-de-salas-de-cinema-em-funcionamento.

Nagib, L. 2003. "Introduction". In Nagib, L. (ed), *The New Brazilian Cinema* London and New York: IB Tauris, pp. xvii–xxvi.

Peron, I. and Martins L. 2018. "Ministério da Cultura diz que Roger Waters não usou Lei Rouanet". *Valor Econômico*. 22 November. www.valor.com.br/politica/5994849/ministerio-da-cultura-diz-que-roger-waters-nao-usou-lei-rouanet.

Pinheiro, A. 2018. "Como mudar os números?" *Revista de cinema* 134 (April), pp. 34–38.

Rêgo, C. 2011. "The Fall and Rise of Brazilian Cinema". In Rêgo, C. and Rocha, C. (eds), *New Trends in Argentine and Brazilian Cinema*. Bristol: Intellect, pp. 35–49.

Rufino, L. 2018. "Filmes brasileiros: causa e efeito. O cenário em 2018 e as perspectivas para 2019". Ancine website. www.ancine.gov.br/sites/default/files/apresentacoes/Apresentac%CC%A7a%CC%83o%20Luana_RioMarket_Filmes%20Brasileiros%20%28004%29.pdf.

Schvarzman, S. 2018. "Cinema brasileiro de grande bilheteria (2000–2016)". In Ramos, F. P. and Schvarzman, S. (eds) *Nova história do cinema brasileiro* Vol 2. São Paulo: SESC, pp. 514–565.

Shaw, L. and Dennison, S. 2007. *Brazilian National Cinema*. London and New York: Routledge.

Sousa, A. P. 2018. "Christian de Castro: o solucionador". *Revista de Cinema* 134 (April), pp. 30–33.

Tendências Consultoria. 2016. *O impacto econômico do setor audiovisual brasileiro*. www.icabrasil.org/2016/files/557-corporateTwo/downloads/LOW_ESTUDO_MPAAL_21x30_06-06-16.pdf.

Trindade, T. N. 2014. *Documentário e Mercado no Brasil: da produção à sala de cinema*. São Paulo: Alameda.

2

ENGAGING WITH AUDIENCES AT HOME AND ABROAD

In Chapter 1 I provided a contextualisation for contemporary film culture in Brazil, looking at key elements of film policy and highlighting a number of issues relating to making, exhibiting and viewing films. While the picture presented was ostensibly one of relatively healthy statistics in terms of Brazilian films beings produced and viewed in the second decade of the twenty-first century, I now want to look in more detail at the films that are engaging with both domestic and international audiences, with a focus on some of the caveats hinted at in relation to these supposedly healthy statistics. The chapter is divided into two parts: part one examines two phenomena connected to box-office success in the domestic film market: popular comedies and films aimed at particular religious groups. The second part focuses on the performance of Brazilian films on the global film circuit, and in particular the film festival circuit.

Section 1: Twenty-first-century box office phenomena

"The Cinema that Speaks Your Language": Globo Filmes and popular comedies

Globochanchadas are light comedies that have dominated national film production and the box offices in Brazil in the twenty-first century. The term, first coined by filmmaker Guilherme de Almeida Prado and increasingly used in both critical and academic circles (Couto 2017; Gregoli 2017; Ribeiro 2016; Schvarzman 2018), if not by the wider cinema-going public, refers to quite a specific set of values afforded the films in relation to their mode of production, style and critical reception, as elaborated below.

The term incorporates the prefix *globo* in reference to one of the world's largest media conglomerates, based in Rio de Janeiro and famed outside of Brazil for its production of internationally best-selling *telenovelas* or soap operas. It was only in 1998 that Organizações Globo set up a film branch (Globo Filmes). This move was timed to take advantage of revisions to how films were being funded and opportunities to screen domestically produced films, through a gradual increase in screens at multiplexes, a growing DVD market and cable TV. Globo Filmes since 1998 has very much strengthened its stake in the Brazilian film industry. From 2000 to 2017, of the ten most successful Brazilian films in box-office terms, nine had some kind of participation from Globo Filmes. And eight of these ten are what can be termed *globochanchadas*.

Secondly, there is the referent chanchadas: the chanchadas were carnival-themed and later parodic comedies of the 1930s, 40s and 50s.[1] In a book published in 2004 entitled *Popular Cinema in Brazil* Lisa Shaw and I sought to demonstrate, inspired by the work on popular culture of William Rowe and Vivian Schelling (1991), that a clear line could be traced from popular home-grown cultural practices such as carnival, the *teatro de revista* or popular music-hall, travelling circus performances (the *circos mambembes*) and the radio, to the hugely popular chanchada tradition with their star comic performers, familiar and often Manichean storylines, archetypal characters, carnivalesque inversions, mistaken identities, irreverence coupled with overtly conservative happy endings, and so on. The chanchadas started off as vehicles to promote particular carnival tunes, such as the popular films starring a pre-Hollywood Carmen Miranda in the 1930s, but eventually the musical dimension ceased to take centre stage and was in many cases absent, and they became more parodic.[2] At the time these films were dismissed as derivative and offensive to elite tastes by drawing attention to, in the case of the blockbuster parodies, the production limitations of the Brazilian version in comparison with the US original. However, Shaw and I have argued (2004; 2007) that many of the later chanchadas provided fascinating snapshots of social life in Brazil at the time: these were films that reached out to migrant populations that were coming from the rural areas of the interior to the cities of the coast, and the chanchadas bore witness to the many challenges of life in the city, for example. We have also argued that, rather than present a flawed and therefore culturally failed version of the nation in their attempts to match big-budget Hollywood hits, the chanchadas parodied Hollywood paradigms and critiqued Hollywood's domination of the Brazilian box-office.

The chanchada films were widely disparaged and largely omitted from the Brazilian film canon, at least until Paulo Emílio Salles Gomes (in Conde and Dennison 2018), and later Robert Stam and João Luiz Vieira (1985), underlined their importance for understanding both audience taste and the socio-political context of urban Brazil in the first half of the twentieth century. A similar process took place in relation to the *pornochanchada*, the soft-core version of the genre which emerged in the late 1960s until the legalisation of screening hardcore porn in specialist theatres in the early 1980s. These were Brazil's "quota-quickies", equally disparaged by critics, in this case for their associations with the dictatorship.[3] A number of *pornochanchadas* with higher-than-usual production values found their way onto Globo's cable channel Canal Brasil, set up in 1998 to screen Brazilian films (and increasingly other domestically-produced audio-visual content), thus helping to foster a nostalgic revision of the sub-genre, whereby the ideologically suspect elements of the films were elided in virtue of their perceived transgressive nature for the times.[4] Recently, Fernanda Pessoa's documentary *Histórias que nosso cinema não contava* (*Stories our Cinema Never Told Us*) received a theatrical release in Brazil (in August 2018) and some discussion in the press and social media. Pessoa's film, whose title is a play on words of another *pornochanchada* title, *Histórias que nossas babás não contavam* (*Stories our Nannies Never Told Us*, Oswaldo de Oliveira, 1979), focuses on revealing the socio-political comment, and particularly on the context of dictatorship, contained in the *pornochanchadas*. There is a whole chapter dedicated to exploring the *pornochanchadas* in Ramos and Schvarzman's updated film history collection *Nova história do cinema brasileiro* (Gamo and Rocha Melo 2018), which in part discusses the low-budget, independent nature of production, and the *pornochanchada's* links with radical filmmakers associated with São Paulo's Boca do Lixo.

To date it has proved much more difficult to make the case for the cultural importance of *globochanchadas*.[5] On the release of *De pernas pro ar II* (*Head Over Heels II*, 2012) consecrated academic and film critic Jean-Claude Bernardet drew a parallel between contemporary comedies and the chanchadas, and warned against dismissing them, as critics had done with the chanchadas in the 1950s (Arthuso, 2013). His post prompted a brief flurry of reactions: more perceptive observers drew attention to both the high-quality production values and mode of production of the contemporary comedies, which they argued made them distinct from the chanchadas and worthy on those grounds alone of being dismissed by critics.[6]

It is not only the *globochanchadas'* bigger budgets and commercial success that trouble critics and scholars,[7] but also their close links to the medium of television. As Eduardo Valente argued succinctly as early as 2003, the films represent:

> an uncomfortable inheritance of an exclusionary elitist pedantry, which is part of a much more grotesque tradition within national thought, according to which everything that comes from an eminently popular tradition, or that is digested by a decent portion of the population with lower incomes and less formal education, cannot have cultural value in its own right. At best, it serves as an exotic product that can be studied sociologically, or accepted when it is absorbed as an influence by an educated "exponent" from within artistic circles […] Since TV reaches from Class A to Class E (and this classification is itself pretentious), it cannot be producing anything of interest to us. Meanwhile cinema, increasingly restricted to Classes A and B (and often only A), is a noble example of extreme cultural value.

Ten years later, film-critic-turned-director Kleber Mendonça Filho, at the time of the release of his first feature-length film *O som ao redor* (*Neighbouring Sounds*

2013), baited Cadu Rodrigues, the then Executive Director of Globo Filmes, in the press on the quality of Globo's film production. Mendonça Filho had commented in an interview with the *Folha de S. Paulo* newspaper:

> They [Globo films] are films made with loads of money and released with loads of money. They spend 6 million reals but it looks like they only spent 800,000 because they use two apartments, four Globo actors, one dog and one cat. I bet that if my neighbour were to release a copy of the video of his BBQ following the Globo Filmes scheme, he'd get 200,000 spectators in the opening weekend.
>
> *(Araújo 2013)*

In response, Cadu Rodrigues challenged the filmmaker to make a film with the full support of Globo Filmes and if it reached an audience of 200,000 he would not charge for Globo's services (Araújo 2013). Mendonça Filho's perhaps predictable rejoinder was to reject taking up the gauntlet thrown down and to state that there were many more important considerations when it came to making films than simple box-office returns (Araújo 2013). The irony here is Globo Filmes is a named producer of Mendonça Filho's follow-up feature film, the internationally critically acclaimed *Aquarius* (2016), discussed in Chapter 10, which reached 300,000 viewers in cinemas.

This polemic requires some further contextualisation. Globo Filmes produces, or has some participation[8] in a very large number of contemporary films, and not just those that break box-office records or are categorised as popular comedies. Many are what could be described as being positioned at the more convention-ally narrated end of non-commercial film production (i.e. those that gain a limited theatrical release): the kind of films that, unlike the *globochanchadas*, receive posi-tive reviews and often screen at film festivals at home and abroad. Films such as the aforementioned *Aquarius*, *Ferrugem* (*Rust*, Aly Muritiba, 2018), which won top prize at the Gramado Film Festival in 2018, Anna Muylaert's widely debated *Que horas ela volta?* (*The Second Mother*, 2015), discussed in Chapter 3, as well as the smash hit and critically acclaimed *Tropa de Elite 2: o inimigo agora é outro* (*Elite Squad II: The Enemy Within*, 2010), discussed in detail in Chapter 8 of this monograph. Eduardo Valente (2003) has suggested a motive for Globo Filmes's involvement in productions less likely to bring good returns at the box-office: that a relatively small financial investment on Globo Filmes' part can translate into cultural capital of the kind that Globo has been deprived of, as a result of the suspicions of televi-sion and its viewers that Valente alludes to above. In turn, filmmakers stand to gain exposure via advertising or even screening of their films on TV. For example, one can argue that Globo Filmes' involvement in *Que horas ela volta?* led to its prime-time screening on TV Globo, enabling it to reach millions of viewers and thus continue important discussions amongst the public about class and social change.

These are not, then, the films that Mendonça Filho was referring to in his cri-tique of Globo Filmes. Hence the need for a term that describes the films that trouble a large part of Brazil's filmmaking class. In my typology I broaden out the definition of *globochanchadas* from just those popular comedies co-produced by or with some kind of significant participation from Globo Filmes to include blockbuster comedies produced by three key production and distribution companies: Downtown Filmes, Paris Filmes and Total Filmes (aka Total Entertainment). I date the phenomenon from 2003 onwards. In 2003 Brazilian films achieved a 21.4% share of the market (Ikeda 2015: 79). It is also the year that Article 3 of the Audiovisual Law was adjusted whereby the Majors were encouraged to co-produce or distribute Brazilian films in return for a reduced tax bill (see Chapter 1). That same year Globo Filmes co-produced seven films using Article 3 that attracted audiences of more than one million (Ikeda 2015: 89).

The first films that date from this time were very much driven by what viewers were responding well to on the different Globo TV channels (terrestrial and satellite/cable subscription channels). *Os normais: o filme (So normal)*, 2003, based on a popular comedy series on Globo TV, produced by Globo Filmes, and with over three million tickets sold, is often cited as the first in this new trend. An essential feature of this new trend, then, is to be a blockbuster (recognised in the Brazilian context as a film that sells more than one million tickets). Most of the films are part of a series (*Os normais II* was released in 2009), usually with a more successful sequel. In this they tap into a tradition of viewers returning to the cinema to see the same familiar characters in action which was popularised, for example, in the hugely successful Jeca series of films released from 1953 to 1980 starring comedian Amácio Mazzaropi, or the large number of films starring the TV quartet the Trapalhões (1965 to the present), or even those starring TV host Xuxa (1988–2009).[9] Together with the chanchadas, *pornochanchadas* and later hard-core porn, these films dominated Brazilian box-offices in the second half of the twentieth century. The earliest notable example of this blockbuster "mini-franchise" phenomenon is *Se eu fosse você* (If I Were You, 2006 and 2009, with the third instalment in pre-production in 2018), a comedy series directed by Daniel Filho, co-produced by Total Entertainment and Globo Filmes and starring stalwart Globo actors Tony Ramos and Glória Pires, based around a battle of the sexes/body-swap storyline and sharing many comedic features in common with the chanchada tradition.

While it is true that a number of the successful *globochanchada* mini-franchises are filmed versions of successful Globo TV series, as indicated with the words "o filme" (the film) appearing in titles,[10] not all such adaptations are successful, and not all franchises can (or should) be dismissed as lazy transmedial outputs. A number of *globochanchadas* indicate a move on the part of producers towards searching out different types of comedy: this is particularly noticeable in the influence of popular theatre on contemporary film screens. Some of the films are based on plays that have performed well, with the most successful franchise to date, the *Minha mãe é uma peça* series, being based on a popular monologue of the same name performed by its creator, Paulo Gustavo.[11] Others seek to tap into the twenty-first-century fascination with new therapies and digital technology, and in particular the points at which these intersect with changes in the status of women, and with the increase

FIGURE 2.1 Tony Ramos and Glória Pires in a still from *Se eu fosse você*
(*If I Were You*, Daniel Filho, 2006)

in consumer power of the growing middle class. These include *Divã I* and *II* (*In Therapy*, 2009 and 2015) and *Cilada.com I* and *II* (*Trap.com*, 2011 and 2013). Notwithstanding this evidence of researching new sources of comedy for adaptation to the big screen, Sheila Schvarzman (2018: 529–530) points to their tried-and-tested aesthetic taken straight from Globo TV.

As was the case of the chanchadas and *pornochanchadas*, a star system of sorts can be identified within the *globochanchada* phenomenon. As well as drawing from Globo's own TV star system,[12] such as the aforementioned case of the *Se eu fosse você* "franchise" and the use of popular veteran Globo soap stars Tony Ramos and Glória Pires, a number of younger stars, all with ties to Globo, and especially Globo's subscription channels (Schvarzman 2018: 521) but also frequently associated with internet comedy such as the critically acclaimed *Porta dos Fundos* series, have successfully translated to the big screen via *globochanchadas*. These stars include Fábio Porchat of *Porta dos Fundos* fame, who has appeared in *Vai que dá certo I* and *II* (*We'll Work it Out I and II*, 2013 and 2016) and *Meu passado me condena I* and *II* (*My Past Condemns Me* 2013 and 2015). What is striking, given that the field of comedy is still very much dominated in Brazil by male performers, is that one of the *globochanchada's* most successful stars is a woman: Ingrid Guimarães, protagonist of the *De pernas pro ar* film series (*Head Over Heels I* and *II*, 2010 and 2012), among numerous other popular comedies.

In the film series Guimarães plays Alice, a married business woman and mother who as a result of finding it difficult to juggle her professional and home life, ends up losing both her job and her husband, and taking over a bankrupt sex shop with her best friend. Cue, then, a series of saucy sex-based jokes, such as when Alice gets stuck in a lift wearing a strap-on, that are reminiscent of the baser aspects of the *pornochanchadas* and in particular their focus on the grotesque. Despite a seemingly modern exploration of women's sexuality, Alice ends the second instalment of the franchise unexpectedly pregnant by her husband (and thus forced back into the home).

This short synopsis signals another difficulty in trying to remap or re-evaluate *globochanchadas*. The films habitually frustrate cultural observers for their perceived endorsement of the social status quo at a time of real desire for change being expressed in a number of sectors, whether those were in tandem with PT (Workers Party) government policies of equality and inclusion pre-impeachment, or as a challenge to Michel Temer's perceived mission to undo such policies post-impeachment. The scant academic material based on close readings of *globochanchadas* (Gregoli 2017; Marsh 2017; Schvarzman 2018)[13] has focused on the women-centred comedy films (*De pernas pro ar* and two films based on cruise liners: *Meu passado me condena: o filme* [2013] and *SOS mulheres ao mar* [*Women Overboard*, 2014]), and while celebrating the extent to which the films demonstrate the inroads made by women into blockbuster filmmaking in the contemporary period (the films star women in key roles and the latter two films were directed by women),[14] this material has highlighted the ultimately conservative nature of the representation of women and gender relations in the films. These films confirm a vision of the world predicated on heteronormative affective relationships and the impossibility of women finding personal fulfilment outside the space of the family.

The most successful *globochanchada* to date is *Minha mãe é uma peça 2* (*My Mother is a Character II*, 2016), with viewing figures reaching over nine million, nearly double the already very successful first outing of the film series, outperforming *Fast and Furious 8* in Brazil, and thus mirroring the kind of success enjoyed by the chanchadas at the height of their popularity. In the films comedy performer Paulo Gustavo plays Dona Hermínia, a sharp-tongued middle-aged divorcée struggling to come to terms with the fact that her children are growing up fast. Like the *Se*

FIGURE 2.2 Ingrid Guimarães in a still from the trailer for *De pernas pro ar* (*Head Over Heels*, Roberto Santucci, 2010)

eu fosse você franchise, we have in the films an example of the carnivalesque element of cross-dressing that is hugely popular in Brazilian culture, from carnival, through the *teatro de revista* and *chanchada* to drag acts and *travestis* (trans women) such as the popular recording artist Pabllo Vittar. It is also worth acknowledging the impressive comic timing of both Gustavo and his supporting cast and Gustavo's drag perform-ance is undeniably charming and beautifully crafted. The series also illustrates the attraction of these kinds of comedy films that is encapsulated in Globo Filmes's slogan: "o cinema que fala sua língua" (the cinema that speaks your language).[15] Rather than focusing on slapstick or amusing situations, much of the comedy in *Minha mãe é uma peça* is predicated on family banter: still witty but often rude and disparaging repartee that characterises much humour in our daily lives. The "behind-closed-doors" nature of the private family unit (the funniest sequences are those shot in the family's apartment) serves as a license for Dona Hermínia to poke fun in ways deemed politically incorrect in the public sphere, such as at her "immensely fat" teenage daughter, ultra-camp son and maid who dares to get above her station. Both films make clear the source text for the Hermínia character: Paulo Gustavo's real-life mouthy but endearing mother Dona Déa (the origin of the title of the films and the monologue on which they are based), as video footage of her appears at the end of each film. Again, this celebration of an anti-intellectual wit and way of speaking of "common" people lay at the heart of the *chanchadas*, announced already in the titles of many of the films.[16]

Gustavo's Dona Hermínia is, above all, a safe performance for his audience, leaving little room for transgression and lampooning of the kind one associates

FIGURE 2.3 Paulo Gustavo cross-dresses in a still from the trailer for *Minha mãe é uma peça*

(*My Mother is a Character*, Andre Pellenz, 2013)

with the grand drag performances of popular cinema (Jack Lemmon in *Some Like it Hot* [Billy Wilder, 1959], or chanchada star Oscarito in *Aviso aos navegantes* [*Calling All Sailors*, Watson Macedo, 1950], for example), or of reflections on gender and identity as witnessed in the performances of Pabllo Vittar, for example, or of trans actress and performer Linn da Quebrada, as discussed in Chapter 4. In terms of his star text, Gustavo goes to great lengths to disassociate himself from a more militant brand of drag performance: he embodies the discreet and therefore "inoffensive" gay man, with conservative views on identity politics, such as questioning the need for Gay Pride parades. And unlike other stars such as Guimarães and Porchat, he was careful not to risk alienating large sectors of his fan base by using social media to criticise the politically reactionary turn in Brazil.[17]

It is worth noting that in the first instalment of the film series, Dona Hermínia's nemesis, her ex-husband's glamorous but decidedly nasty new girlfriend Soraia, is played by Ingrid Guimarães. One could argue, then, that *Minha mãe é uma peça* destroys the myth of the quirky but loveable modern woman as played by Guimarães in films such as *De pernas pro ar*, to endorse instead the stereotypical old-fashioned mother type with no interest in appearing modern or sophisticated, and one played by a man, Paulo Gustavo. The third instalment of the film series is expected in 2019.

Million-dollar niches: blockbuster religious films

As highlighted previously, the commercial success of domestic film production since 1970 and the creation of Embrafilme (1969–1990) has most commonly been measured by numbers of tickets sold in film theatres, with charts being regularly updated and released by Filme B, Brazil's foremost film industry portal. There are limitations to focusing on tickets sold rather than revenue from the many different outlets for movies now available to producers (TV, DVD, VOD), as well as other ways of viewing films (legal and illegal uploads and downloads, and so on). Setting aside these limitations, it can be argued that focusing on "bums on seats" in the formal setting of a film theatre offers both a sense of the financial success of films (important in making the neo-liberal case for the importance of film within the cultural industries) *and* a sense of domestic film's ability to reach and communicate with audiences. It above all has offered a reliable way of gathering useful data on films, facilitating helpful year-on-year comparisons for both the industry and scholarship on film, and gaining some kind of sense of audience taste in a context of few or no studies on film reception.

Two films have, however, recently raised the question of the usefulness of the ticket sales statistics. The films, *Os dez mandamentos: o filme* (*The Ten Commandments: The Movie*, Alexandre Avancini, 2016) and *Nada a perder – contra tudo. Por todos* (*Nothing to Lose*, Alexandre Avancini, 2018) outsold all other domestic films in the year of their release, with *Nada a perder* recording the highest number of presales (four million before the film was released) and the record number of box-office tickets sold (11,226,127) since statistics began in 1970. *Os dez mandamentos*, which was released in 1,000 theatres in Brazil (Schvarzman 2018: 541), comes in a close second with 11,183,219 tickets sold. Both films were produced with the support of the Igreja Universal do Reino do Deus (IURD), the Universal Church of the Kingdom of God or UCKG in English, one of the world's largest, wealthiest and often controversial global neo-pentecostal churches set up in Brazil by the self-declared Bishop and now billionaire Edir Macedo in 1977. *Os dez mandamentos*, the church's first incursion into feature filmmaking,[18] was based on the UCKG-owned TV Record's popular miniseries of the same name and directed by the "in-house" and Globo-trained Alexandre Avancini. The feature film was pieced together almost entirely from scenes from the 176-episode TV series (Douglas 2016).

Suspicions were roused about the success of *Os dez mandamentos* when sell-out screenings were reportedly playing to half-empty theatres: reporters from broadsheets and tabloids were dispatched and confirmed the lack of "bums on seats", despite the astronomical ticket sales. *Nada a perder*, based on the best-selling biography of the same name, recounts the early life and career of Edir Macedo. It too was released in over 1,000 cinemas in Brazil and also allegedly played to sur-prisingly depleted audiences. Macedo and his church have denied any wrong-doing or statistical manipulation: they have denied accusations of buying up tickets for publicity and giving them away for free to church members, despite reports to the contrary in relation to both films from filmgoers themselves (Domingos de Lima 2018). *Nada a perder* was released on Netflix worldwide three months after its the-atrical release in Brazil. It would be churlish, therefore, to question the claim of impressive viewing figures for the movie.

Nevertheless, the perceived statistical manipulation of the box-office has clearly troubled cultural commentators, with more newspaper copy and blog space being taken up discussing numbers than reviews of the two films (which are almost without exception damning in the extreme). It is fair to say that Globo seems par-ticularly troubled by the phenomenon: for example, *Nada a Perder*'s inexplicably high IMDB rating has a whole article dedicated to it in *O Globo* newspaper (2018). As we will see, Globo Filmes has a vested interest in all other religion-inspired blockbuster films in the twenty-first century.

The authorised biopic *Nada a perder* does not shy away from discussing Edir Macedo's high-profile (unsuccessful) prosecution on grounds of charlatanism in 1992: his arrest and trial opens and closes the film, which is set to have a sequel (due 2019) and continue the story of Macedo and the growth of the church. The prosecution is thus read as *persecution* by an unsympathetic state (in the guise of the Catholic Church) troubled by Macedo's growing power and influence and threat to the status quo. This is deeply ironic, of course, given the accusations of lawfare at the time of the film's release being aimed, and not without just cause, at lawmakers in Brazil as a result of both the impeachment of Dilma Rousseff and the imprisonment of former president Lula and his disqualification from standing in the 2018 presidential elections.

And the similarities with Lula do not end there, particularly if we consider the notorious 2009 biopic depicting the then president (*Lula, filho do Brasil* [*Lula Son of Brazil*], Fábio Barreto).[19] Both films are based on acritical popular biographies, and both set out to tell the story of a determined, charismatic, visionary man who overcomes financial and personal difficulties to help the needy, and by doing so threatens to undermine the socio-political bedrock of the Brazilian nation.

Perhaps surprisingly, Macedo comes across as more complex a character than Lula as depicted in Fábio Barreto's biopic. The Macedo character, played by Petrônio Gontijo, is rather unlikeable. He appears obsessive and prickly, rather than holy or spiritual. The film acknowledges that he behaves badly towards his then fiancé (Ester Bezerra, played by Day Mesquita): he is controlling and impatient and she draws his attention to this. He apologises and explains his actions by describing his ambitious vision for both of them. There is no clear suggestion, then, that the controlling and impatient behaviour subsided after her threat not to marry him. Both Macedo and his wife are depicted as feeling revulsion towards their baby daughter who was born with a hare lip and cleft palate: the spontaneous love for a newborn, regardless of their physical condition, that one would expect from a hagiographic biopic is replaced with a sense of disappointment and burden of having a facially deformed child. Likewise the filmmakers thought nothing of showing a scene where Macedo manhandles the wife of a friend who is behaving erratically in order to oust an evil spirit from her. Where this need to exorcise came from (i.e. this was not part of his Catholic upbringing *per se* but is a significant and very controversial aspect of the church's activities) is not fully explained. Furthermore, when Macedo gives up his job to dedicate himself full-time to the church, or when he has plans to expand the church, the funding for these schemes falls firmly within the well-worn "God Will Provide" explanation. Thus, there is no discussion of tithes, another key polemical issue with the UCKG. The film completely sidesteps the UCKG's prosperity theology dimension, both in terms of wealth of the church and the wealth (or at least the promotion of the ambition of wealth) of its congregation.

The UCKG blockbuster phenomenon did not appear from nowhere: it built on TV Record's success both in terms of media evangelising (the success of the TV

FIGURE 2.4 Petrônio Gontijo plays Bishop Macedo in a still from the trailer for *Nada a perder*

(*Nothing to Lose*, Alexandre Avancini, 2018)

pastors such as future Mayor of Rio Marcelo Crivella) and the increasing narrative ability of its regular soap operas (Araújo 2016). It also appeared in the wake of a number of other box-office hits of the twenty-first century promoted by religious denominations. In terms of blockbuster films supported by religious groups, it is the Allan Kardec-inspired *espíritas* (spiritists) who have made the most consistent inroads into the Brazilian box-office.[20]

Brazil is home to the world's largest population of spiritists: according to the 2010 census, 3.8 million Brazilians described themselves as *espíritas* (2% of the population) (Cánepa and Suppia 2017: 81). *Espíritas* believe in the immortality of spirits and their ability to communicate with mortals on earth via mediums. Inspired in large part by Allan Kardec, the nineteenth-century French philospher and codifier of spirits, the spiritist movement was formalised in Brazil with the founding of the Federação Espírita Brasileira (the Brazilian Spiritist Federation) in 1895 (Cánepa and Suppia 2017: 82). The federation's first president, the medical doctor Bezerra de Menezes, is the subject of the film *Bezerra de Menezes: O diário de um espírito* (*Bezerra de Menezes: Diary of a Spirit*, Glauber Filho and Joel Pimentel, 2008). This low-budget bio-pic produced by a spiritist association Estação Luz, based in the northeastern state of Ceará, was something of a surprise hit, with nearly 800,000 tickets sold (Cánepa and Suppia 2017: 86). This film arguably set the scene for two spiritist mega-productions that would follow in 2010: *Chico Xavier* (also made with the support of Estação Luz [Cánepa and Suppia 2017: 87]) and *Nosso lar* (*Astral City: A Spiritual Journey*).

Chico Xavier (1910–2002) was responsible for popularising espiritism in Brazil (Cánepa and Suppia 2017: 82). His "psychographed" works, communicated to him by the deceased, continue to sustain a large part of Brazil's publishing market (Cánepa and Suppia 2017: 83). There was thus already a strong tradition in the Brazilian cultural landscape of spiritism-inspired books, plays that are capable of attracting hundreds of thousands of spectators, philosophical treatises and even poems by consecrated Brazilian poets that that were said to be "psychographed" by Chico Xavier.[21] The biopic of the same name was directed by Daniel Filho through his Lereby Productions (*Se eu fosse você*), and was scripted by Marcos Bernstein (*Central do Brasil/Central Station*, 1998) and co-produced by Globo Filmes. With half-decent reviews even from the broadsheets, the film sold 3.4 million tickets. Likewise, the big-budget *Nosso Lar*, by Wagner de Assis,[22] and made through his own production company Cinética and with co-production from both Globo Filmes and Magda Filmes (responsible for the *globochanchadas Minha mãe é uma peça I and II*), attracted four million viewers. *Nosso Lar* is based on one of Chico Xavier's best-known psychographed texts (and then best-selling book) which was dictated to him by the spirit of André Luiz in 1944, in which he describes in detail the afterlife. As in the later case of *Os dez mandamentos*, the costly special effects were highlighted in the fim marketing, with much being made of both the futuristic design of the "astral city" in the afterlife, and the input of a Canadian SFX company (Intelligent Creatures). Together with *As mães de Chico Xavier* (*The Mothers of Chico Xavier*, 2011) and *E a vida continua* (*And Life Goes On*, 2011) the so-called spiritist films led to a surge in interest in spiritism. Furthermore, Cánepa and Suppia (2017: 81) have argued that these films encouraged an interest in horror and science fiction film more broadly:

> In their attempt to overcome multiple contradictions (the problematics of faith, the dualism between body and spirit, political conservatism, and so on) the spiritist film appears to roam between two worlds, halfway between the niche of converts and the public at large, between indoctrination and spectacle.

They contextualise their argument by explaining that global hits that deal with spirits and the afterlife, such as *Ghost, Flatliners, The Sixth Sense* and *The Others* traditionally fare very well at the Brazilian box-office (83).[23] It is worth adding here, as we discuss the broad topic of faith and the cinema, that biblical adaptations, such as Mel Gibson's *The Passion of the Christ* (2004) and Darren Aronofsky's *Noah* (2014) also perform particularly well in Brazil. As well as the big-budget movies produced in Hollywood, Brazil screens the increasingly popular and mostly US sub-genre known as the Christian film via the annual National Christian Film Festival (in Rio de Janeiro since 2013). Other faith-led films have screened at the Transcendental Film Festival in Brasilia and Ceará since 2011.[24]

While the large number of self-declared *espíritas*, coupled with a considerable number of *simpatizantes*, or those sympathetic to the spiritist cause, might be impressive, and while the Brazilian neo-pentecostal movement is the fastest growing in the world (22% of the population, according to an unofficial poll – Datafolha 2016), Roman Catholicism continues to be Brazil's most popular religion (64.6% according to the latest census), and Brazil continues, therefore, to be the largest Catholic country in the world. Although it was arguably slow off the ground in terms of embracing the audio-visual media to both evangelise and keep the faithful, the Catholic church, and in particular the charismatic movement within the church (the Catholic Charismatic Renewel or CCR), has been actively engaging in promotional work via the mass media. The "telegenic CCR superstar" (Chestnut 2013) Father Marcelo Rossi has for decades been the "poster boy" for the movement, rising to fame first as a "singing priest" (he is one of Brazil's most successful recording artists). He has also maintained strong strategic links with Globo: he conducts mass that is broadcast live on TV Globo on Sunday mornings and has radio programmes and book contracts affiliated to the Globo organisation. In the Catholic church's first officially sanctioned feature film, *Maria mãe do filho de Deus* (*Mary, Mother of the Son of God*, Moacyr Goés, 2003), Father Rossi makes an all-important appearance, both as himself and the angel Gabriel. Despite his relatively small role, he also features distinctively on the film poster and advertising.

While the UCKG's first foray into filmmaking related the ecumenical tale of God communicating the ten commandments to Moses, the charismatic movement within the Catholic church opted for an adaptation of a biblical story disputed by protestants: the influence of Mary and her place on par with the Holy Trinity (as suggested by the film's very title). It is unsurprising, then, that the film was regarded as a "counter-attack" (Dantas 2003) against the wave of neo-pentecostal churches sprouting up all over the country and poaching the erstwhile ultra-loyal Catholic flock. The film was a box-office hit, with 2.5 million ticket sales. A follow-up film, *Irmãos da fé* (*Brothers of the Faith*, 2004), also starring Rossi, just fell short of one million spectators.

More recently (2010), the big-budget *Aparecida*, based on the history of devotion to Our Lady of Aparecida, the patron saint of Brazil, was co-produced by Globo Filmes and directed by Tuzuka Yamazaki, a director who made the critically acclaimed *Gaijin* (*Gaijin, a Brazilian Odyssey*, 1980) on Brazil's Japanese diaspora (the largest outside of Japan and of which Yamazaki is herself a member) but whose films consist mostly of commerically driven fare (a number of Xuxa vehicles, for example).

Both *Maria, mãe do filho de Deus* and the later *Aparecida: o filme* deploy the narrative strategy of telling parallel tales: the story of Mary and the miracle of Aparecida respectively, alongside a contemporary tale of redemption and renewal of Catholic faith, in an open gesture signalling the evangelising role of the film, as well as a desire to entertain.[25] *Aparecida* was filmed at the pharaonic Our Lady of Aparecida Basilica, the national shrine to the saint, the second largest cathedral in the world and visited by every pope since it was built in 1980. The film, with its equally pharaonic ambitions, was a box-office flop, despite being vigorously promoted by the Brazilian Conference of Bishops. It was summarily dismissed by influential critic Inácio Araújo (2012) as a front-runner for the award of worst film of the century. He pondered at the time of its release: "How the Catholic Church, with all its wise men, can be behind such a load of nonsense, is a great mystery".

Section 2: The circulation of Brazilian films abroad

While Brazil is perhaps best known in twentieth-century cinephilia for *Cinema Novo*, the avant-garde and politically inflected filmmaking movement that took the European art-house and festival circuit by storm in the 1960s, Brazilian cinema first made its mark in the festival circuit in 1953 with Lima Barreto's "Western" *O cangaceiro* (*The Bandit*), the first Brazilian film to win at Cannes (the "Best Adventure Film" category). And even into the 1960s, when it is true to say that *Cinema Novo* dominated, in terms of Brazilian film production, the "big three" European festivals (Cannes, Berlin and Venice), it was Anselmo Duarte's 1962 popularly-inflected *O pagador de promessas* (*The Given Word*) that secured for Brazil its one and only Palme d'Or. Luiz Zanin (2012) argues that it is a mystery how *The Given Word* ever won this award, given that it faced stiff competition from films by Buñuel, Antonioni and Bresson, among other consecrated names. Zanin astutely hints at its "charming whiff of the Third World" (2012) as a possible draw for jury members of the ilk of François Truffaut, as well as the excellent interpretations of the cast, and its technical quality, provided by H. E. (Chick) Fowle, the British photographer renowned for his work on such iconic early British documentaries as *Night Mail* (1936), and brought over to Brazil in the 1950s to work at the Vera Cruz film studios. In fact, Chick Fowle worked on five Brazilian films between 1951 and 1962 that competed at Cannes, all of which predated *Cinema Novo*'s success abroad.

With the demise of the *Cinema Novo* in the early 1970s, Brazilian cinema did not simply disappear from global screens. In 1969 the majority State-owned distribution and production company, Embrafilme, had been set up with the express purpose of increasing the market share of Brazilian films both at home and abroad. And it was under the headship of Roberto Farias (1974–1979) that Embrafilme's budget was substantially increased and an aggressive policy of selling films abroad began (Gatti 2008: 46), with sales agents established in New York and Paris, and significant support offered for festival attendance by directors, for example. Successes at this time shifted decidedly away from the "whiff of the Third World" referred to above,[26] and instead highlighted the sensual and carnivalesque side to Brazilian culture. Films included the light-hearted *Dona Flor e Seus Dois Maridos* (*Dona Flor and Her Two Husbands*, Bruno Barreto, 1976), starring the "bombshell" Sônia Braga, a phenomenal success at home and subsequently distributed in the US. It was nominated for a Golden Globe (Best Foreign Film) in 1978 and was remade by Hollywood with the title *Kiss me Goodbye* (Robert Mulligan, 1982), starring Sally Field and James Caan.

Even in the 1980s – a filmmaking period dominated in Brazil by soft and hard-core porn production, and one that has been largely edited out of Brazilian film history – one or two Brazilian films continued to be selected for the major European festivals almost every year, along with a healthy number of features screening and winning prizes at the increasingly important Havana Festival of Latin American Film. Remarkably, in the second half of the 1990s, with the return to production and State support for the film industry after the lost years of the ill-fated Collor administration (see Chapter 1), regular appearances by Brazilian films on the international festival circuit were complemented by the much-sought-after Oscar nod. In this period Brazil secured three nominations in the space of four years for best foreign language Oscar, and *Cidade de Deus* (*City of God*, Fernando Meirelles and Kátia Lund, 2002) was nominated in four different categories shortly after in 2004, demonstrating not only a return to strength of the industry after it practically ground to a halt in 1990, but also the increased influence and lobbying power of certain Brazilian directors and film producers within Hollywood.

With the growth of the film festival circuit from the 1990s onwards, and particularly of festivals championing more independent productions, such as Rotterdam and Sundance, Brazilian films have continued to be successful. Both Rotterdam and Sundance (both the festivals and their associated film funding schemes) have been generous to Brazilian film,[27] helping to cement the industry's reputation as a World Cinema player. In August 2018 Sundance worked in partnership with the Cinema do Brasil initiative and the Brazilian Foreign Ministry on Encontros do Cinema Brasileiro (Encounters With Brazilian Cinema), whereby Sundance representative Heidi Zwicker viewed 11 independent Brazilian films "in situ" (during the CineBH festival in Belo Horizonte). Previous editions of the Encounters programme brought commissioners from the festivals of Cannes, Venice, Toronto, Roterdam, Berlim, Locarno, Havana and Rome.

The so-called Sundance Labs are of increasing importance in the creation of successful World Cinema films: in 2011, for example, six out of the twenty feature films in competition at the Sundance film festival came through the Sundance Institute's workshop programme. Writing in 2006, Lúcia Nagib argued that "It is not mere coincidence that several of Brazil's most successful films abroad, such as *Central Station* (Walter Salles, 1998), *Me You Them* (Andrucha Waddington, 2000) and *City of God* have received Sundance support for their films" (96–97). In her essay, Nagib argues that festival labs such as Sundance are influencing the kinds of stories being told by World Cinema in the twenty-first century, a cinema that is aimed at a new audience which is enlightened, comfortable with subtitles, keen to be instructed, but not necessarily fans of the experimental and less commercial end of arthouse production à la the late Portuguese filmmaker Manoel de Oliveira (Nagib 2006: 96–97). In this context she discusses Walter Salles's *Central Station*, which underwent numerous rewrites at the Sundance lab before emerging to claim its place as one of the most striking World Cinema films of the late 1990s. Nagib points to the need for further discussion of the impact of seeking co-production funding and chasing festival opportunities on Brazilian (and by extension, other World Cinema) film production. She warns: "The recipe of the private hero, in a national cultural context, who goes through the experience of the improbable made convincing by a wisely constructed script generates interesting questions of authorship and nationality which deserve further attention" (Nagib 2006: 98).

Film critic turned director Kleber Mendonça Filho has expressed concern over a certain type of script lab (Sundance, one imagines) whereby too much input changes original ideas beyond recognition and transforms them into standard "World Cinema", a concept which he confesses gives him "the creeps", since it does away with the "honest, personal approach" that makes cinema great (2017). "The World Cinema script-writing machine […] is just as bad as going to some multiplex to watch the latest comic-book blockbuster. […] They both try too hard to please a certain kind of audience" (2017).[28]

But the links between Sundance and the Brazilian film industry run deeper than what could be superficially appraised as a rather condescending meddling in plots, via funding and lab opportunities, with a view to producing some kind of homogenous global narrative. The number of high-profile Brazilian directors, producers and films connected to Sundance is striking, and suggests, in counterpoint to Nagib's argument, that film industry personnel from the former Third World can enjoy a symbiotic relationship with the Institute. By way of example, José Padilha, now widely known outside of Brazil as the director of the 2014 remake of *Robocop*, and creator of the Netflix smash hit series *Narcos*, began a close relationship with Sundance, which arguably set him on course for international recognition, when his debut feature documentary *Ônibus 174* (*Bus 174*, with Felipe Lacerda, 2002) featured at the festival. His 2010 documentary *Secrets of the Tribe* also screened at Sundance (Brazilian documentaries are a regular feature at the festival) and elicited further invitations: to hold the international premiere of his domestic box-office smash *Tropa de elite: o inimigo agora e outro* (*Elite Squad: The Enemy Within*, 2010) there, as well as to serve on the festival jury.

As a result of the success of *Central Station* Robert Redford, founder of the Sundance Institute, encouraged Walter Salles to direct in 2004 the first filmic adaptation of Che Guevara's *Motorcycle Diaries* (Williams 2007: 11), one of the most successful co-productions to come out of Latin America and arguably the next step for Salles, after filming two successful road movies (one national, one transnational) towards road-movie gold in the form of the opportunity to adapt Jack Keroac's *On the Road* (2012). It is worth noting that both Walter Salles's *On the Road* and the Brazilian co-produced *Frances Ha* (Noah Baumbach, 2012) are Cinco vezes regular features on Sundance Television schedules.

One of the biggest filmic talking points in Brazil of the last few years, Anna Muylaert's *Que Horas Ela Volta?* premiered at Sundance in 2015 and picked up acting awards for the two leads, Regina Casé and Camila Márdila. It went on to pick up two more awards in out-of-competition sections of the Berlin film festival, a festival that has, since *Central Station* won the Golden Bear back in 1998, screened a large number of Brazilian films and has awarded prizes to José Padilha's *Tropa de Elite* (*Elite Squad*, 2008) – Golden Bear, and Teddy awards ("the official queer award") to *Hoje eu quero voltar sozinho* (*The Way He Looks*, Daniel Ribeiro, 2014), Anna Muylaert's follow-up to *The Second Mother*, *Mãe só há uma* (*Don't Call Me Son*, 2016) and two Brazilian films in 2018: best feature film for *Tinta bruta* (*Hard Paint*, Felipe Matzembacher and Márcio Reolon, 2018) and best documentary for *Bixa Travesty* (Claudia Priscilla and Kiko Goifman, 2018) (see Chapter 4). Twelve Brazilian films screened at the Berlinale in 2017, and seven films came away with prizes from the 2018 edition of the festival, including Berlin-based Karim Ainouz's German-Brazilian co-production *Central Airport* (2018) and Netherlands-based Maria August Ramos's Brazilian-Dutch co-production *O processo* (*The Trial*, 2018), discussed in Chapter 3.

Brazilian players and global film production

Directors such as Walter Salles and Fernando Meirelles are, to borrow Deborah Shaw's description of transnational directors, "fluent in transnational modes of narration, and are physical embodiments of cultural exchange" (Shaw 2013: 60). As defined by Shaw, they form part of a group of directors in Latin America "who work and seek funding in a range of national contexts, while they have their films distributed in a global market" (60–61). But while these "celebrity" transnational directors share company with the likes of Mexicans Alejandro González Iñárritu, Afonso Cuarón and Guilhermo del Toro, we can also look elsewhere, to the producers, for example, for noteworthy examples of industry players taking on the globe. By way of example, in an article tellingly entitled "Brazil's RT Features Gives US Independent Films a Boost", John Hopewell (2016), *Variety's* chief international correspondent, declared that "to find one of the biggest impact players on the American indie scene, you have to go to Sao Paulo". Hopewell was referring to RT Features, the Brazil-based production company fronted by Rodrigo Teixeira,[29] whose list of recent indie credits is impressive, as Hopewell recognises, for any producer of any nationality: the aforementioned *Frances Ha*, *The Witch* (Robert Eggers, 2015), *Mistress America* (Noel Baumbach, 2016), and the mulit-award-winning *Call Me By Your Name* (2017), to name only four from a long list of productions, both of US and Brazilian origin.

The success of RT Features, and other production companies in Brazil with international as well as national profiles, such as Salles' Videofilmes (*On the Road*; *Jia Zhangke: A Guy from Fenyang*, 2014) and Meirelles" O2 Filmes (*Blindness*, 2008; *360*, 2011, *Exodus*, 2017) highlight the danger in drawing the easy conclusion that producers based in emerging nations engage in international film co-production only when they need the financial support from more powerful partners based in Europe or (much less frequently) the USA to make local movies. By way of example of such a relationship, consider the influence of El Deseo (Spain), the Almodóvar brothers' production company that co-produces with key auteurs such as Argentine Lucrecia Martel and Mexican Paul Leduc in Latin America. According to Marvin D'Lugo (2013) El Deseo produces films with an "ambitious transterritorial aesthetic that seeks to engage audiences in Spain and Latin America in [...] the co-production of a transnational Hispanic identity" (D'Lugo 2013: 113). One of the motivating factors in this, far from a straightforward financial transaction, is a "special affinity with Latin America" (D'Lugo 2013: 131), but what is clear is that this exploration of transnational Hispanic identity and special affinity appears to be, or at least it is most commonly read as, the prerogative of Europeans (the ex-colonial rulers, if you like). Similar arguments have been levelled against Ibermedia, the Hispanic and Latin American film production funding pool (Falicov 2013) modelled on Eurimages, and the Cine en Construcción post-production funding competition for Latin American films associated with the San Sebastian and Toulouse film festivals (Toribio 2013), whereby as a result of a sense of correcting a historical debt to the erstwhile colonies with their struggling film industries, Spain (the biggest funder in both initiatives) enables Latin American films to be made.

An excellent example of inversion of the supposed one-directional co-production power flow is Brazilian production company Conspiração Filmes and their key involvement in the "Spanish" film *Lope* (Andrucha Waddington, 2010). I use scare quotes here deliberately, as this, to all intents and purposes, is an excellent example of national cinema: a lavish, big-budget period film that recounts the adventures of one of the indisputable symbols of "Hispanidad" or Spanishness: Lope de Vega, the Golden-Age author. The film was nominated for a Goya, the principal Spanish film gong, in six different categories. Brazilian Conspiração contributed to the production with 20% of the budget and crucially provided the (Brazilian) director, Waddington. Interestingly, Lucrecia Martel's 2018 big-budget historical drama *Zama* is an eleven-way co-production: El Deseo co-produced but top production credits in the film belong to the Brazilian Bananeira Filmes.

FIGURE 2.5 Argentine-born Alberto Ammann in a still from the trailer for the Spanish-Brazilian co-production *Lope*

(Andrucha Waddington, 2010)

Brazil and international co-productions[30]

In Brazil, while the raw co-production numbers compare quite favourably to other Latin American countries (22 in 2017 and a remarkable 35 in the period 2013–2014, for example), we need to bear in mind that over 100 Brazilian films are released every year, and of these, only on average 10% are international co-productions. We must also recognise that a large number of films are never released: their exhibition is limited to festivals, specialist TV channels, VOD platforms, and so on. In the period 2005–2014, most co-productions were made with Portugal (25), followed by France and Argentina (16 each) and then Spain (15) (Rocha and Ibiapina 2016: 102–103). According to statistics from Ancine, of the 116 co-productions to be released in Brazil between 2009 and 2017, the three top co-producing partners were from Portugal, Argentina and France. It is worth reflecting on the co-production relationship between Brazil and Portugal as facile assumptions can be made about the pull of old colonial ties in terms of contemporary cultural production, and in particular at a time when transnational/migratory stories are very much in vogue. It is likely that these assumptions are based partly on our understanding of the relationship which many film industries of former Spanish- and French-language colonies have with producers based in Spain and France. However, unlike the French and Spanish cases, there is a dearth of films that depict relations (historical or contemporary) between Portugal and its former South American colony. In fact, in terms of industry relations and transnational story-telling, there is much greater resemblance between Portugal''s relationship with its former African colonies, and Francophone and Hispanophone cultural relations. Rather than pointing to a body of work that indicates cultural exchange, as promoted on paper by many of the State funding opportunities available to Brazilian and Portuguese filmmakers, many of the Brazilian/Portuguese co-productions of the last few years are opportunistic in nature, with finished products that rarely travel beyond the territory making the majority investment.[31] Industry expert André Sturm suggests that Brazilian funding for such initiatives is relatively easy to secure (via funding calls that are far from competitive), and that after securing the funding it is equally easy for directors and producers to circumvent any stipulations regarding "cultural exchange" (in Rocha and Ibiapina 2016: 145–146). They simply need to have contacts in the Portuguese film industry, something that is inevitably facilitated by a common language, and perhaps attractive for those who are less adventurous when it comes to transnational film financing. For while film directors such as Walter Salles, Kleber Mendonça Filho, José Padilha, Maria Augusta Ramos and Karim Ainouz, for example, navigate the international film scene effortlessly with their impeccable language skills acquired through living abroad, there are a great many cultural producers in Brazil who lack the confidence and experience to do business in any language other than Portuguese.

Since the "Cinema do Brasil" film promotional programme was set up in 2006, there has been a marked growth in both international co-productions and Brazilian film exhibition abroad. The programme's creator, André Sturm, appears to have been inspired to set up the initiative, which is run through Brazil's export agency APEX, after drawing the conclusion that big-screen exposure on the European festival for countries such as Argentina was a direct result of making international co-productions with key players in Europe such as France, Spain and Germany (Rocha and Ibiapina 2016: 87).

As Brazil finds itself in one of its worst ever economic crises, and given the turn away from State support for the Arts hinted at by the country's future president at the time of writing, it is questionable as to whether the level of investment in co-production will continue, particularly given the negligent results in terms of building a market for Brazilian product in Portugal for example. The figures provided by Ancine for the number of tickets sold for Brazilian films in key markets such as Portugal, Argentina and Germany are very low. And we must also question the attraction of small amounts of Brazilian funding for foreign directors and producers to film in Brazil via co-production arrangements. It seems that even where formal coproduction treaties exist, film business can be hard to conduct in Brazil. The celebrated Argentine cineaste, Daniel Burman, said the following of his experience of working in Brazil:

> Speaking as a director and author, working in Brazil is both natural and fruitful. But, speaking as a producer, I don't know if I'll make any more co-productions. My two experiences of working in Brazil revealed a huge asymmetry between administrative processes in Brazil and Argentina. In Brazil, everything takes so long, everything seems so much more difficult. I don't want to say bureaucratic, but the time it takes to produce anything in Brazil means I'd rather stick to Argentina.
>
> *(Miranda 2014)*

There are two final issues that need to be borne in mind in relation to this panorama of Brazilian cinema's "presence" in the global marketplace. First of all, in terms of State legislation and support for the film industry, the priority is and has always been promoting film within the domestic market. The success of popular comedy films, such as those produced by Globo Filmes, signals that the internal market is large enough to provide considerable commercial success. This in great part explains why we have, for example, seen no significant attempt by Globo Filmes to break into foreign markets, such as Portugal, where Globo TV soap operas continue to reign supreme.

Secondly, evidence suggests that legislators themselves in Brazil do not view Brazilian film culture's global presence as described above as in any way significant (Rocha and Ibiapina 2016: 169; Dennison and Meleiro 2017). As I have argued elsewhere, despite the presence of Brazilian films abroad, at least on the festival circuit, Brazil lacks a national film brand (Dennison and Meleiro 2017). Given the transnational profile of some of Brazil's key players (José Padilha; Walter Salles; Fernando Meirelles; Rodrigo Teixeira; Andrucha Waddington, Vania Catani, for example), who are "hotwired into an international framework of distribution as never before" (Brookes 2002) and given the less than effective legislation and funding in place to encourage a more consolidated international dissemination of Brazilian films, this is not entirely surprising. What we can say with confidence is that Brazil is actively contributing to twenty-first century World Cinema culture.

Notes

1 The origin of the term is unclear but it is usually ascribed a pejorative meaning along he lines of leftovers or unfit scraps. For a reading of the chanchada see Dennison and Shaw (2004); and Shaw and Dennison (2007: 70–77). Chanchada has remarkably made its way into the *Oxford English Dictionary*: hence the lack of italics when used in this monograph.

2 For example, the chanchada parody of Fred Zinneman's 1952 *High Noon*, *Matar ou correr* (*Kill or Run*, Carlos Manga, 1954), was released within six months of the original being screened in Brazil.

3 This partly had to do with how the films were funded, partly because of their tendency to self-censor in order to avoid delays with exhibition, and partly because of the resulting morally conservative message the films tended to espouse.

4 See Dennison 2009.

5 Worthy of note is *Folha de S. Paulo* film critic Sergio Alpendre's short course on new film comedies as *genre* conducted at the Instituto Itaú Cultural in São Paulo in September 2013.

6 See for example Arthuso (2013).

7 Lúcia Nagib (2017: 33), for example, dismisses the current Globo-driven boom in production as commercial, in contradistinction to the creative boom of the *retomada*, while Sheila Schvarzman (2018) is also disparaging in her analysis of contemporary popular comedies.

8 Globo Filmes' co-production in some instances involves cross media initiatives, such as product placement and "plugs" during commercial breaks in Globo TV programming. In others it offers "artistic supervision", for example script consultation and advising on cast, or permitting contracted Globo stars to appear in films (Ikeda 2015: 90–92).

9 For more information on these films, see Dennison and Shaw 2004.

10 For example, *Os normais, o filme* (*So Normal*, 2003); *A grande família, o filme* (*Big Family*, 2007); *Meu passado me condena, o filme* (*My Past Condemns Me*, 2013) and *Vai que cola, o filme* (*It Might All Work Out*, 2015).

11 It is worth acknowledging here that Gustavo worked on Globo's subscription channel Multishow and starred in a *globochanchada*, *Divã* (*In Therapy*, José Alvarenga Jr, 2009) in between making his mark with his stage performances and the making of the film version of *Minha mãe é uma peça*.

12 See Johnson 2017.

13 Andrea Ormond provides detailed readings of a number of *globochanchadas* on her blog: *Estranho encontro*.

14 Julia Rezende and Cris D'Amato respectively. Rezende will direct the third instalment of the *De pernas pro ar* franchise (due December 2018).

15 On the subject of language, Schvarzman (2018: 521) highlights the growing number of younger cinema-goers who eschew subtitles (traditionally more common than dubbing in relation to cinema releases in Brazil), which may be encouraging an interest in domestic productions.

16 For example, *A dupla do barulho* (*The Terrible Twosome*, Carlos Manga, 1953) and *Metido a bacana* (*A Cut Above the Rest*, J. B. Tanko, 1957).

17 To his credit, he did make a short, last-minute video in October 2018 stating he would not vote for a homophobic presidential candidate.

18 Record Filmes was set up in order to co-produce, with Paris Filmes, *Os dez mandamentos* and *Nada a perder*.

19 Notorious because the film was directly funded by a range of big businesses, many of which would later be implicated in the Operation Car Wash grafting scandal. See Dennison and Meleiro (2017). *Lula, filho do Brasil* cost 17 million Reals and was seen in cinemas by 848,000 spectators (Trindade 2014: 111). It controversially represented Brazil in the Oscars Foreign Film category in 2010.

20 See Laura Cánepa and Alfredo Suppia's study of the Brazilian spiritist film (2017).

21 For more information on Chico Xavier, see his obituary in *The Guardian* (Bellos, 2002).

22 Best known for writing a number of films starring Xuxa.

23 Cánepa and Suppia (2017) discuss *White Noise* starring Michael Keaton. The film was a global flop but it fared well in Brazil. As a result *White Noise – The Light*, a sequel made straight-to-DVD, was released theatrically in Brazil.

24 The only other spiritist film festival took place in Australia's Gold Coast in 2017, with mostly Brazilian films in the feature film section.

25 Similarly, in the spiritist film *Bezerra de Menezes*, archive footage and statements from the faithful run parallel to the final credits (Cánepa and Suppia 2017: 86)

26 There are, of course, always exceptions that prove the rule, and one worth mentioning here is Hector Babenco's Embrafilme-distributed and Gloden Globe-nominated *Peixote: A Lei do Mais Fraco* (*Pixote*, 1980), which dealt with the tough lives of street kids.

27 Fifteen Brazilian films were selected to screen at Rotterdam 2017, and a remarkable five feature films made the prestigious Tiger and Bright Future competitions in 2018.

28 In this context it is worth noting that Schvarzman (2018: 527), in her analysis of contemporary home-grown popular comedies, emphasises the input of the co-producing Majors in script development.

29 Not to be confused with the "other" Brazilian Rodrigo Teixeira, co-creator of Magnopus and successful special effects consultant based in Los Angeles.

30 For a more detailed description of the co-production scenario in Brazil, and in particular in terms of government initiatives and legislation, see Dennison and Meleiro (2017); Ancine (2018).

31 There are, of course, exceptions to this rule: take, for example, Zezé Gamboa's *O grande kilapy* (The Great Kilapy, 2012), an innovative co-production between Brazil, Portugal and Angola that took advantage of targeted funding for Brazil/Portugal co-productions.

References

Ancine. 2018. "Anuário estatístico do cinema brasileiro". https://oca.ancine.gov.br/sites/default/files/repositorio/pdf/anuario_2017.pdf.

Araújo, B. B. M. 2013. "Crítica de Kleber Mendonça Filho incomoda executivo da gigante Globo Filmes". *Jornal do Comércio Online*. 22 February. https://jconline.ne10.uol.com.br/canal/cultura/cinema/noticia/2013/02/22/critica-de-kleber-mendonca-filho-incomoda-executivo-da-gigante-globo-filmes-74261.php.

Araújo, I. 2012. "Filme *Aparecida: o milagre* é uma grande bobagem sobre recuperar fé". *Folha Ilustrada*. 7 November. www1.folha.uol.com.br/ilustrada/1181345-critica-filme-aparecida-o-milagre-e-uma-grande-bobagem-sobre-recuperar-fe.shtml.

Araújo, I. 2016. "Título do filme deveria ser *Os dez mandamentos: o pesadelo*". *Folha ilustrada*. 30 January. https://www1.folha.uol.com.br/ilustrada/2016/01/1735069-titulo-do-filme-deveria-ser-os-dez-mandamentos---o-pesadelo.shtml.

Arthuso, R. 2013. "Jean-Claude Bernardet e as comédias". *Revista cinética*. 16 July. http://revistacinetica.com.br/home/jean-claude-bernadet-e-as-comedias/.

Bellos, A. 2002. "Chico Xavier". *Guardian*. 11 July. www.theguardian.com/news/2002/jul/11/guardianobituaries.booksobituaries1.

Cánepa, L. and Suppia, A. 2017. "O filme espírita brasileiro: entre dois mundos". *Alceu* 17:34, pp. 81–97.

Chestnut, R. A. 2013. "How the Charismatic Movement Conquered Brazil". *Catholic Herald*. 26 July. https://catholicherald.co.uk/news/2013/07/26/how-the-charismatic-movement-conquered-brazil/.

Conde, M. and Dennison, S. (eds) 2018. *Paulo Emílio Salles Gomes: On Brazil and Global Cinema*. Mleksham: University of Wales Press.

Couto, J. G. 2017. "Além da globochanchada". *Blog do IMS*. 29 September. https://blogdoims.com.br/alem-da-globochanchada/.

Dantas, E. 2003. "Os católicos contra-atacam". *Revista época* 28 July. http://revistaepoca.globo.com/Epoca/0,6993,EPT574696-1664-2,00.html.

Datafolha. 2016. Datafolha Institute. www1.folha.uol.com.br/poder/2016/12/1844365-deixam-de-ser-catolicos-ao-menos-9-milhoes-afirma-datafolha.shtml.

Dennison, S. 2009. "Sex and the Generals: Reading Brazilian Pornochanchada as Sexploitation". In Tierney, D. and Ruetalo, V. (eds) *Latsploitation, Exploitation Cinemas and Latin America*. New York: Routledge, pp. 230–244.

Dennison, S and Meleiro, A. 2016. "Brazil, Soft Power and Film Culture". *New Cinemas* 14:1, pp. 17–30.

Dennison, S and Shaw, L. 2004. *Popular Cinema in Brazil*. Manchester: MUP.

D'Lugo, M. 2013. "Pedro Almodvar's Latin American 'Business'". In S. Dennison (ed.), *Contemporary Hispanic Cinema: Interrogating the Transnational in Spanish and Latin American Film*. London: Tamesis, pp. 113–135.

Domingos de Lima, J. 2018. "*Nada a Perder* e os 'recordes' de bilheteria do cinema evangélico". *Nexo*. 10 April. www.nexojornal.com.br/expresso/2018/04/10/%E2%80%98Nada-a-Perder%E2%80%99-e-os-%E2%80%98recordes%E2%80%99-de-bilheteria-do-cinema-evang%C3%A9lico.

Douglas, B. 2016. "The Ten Commandments: Film Set to Be Biggest Box-office Hit in Brazil History". *Guardian*. 29 January. www.theguardian.com/world/2016/jan/29/the-ten-commandments-film-biggest-box-office-hit-brazil.

Gamo, A. and Rocha Melo, L. A. 2018. "Histórias da Boca e do Beco". In Ramos, F. P. and Schvarzman, S. (eds) *Nova história do cinema brasileiro*. Vol 2. São Paulo: SESC, pp. 322–359.

Gatti, A. P. 2008. *Embrafilme e o cinema brasileiro*. Centro Cultural Sao Paulo: E-book.

Globo. 2018. "Mal recebida pela crítica, *Nada a perder* tem nota alta no IMDB". *O Globo* 9 April.

Gregoli, R. 2017. "De Pernas pro Ar: A Revolution Confined to the Bedroom". *Revista observatório* 3:1, pp. 131–160.

Hopewell, J. 2016. "Brazil's RT Features Gives US Independent Films a Boost". *Variety*. 12 February. Available at http://variety.com/2016/film/global/brazil-production- company-rt-features-1201701634/

Ikeda, M. 2015. Cinema brasileiro a partir da retomada: aspectos econômcios e politicos. São Paulo: Summus Editorial.

Johnson, R. 2017. "Television and the Transformation of the Star System in Brazil". In Delgado, M. M., Hart, S. M. and Johnson, R. (eds), *A Companion to Latin American Cinema* Chichester: Wiley Blackwell, pp. 21–35.

Marsh, L. L. 2017. "Women, Gender and Romantic Comedy in Brazil: Love on the High Seas". In *Meu pasado me condena* (2013) and *S. O. S. mulheres ao mar* (2014). *Feminist Media Histories* 3:2, pp. 98–120.

Mendonça Filho, K. 2017. Interview with the author. March.

Miranda, A. 2014. "*O mistério da felicidade* é a segunda coprodução de Daniel Burman com o Brasil; e pode ser a última". *O Globo*. 8 October. Available at: http://oglobo.globo.com/cultura/filmes/o-misterio-da-felicidade-a-segunda-coproducao-de-daniel-burman-com-brasil-pode-ser-ultima-14173583#ixzz4Ve9rL58Y.

Nagib, L. 2006. "Going Global: The Brazilian Scripted Film". In S. Harvey (ed.), *Trading Culture: Global Traffic Local Cultures in Film and Television*. Eastleigh: John Libby, pp. 95–103.

Ormond, A. n/d. *Estranho Encontro* (film blog). http://estranhoencontro.blogspot.com/.

Rocha, F. and Ibapina, D. 2016. *Cinema Brasileiro e Co-produção Internacional*. Curitiba: Appris.

Rowe, W. and Schelling, V. 1991. *Memory and Modernity: Popular Culture in Latin America*. London and New York: Verso.

Schvarzman, S. 2018. "Cinema brasileiro de grande bilheteria (2000–2016)". In Ramos, F. P. and Schvarzman, S. (eds) *Nova história do cinema brasileiro* Vol 2. São Paulo: SESC, pp. 514–565.

Shaw, D. 2013. "Deconstructing and Reconstructing Transnational Cinema". In Dennison, S. (ed.). *Contemporary Hispanic Cinema: Interrogating the Transnational in Spanish and Latin American Film*. London: Tamesis, pp. 47–65.

Shaw, L. and Dennison, S. 2007. *Brazilian National Cinema*. London and New York: Routledge.

Stam, R. and V. J. L. 1985. "Parody and Marginality: The Case of Brazilian Cinema". *Framework: The Journal of Cinema and Media*. 28, pp. 20–49.

Toribio, N. T. 2013. "Building Latin American Cinema in Europe: Cine en Construcción/Cinéma en construction". In Dennison, S. (ed) *Contemporary Hispanic Cinema: Interrogating the Transnational in Spanish and Latin American Film*. London: Tamesis, pp. 89–112.

Trindade, T. N. 2014. *Documentário e Mercado no Brasil: da produção à sala de cinema.* São Paulo: Alameda.

Valente, E. 2003. "Freud explica? A Globo Filmes e o fetiche-cinema". *Contracampo* 57.

Williams, Claire. 2007. "Los Diarios de Motocicleta as Pan-American Travelogue". In Shaw, D. (ed.), *Contemporary Latin American cinema: Breaking into the Global Market.* Plymouth: Rowman and Littlefield, pp. 11–27.

Zanin Oricchio, L. 2012 "50 anos da Palma de Ouro a *O Pagador de Promessas*". *Estadão Cultura.* 24 May. http://cultura.estadao.com.br/blogs/luiz-zanin/50-anos-da-palma- de-ouro-a-o-pagador-de-promessas/.

3

WOMEN AND FILM CULTURE IN BRAZIL

> In one generation, Latin American women's cinema has evolved from the singular achievement of isolated films, discovered and viewed only with difficulty, into a mature corpus of work that has created a field of its own. And yet, the history-making women of Latin American cinema remain outsiders to the Latin American and even Anglophone canon, under-recognised and still urgently in need of champions.
>
> (Rich 2017: xv)

It is thus that B Ruby Rich introduces Deborah Martin and Deborah Shaw's collection of essays on Latin American women's filmmaking, published in 2017. Martin and Shaw's book, which contains a number of chapters on Brazilian cinema, is one of a mere handful of texts published in English over the last twenty years which deals with the subject of women's filmmaking in Brazil.[1] What is more surprising than this dearth of material, however, is the lack of publications on the subject in Brazil. Karla Holanda and Marina Cavalcanti Tedesco's collection *Feminino e plural: mulheres no cinema brasileiro*, also published in 2017, is ground-breaking in this sense: it is the first Portuguese-language collection dedicated to the analysis of films directed by women.

Twenty years ago the isolated films to which B Ruby Rich refers would at best be referred to in passing in essays, and these would almost exclusively be feature-length films: the work of Carmen Santos, a pioneering producer from the 1920s,[2] the equally "pioneering" Gilda de Abreu and her box-office smash *O ébrio* (*The Drunkard*, 1946),[3] the three films from the 1970s and 80s by Ana Carolina[4] (certainly one of the most written-about directors in English-language texts), the then single feature-length film by Suzana Amaral (the critically acclaimed *A hora da estrela* (*The Hour of the Star*, 1986),[5] and very little else. There was practically no mention, for example, of an important work made by Afro-Brazilian filmmaker Adélia Sampaio in 1984, *Amor maldito* (*Damned Love*) the first feature film made by an Afro-Brazilian woman.[6] The other largely unheard of or forgotten but undoubtedly remarkable films, from the 1920s through to the 1990s, including short and low-budget documentary films discussed in detail in a number of the essays in *Feminino e plural*, negates the well-worn argument that the historical dearth of academic material on the subject is simply a reflection of a dearth of production of films by women. And while both edited books mentioned above, along with Leslie Marsh's important study *Brazilian Women's Filmmaking: From Dictatorship to Democracy* (2012), celebrate the boom in filmmaking by women in Brazil in the twenty-first century, they still comprise isolated examples of detailed discussions in academia of this boom.

Given the focus of this monograph on film culture, what this chapter seeks to do is highlight the conditions in which women make films in Brazil in the twenty-first century, with particular focus on the last four years (President Dilma's Rousseff's second term of office [2014–2016], impeachment, and the run-up to elections in 2018, to be precise). The aim is to provide a snapshot of these conditions: structural (in the sense of access to state funding and women-centred organisations), political (the impact of the impeachment of Brazil's first female president) and cultural (the impact of global movements such as #metoo, and those closer to home, such as a misogynist backlash and the #elenao campaign, for example).

Brazilian women filmmakers' spring?

At first glance there appears to be a great deal to celebrate in relation to women's filmmaking in the twenty-first century. Lúcia Nagib (2017: 32) points to the *retomada*, the so-called renaissance of Brazilian filmmaking post-1994,[7] and the gradual widening participation in terms of access to financial support for making films, as the point at which women began to increase their presence in the film industry: "among 90 filmmakers active between 1994 and 1998, 17 were female, that is, nearly 19%, a significant rise compared with the less than 4% female presence in the pre-Collor [1989–1991] years" (33). And while Nagib argues that the percentage did in fact decrease in the post-*retomada* period, the truth is that the figures are prone to fluctuation: 24% of audio-visual works of 2012 were made by women, while only 10% were in 2014, averaging out over the twenty-first century at around 17%. This figure is still very low, given that 52% of the Brazilian population is made up of women, but it does demonstrate considerable growth, and particularly if we compare it to other influential professional sectors such as politics. The volume of audio-visual material (film and TV) being made in Brazil annually has also risen exponentially.

While there are those that argue that the diversity and cultural inclusion agenda introduced during Lula's two terms of office took a bit of a back seat under Dilma Rousseff (Amadeu da Silveira et al. 2013; Fagundez and Mendonça 2016), there was arguably still enough momentum to keep alive the mission of opening more spaces to creative women, both within Rousseff's second mandate, and post-impeachment.

In 2018 Ancine (2018b) reported that through the FSA (Audiovisual Sector Fund) it had received more than 800 applicants to its first gender and race-based quota competition for feature-length films, and that 10 out of the 11 public calls from its first raft of funding for 2018 had earmarked 50% of funds for female applicants (cis and transgender).

By 2018 over 40% of films put forward to the national selection process to choose Brazil's entry for the Oscar Best Foreign Film 2019 were directed by women. These included *O caso do homem errado* (*The Case of the Wrong Man*, 2017) a documentary by first-time Afro-Brazilian director Camila de Moraes. The film, co-produced by de Moraes and fellow Afro-Brazilian Mariane Ferreira, gained a theatrical release in August 2018 to positive reviews in Brazilian broadsheets. The fifty-first edition of the Brasília film festival in September 2018 was very much the year of women in film. Of the 21 films in competition, over half (13) were directed by women. Beatriz Seigner was awarded the Best Director prize for *Los silencios*, a Brazilian-Colombian-French co-production which had premiered to rave reviews at the Directors Fortnight in Cannes. Afro-Brazilian Glenda Nicácio achieved the remarkable feat of two award-winning feature-length films (co-directed with Ari Rosa) in two consecutive festivals (*Ilha* [*Island*] in 2018 and *Café com canela* [*Coffee with Cinnamon*] in 2017). And Susanna Lira's *A torre de donzelas* (*The Tower of Maidens*, 2018), a film featuring accounts of torture by a number of female survivors of the most brutal days of the dictatorship over 40 years earlier, and which includes an appearance by Dilma Rousseff, won the Special Jury Prize and stole the show with the post-screening participation of the women involved (except Rousseff).

Brazil's female film producers, identified by Nagib as larger than usual in number, continue to grow in strength and impact: in 2016 they totalled 41%.[8] While many producers make only one or two short films with low impact, and the largest companies such as Paris, Downtown, Total Entertainment and Conspiração are male-dominated enterprises, there are a number of influential women producers currently working in the film industry in Brazil. A woman, Silvia Cruz, founded and runs one of Brazil's most successful independent film distribution companies, Vitrine Filmes. Vania Catani is behind the prolific Bananeira Filmes, co-producer of Argentine director Lucrecia Martel's critically acclaimed *Zama* (2017), and the long-established Mariza Leão of Morena Filmes is responsible for a wide range of popular movies such as the *globochanchada* series discussed in Chapter 2, *De pernas pro ar* (*Head Over Heels*, Roberto Santucci, 2010). There are also the films directed by Leão's daughter, Julia Rezende, such as *Meu passado me condena* (*My Past Condemns Me*, 2013). Rezende, along with fellow *globochanchada* director Cris D'Amato and filmmakers such as Gabriela Amaral, director of horror films including the acclaimed *O animal cordial* (*Friendly Beast*, 2017) can be cited as examples of filmmakers working in genre film, and as evidence of how women directors are no longer corralled into the traditions of arthouse, independent, short or documentary film-making.

There are examples in abundance of women in film organising themselves to promote their work and to combat institutional sexism, from websites such as *Mulheres do cinema brasileiro* (Women of Brazilian Cinema), the formation of Elviras, a collective of female film critics, to the launch in 2018 of Elas, a network under the umbrella of distributors Elo Company, of filmmakers and executives whose purpose is to promote female-driven film production. Social-media-centred international lobby groups that have gained a high profile thanks to the involvement of women working in the film industry (and Hollywood in particular), such as the #metoo campaign, have impacted on the cultural industries and society at large in Brazil, drawing attention to a series of unresolved issues that debunk the notion that more funding and quotas is all that it takes to achieve gender equality. In fact Brazil has its own hashtag that predates the rise to fame of #metoo: #meuprimeiroassedio (my first [sexual] harassment), a hugely successful social media campaign created by the influential Think Olga NGO (Xavier 2015) which a number of high-profile film and TV actresses supported. The success of the campaign arguably led to the decisive action on the part of TV Globo to suspend actor José Mayer in 2017 for sustained inappropriate behaviour in relation to soap "extra" Sus Tonani. Thus the audio-visual "sorority" can be seen lending its weight and visibility to campaigns likely to have a positive impact in terms of consciousness-raising among women in Brazil. The same can be seen in relation to the hashtag #elenao (not him): film and TV stars, both female and male, with millions of followers on social media lent their support to the women-led campaign to discourage voting in the 2018 presidential elections for Jair Bolsonaro, a politician known for his sexism and homophobia. As Heloísa Buarque de Holanda (2017: 7) has observed in relation to Brazil:

> Today the young feminist movements, black feminism, trans feminism and many others are moving centre-stage and gaining the visibility they deserve. The movement is animated: the streets have already demonstrated what women want, the internet is a huge laboratory for the creation of an inclusive and alert activism.

However, the upworthy news regarding women's participation in the film industry needs nuancing. As discussed elsewhere in this monograph, funding calls issued by the national government agencies such as Ancine tend to be oversubscribed and/or bureaucratic, subject to the ideological whims of those who lead them, and Ancine's decision in 2018 to grade filmmakers according to their success with the public is likely to have a detrimental effect on first-time directors, among others (Lima, 2018). Only six female directors scored the highest mark (10) in Ancine's first grading in 2018. Women still make predominantly short, low-budget films with low-key engagement with the public. As Ancine (2018a) has revealed through its snapshot investigation of the conditions of women in the audio-visual sector in 2016, the more expensive a film, the fewer the number of women working on it will be.

While an admirable 40% of the entries to the Oscar selection competition in 2018 were women, the nod went to veteran (male, white) director Carlos Diegues with *O grande circo místico* (*The Great Mystical Circus*, 2018). Diegues, as well as being the most selected filmmaker for Academy Award competition (he has never won), was recently welcomed to the ranks of the so-called *imortais* or immortals of the Brazilian Academy of Letters, itself still dominated by white men and associated with patriarchal tradition. Diegues took up the seat left vacant by fellow *cinemanovista*, the late Nelson Pereira dos Santos.

According to Lúcia Nagib (2017: 32), "the most decisive contribution brought about by the rise of women in Brazilian filmmaking has been the spread of team-work and shared authorship, as opposed to a mere aspiration to the auteur pan-theon, as determined by a notoriously male-oriented tradition". As admirable as this contribution might be, it does not square with the perhaps unconscious process of privileging solo directors both within academia and within the film industry, itself a reflection of a certain obsession on the part of film studies academics, film critics and funders with an auteurist filmmaking tradition. As Knott (2014) argues:

> In cinema, as in many other industries, women are pushed towards collabora-tive, supportive roles, while men are encouraged to be leaders. The qualities associated with the hallowed director figure – leadership, authority, creative genius – are codified in our society as male.

One recalls the dropping of the name of Kátia Lund in relation to the international hit *Cidade de Deus* (*City of God*, 2002), purportedly to enable the film to compete at the Oscars (under the name of Fernando Meirelles), where co-direction is not recognised. The result was the erasure of Lund's contribution in the long term, not only to *Cidade de Deus* but also to the spin-off TV series *Cidade dos homens* (*City of Men*, 2002–2005). Lund later stated in relation to the Oscar oversight:

> A year of preparation. Sitting on the set next to Fernando. Going to the edit. I was not there just to hold his hand. It puts me in a very awkward position. I worked on the script from the 4th to the 12th draft. I supervised the crew. I know I was there working with Fernando to construct the vision and style of this film. If I was not directing, what was I doing?
>
> *(Knott 2018)*[9]

Likewise filmmaker Daniela Thomas's co-direction of films involving the much more high-profile Walter Salles is not always acknowledged.

A woman's film for our times? Anna Muylaert's *Que horas ela volta?*

Anna Muylaert's *Que horas ela volta?* (*The Second Mother*) was released in 2015 to both critical and popular acclaim. Muylaert's first feature film since her 2009 *É proibido fumar* (*Smoke Gets in Your Eyes*), it performed well on the film festival cir-cuit, with awards from Sundance and Berlin, and it was a box-office success (over half a million spectators, including both domestic and international screenings). Muylaert was only the second Brazilian woman to have a film put forward for the

Academy Award for Best Foreign Film competition (after Suzana Amaral in 1986 with the aforementioned *A hora da estrela*). In *Que horas ela volta?* Val, played by popular TV presenter and comedian Regina Casé, is a northeastern woman who works as a live-in maid in a middle-class home in São Paulo. Out of the blue, her teenage daughter Jessica, whom she had left in the Northeast with grandparents 10 years previously (thus mimicking the trajectory and life experience of so many poor women from the interior),[10] announces that she is coming to stay so that she can take the entrance exam to a prestigious university (The School of Architecture of the University of Sao Paulo). At first the family is accommodating, but tensions ensue as a result of Jessica's "behaviour" (her disconcerting self-assurance and non-conformity with class-related expectations), and as a result of the fact that she is more successful in her studies than the family's son, Fabinho.

Like so many Brazilian films *Que horas ela volta?* highlights the dichotomy of experience between poor northeasterners and their wealthier counterparts in the centre-south – and between generations –, but the film stood out at the time of its release for daring to suggest that times are changing. The presence of Jessica, unaccustomed and unaccepting of decades-old unwritten rules about co-habitation between Brazilians of different classes, debunks the supposedly natural order of things, whereby the middle-class family, and in particular the *patroa* (the female head of household), is unable to accommodate her, given that these unwritten rules were not drawn up with the possibility of social ascension in mind.

So greater access to education, one of the cherished *conquistas sociais* or social conquests of the Workers Party government through initiatives such as affirmative action and the creation of new universities,[11] have quite serious implications for the pillars of Brazilian so-called cordiality,[12] which are seen in the film to wobble and eventually come tumbling down. The undoing of this false intimacy (Barbara tells Val she is "almost family", for example), an intimacy designed to cloak injustice and

FIGURE 3.1 The maid Val (Regina Casé) foregrounded in the kitchen, with the mistress Bárbara (Karine Teles) in the dining room. Still from *Que horas ela volta?*

(*The Second Mother*, Anna Muylaert, 2015)

lack of equal opportunities in a uniquely Brazilian form of cordiality, is the highlight of Muylaert's film for many, both in terms of viewing pleasure and the extent to which it contributed to on-going debates about social relations. The latter point is of vital importance, and it needs to be perhaps more central in our interpretation of film culture: the extent to which the film found a wide audience,[13] and in politically very polarised times, that was prepared to engage constructively with its central focus: the shift in relations between the *patroa*, the traditional figure of the female head of the household, and the *empregada*, or the maid, and particularly in light of the so-called PEC das Domésticas (PEC 66/2012), the hard-fought-for and inevitably controversial constitutional amendment which limited the number of hours maids could work.[14]

It is interesting to note that Viviane Ferreira, one of a number of Afro-Brazilian filmmakers beginning to make a mark on the short film scene in Brazil, included a similar reference to greater access to education for traditionally marginalised groups in her award-winning short film *O dia de Jerusa* (*Jerusa's Day*, 2014). In the film, an impatient young market researcher, Silvia (Déborah Marçal), is barely tolerant of the older Jerusa (Léa Garcia) and her insistence on telling her tales of her life rather than answering her market research questions on soap powder. That is, until she receives the news while in Jerusa's home that she has passed the state university entrance exam. Like Jessica in *Que horas ela volta?*, the success of Silvia in getting a place at University serves in the film as a catalyst for rethinking her relationship with both the established order, and those around her. Silvia can suddenly appreciate what she has in common with Jerusa, rather than what separates the two of them. Viviane Ferreira is currently working on a feature-length version of this tale: its importance cannot be underestimated, given that it is nearly 35 years since the last feature-length fiction film was made by an Afro-Brazilian woman as sole director. As Ferreira has observed: "Making the feature film *Jerusa's Day*, with a budget of half a million dollars, will be a historic responsibility for me, and I am aware that if the film was being directed by a white man, it would likely have a much higher budget" (in Mutch-Vidal 2017)

Returning to *Que horas ela volta?*, the choice of the much-loved Regina Casé to play the role of the maid, and in a comedic way, enabled the audience to find a safe point of identification in a plot that might otherwise have been naively read and dismissed as political propaganda. Casé's (uncredited) input into the script will doubtless have contributed to the sense of identification with her plight that many audience members were able to forge. The choice of a light-skinned actress to play the maid's daughter Jessica provoked some criticism, for example from Geledés, one of the most important and most cited Afro-Brazilian feminist internet sites in Brazil (2015). But arguably this choice enabled the filmmaker to disambiguate the issues of class and race, and while it really should be anathema to do so in the Brazilian context, it did arguably enable more conservative members of the audience to focus on questions of intimacy, cordiality and other outmoded social relations without risking making facile, ill-informed and erroneous assumptions about race, as they have historically been prone to do.

That said, one scene in particular does offer another reading for racially con-scious viewers. After Jessica ignores her mother's warnings and takes a dip fully clothed in the family's swimming pool with Fabinho, the *patroa* Barbara drains the pool. It is hard not to recall the probably apocryphal but still very potent and widely heard tale of a swimming pool in Las Vegas being drained after African-American star Dorothy Dandridge dipped her toe in the water. The film was also made on the fiftieth anniversary of the widely covered and widely remembered incident in Florida where, in a protest by integrationists in a motel pool, the motel manager poured acid on black bathers.

When Regina Casé's character Val leaves the middle-class home she breaks the pattern of *agregados*, or social dependants, traditionally at the heart of much of Brazilian social life and highlighted by literary critic Roberto Schwarz as symp-tomatic of Brazil's backwardness (2005). When Val leaves the home she continues her role as nurturer, but now it is her own family and her own home (again, an important element of the Workers Party political programme), rather than someone else's home, that she takes care of.[15]

"What the f*** is women's cinema?"

Throughout 2015 Anna Muylaert was tireless in her promotion of *Que horas ela volta?*, accepting invitations to debates with high-profile politicians, charity workers, representatives of domestic workers associations, and so on, and taking part in Q & As to accompany the launch of the film in different states in Brazil.[16] One such Q and A, after the film's premiere in the northeastern state of Pernambuco (from where the character Val hailed in the film), drew the attention of the national press and provided the catalyst for important reflections on everyday acts of chauvinism experienced by Brazilian women.

At the event, in the Cinema da Fundação, one of the state capital Recife's prem-iere arthouse cinemas, two well-known Pernambucan cineastes, Claudio Assis and Lírio Ferreira, friends of Muylaert, made headline news for their drunken behav-iour. As reported in *O Globo* newspaper (2015), during the Q & A, Assis, who has a reputation for provocative behaviour, referred to actress Regina Casé as fat, and delayed proceedings by insisting that Muylaert chose her own seat on stage. According to the same source, Ferreira was so drunk that he was unable to formu-late a question, and constantly interrupted the debate. The film's art director, Thales Junqueira, commented on the occasion on social media: "I spoke out about my discomfort and how absurd it was to see so many people who were interested in the film abandoning the debate [...]. A spectacle of chauvinism, sexism and body-shaming" (*Globo* 2015).

The filmmakers in question were quick to apologise via social media, blaming excess alcohol for their behaviour, but the Fundação Joaquim Nabuco, the State-sponsored cultural foundation that runs the cinema, with the blessing of the Ministry of Culture, took punitive action against them, and in an official note banned them and their films from the cinema for one year. Focus then shifted away in part from the perceived misogyny of the filmmakers' actions to the question of censorship and freedom of expression, with Ferreira announcing that he would seek legal advice, and Muylaert herself stating that while she did not condone the behaviour of her friends, their films, the making of which will have involved a collective effort, should not suffer as a result of their actions. "This is fascism!", exclaimed a frustrated Assis on social media. "Art is freedom. Art is much bigger than me. I might be a complete prick, but art has nothing to do with this" (Pelli 2015). Assis and Ferreira clearly failed to appreciate the irony of claiming censorship as a result of their own obstruction of a debate after the screening of the film.[17]

Cláudio Assis and Lírio Ferreira, along with directors Paulo Caldas and Marcelo Gomes, among others, belong to a generation of filmmakers from the state of Pernambuco that rose to national and international prominence during the *retomada* period and early twenty-first century, with iconic films such as *Baile perfumado* (*Perfumed Ball*, Caldas and Ferreira, 1997), *Amarelo manga* (*Mango Yellow*, Assis, 2002) and *Cinema, aspirinas e urubus* (*Cinema, Aspirins and Vultures*, Gomes, 2005). This almost exclusively male (and white) group of filmmakers were, and continue to be for many, a source of pride for the region, both as a symbol of strength of filmmaking beyond the centres of Rio and São Paulo, and as an example of close bonds and a spirit of professional teamwork and mutual support. This spirit even gained an affectionate moniker: *brodagem*, a play on the term *broder*, which is a Brazilianised version of the English word brother. The term *brodagem* has only in the last few years been discussed in terms of its gendered nature: when it appeared, it was celebrated as a gender-neutral term, given that a number of women were also involved in the filmmaking scene.[18] The fact that it was only in 2013 that the first feature-length film by a woman from Pernambuco was made, Renata Pinheiro's *Amor, plástico e barulho* (*Love, Plastic and Noise*), points to the secondary roles assumed by women in this scene.[19]

In March 2015 five female filmmakers based in the state of Pernambuco organised a mini-festival of films made by women.[20] According to the organisers, the purpose of the festival was both to give women filmmakers for the first time in Pernambuco the opportunity to have their films discussed, and to contribute towards audience-building: the setting, once again the prestigious Cinema da Fundação in Recife, seemed ideal for both. However, their plans were scuppered by the remarkably strong reactions on social media on the part of the filmmaking establishment to the choice of title for the event: Mostra Cinema de Mulher (literally woman's film festival, but with connotations that suggest a [playful and ironic] dismissiveness of women). The catalyst for the subsequent social media storm came from a post by Thales Junqueira, the same art director who five months later would seek to defend Muylaert and her audience from the misogynist antics of Assis and Ferreira. Junqueira aggressively asked "O que porra é cinema de mulher?" ("What the f★★★ is women's cinema?"). Junqueira would later delete the post and the hundreds of comments it received.[21]

Many of the aforementioned *broders* commented on the post, some sarcastically, others using sexist and homophobic language, and when questioned, their and others' defence was that they were only taking issue with the name of the festival. However, some commentators, including a number of women, did question the need for a festival of films made by women, claiming that they risked ghettoising their work.

One of the organisers of the festival, Séphora Silva was warned to expect heckling from the audience during screenings, which in the end were practically boycotted by members of the local film industry (Wanderley, 2016: 99; 103).

> The debate on Facebook was awful: extremely aggressive, misogynist, prejudiced, angry and it impacted on the festival [...] the public that went to the festival was attracted by the debate on Facebook. And the debate on Facebook wasn't about our films. [...] We wanted to screen our films and discuss our films. And we didn't get that opportunity [...] The level of discussion was of the same level as the Facebook comments: empty and aggressive. [...] That revolting debate on Facebook took away any pleasure from organising the festival.
>
> *(Liana Cisne in Wanderley 2016:103)*

The difference in reaction to these two instances of misogynist behaviour, only five months apart, is striking, and it can be explained in part by a culture of fear of rocking the boat, in a region (the Northeast) which is understood to be intractably sexist.[22] As filmmaker Renata Pinheiro has stated:

> We [women] are taught to remain silent when we are attacked. It is naturalised, as if that's the way it's meant to be. So many women haven't taken forward their own film projects because it is easier to be part of a man's team. It's more accepted. But times are changing.
>
> *(Ximenes n/d)*

While accepting Assis and Ferreira's apologies, and while defending their right to have their own films screened, Muylaert did make the following keen observation:

> What is more important than discussing what happened [at the Q & A] is the opening up of debate about how society might learn to accept situations in which women are protagonists and men the supporting cast. [...] One of the themes of my film that we were discussing that day is precisely invisible social rules that we abide by, often without realising.
>
> *(G1 2015)*

As a result of Muylaert's interrupted Q and A, feminist collectives issued formal critiques of what on this occasion was identified as chauvinism: one such critique co-signed by a number of entities and published in the *Diário de Pernambuco* broadsheet (2015) made ample reference to the Mostra Cinema de Mulher debacle and linked the two events as examples of the kind of chauvinism that was a common feature of the audio-visual sphere in Pernambuco, and that needed to be vigorously challenged. And within weeks the pressure group Quebrando Vidraças (Breaking Glass) had been formed by women working in a range of professions linked to the audio-visual industry in Pernambuco. This in turn led to a number of initiatives, such as state-government support for women-centred workshops attached to film festivals, for example Festcine in 2016. And an international women's film festival, FINCAR was successfully staged in 2016, although interestingly, none of the women who organised the fateful Mostra Cinema de Mulher were involved in this festival.

Maria Augusta Ramos and the trial of Dilma Rousseff

When it comes to documenting lesser-known identities and life experiences, women are behind some of the most innovative and thoughtful films coming out of contemporary Brazil. Take, for example, the work of Maria Augusta Ramos. Ramos's films are renowned for their ability to demystify certain spaces and processes, through which audiences can nuance their understanding of, for example, the judicial system and how its unwieldy nature impacts on the lives of those that pass through it, as in the case of *Justiça* (*Justice*, 2004), the penal system and how its design means it could never successfully serve as either a form of deterrent or a method of individual reform, in the case of *Juízo* (*Behave*, 2007), the recent and ultimately failed attempt to "pacify" Rio de Janeiro's notorious slums in *Morro dos Prazeres* (*Hill of Pleasures*, 2013), or the impact of what can feel like quite impersonal mass demonstrations on the individual lives of Brazilians from different walks of life, as in *Futuro junho* (*Future June*, 2015).[23]

Looking first at *Morro dos Prazeres*, the film takes its name from the favela or hill-side slum in the Santa Teresa neighbourhood of Rio de Janeiro and it captures the daily routine of a few of those who work and/or live in the favela: members of the newly created UPP or Pacifying Police Force, the local postman and trainer of a women's football team, the guy who sells books, a bisexual teen who cares for her grandmother but struggles to stay out of trouble with the law, and so on. *Morro dos Prazeres* premiered at the Brasilia film festival in 2013, the same year Tiago Campos Torres's *O mestre e o divino* (*Master and Divine*, 2013), won the best documentary category (see Chapter 6). This victory is likely the result of the fact that *O mestre e o divino* was less problematic to get behind in terms of a cause being represented (the increased access of indigenous groups to technology and new media and the positive impact this has on their sense of identity and social consciousness). In the case of *Morro dos Prazeres*, Ramos's brilliantly executed observational style did not provide a good news story that could be embraced by left and right, given that it highlighted both the fear and the frustration of the police officers in their roles (the new police force is made up in large part of women), as well as the dangers posed by the occupation of the favela to the strong sense of community, and the inherent lack of support services which were supposed to accompany the UPP into the favelas and whose absence, we could argue, ultimately resulted in the failure of the occupation exercise.

Maria Ramos's latest documentary, released in 2018, represents a departure, in the sense that her views on what she is filming are unavoidably made clear. Encouraged by friends and colleagues, and clearly driven by an admirable sense of civic duty and deep frustration at the impeachment process, Ramos spent months in 2016 in her home city of Brasília filming behind the scenes at the Senate Committee Chamber and with Rousseff's impeachment defence team. The name of the film, *O processo* (*The Trial*), is self-explanatory for anyone who followed, in 2016, the Kafkaeque process of replacing, with the most wafer-thin veneer of legitimacy imaginable, President Rousseff and her Worker's Party with her Vice-President of the right-wing MDB party, Michel Temer. Ramos's film was awarded post-production support from the Berlin Film Festival World Cinema Fund, and had its premiere at the festival in 2018 (it was enthusiastically received by a mostly ex-pat audience and won third place in the Panorama Audience Award). With its general release in Brazil ahead of the 2018 elections, it has contributed to political debates, if not by changing hearts and minds then at least by galvanising support for the Workers Party within sectors of the public used to watching political documentaries in film theatres.

The notional grounds for impeaching President Rousseff were as a result of perceived crimes of fiscal responsibility, and specifically "fiscal pedalling" in her administration. The Rousseff Administration's budgeting allegedly used this so-called pedalling to improve its fiscal outcomes and make the surplus for the years 2012 to 2014 appear larger. Regardless of what one might think in relation to

FIGURE 3.2 A female officer in Rio's Pacification Police (UPP) laments the low esteem in which the police are held. Still from *Morro dos Prazeres*

(*Hill of Pleasures*, Maria Augusta Ramos, 2012)

both her culpability and the need to call for impeachment and thus overthrow a government over the relatively common practice, it is perhaps worth bearing in mind that unlike a huge number of her fellow politicians, no claim has ever been made in relation to Dilma Rousseff, a militant in her youth who was imprisoned and tortured during the military dictatorship, that she used her political position to generate personal wealth.

What becomes clear in the footage of her trail is that her culpability or otherwise is of little importance. What we witness is a kangaroo court in action, but one for which the defence team is still expected to spend a large amount of time and resources in the ultimately pointless preparation of countering claims of illegality. It is little wonder, then, that many supporters of Rousseff and the Workers Party have found the film distressing to watch.

Few objective observers nowadays deny that the ousting of Rousseff in 2016 was tantamount to a parliamentary coup, and watching this documentary certainly leaves very little room for doubt. Where the nation remains divided is over whether her removal was in fact the right thing to do for the long-term good of the country. Some claim that the use of lawfare was justifiable in order to rid the nation of what had become a very unpopular leader, given the deep economic recession into which Brazil had been plunged after years of riding the high of a commodities boom. Others argue that Rousseff's removal mid-term was part of an on-going process on the part of Brazil's elites to both halt the progress made in Brazil in terms of social justice, and to scupper the chances of the Workers Party being re-elected in 2018, and what the film clearly suggests was a diversionary tactic to halt the Lava-jato grafting investigation (Operation Car-wash).

As critic Luciana Veras (2018) has stated, *O processo* is about "the year that never ends". And here the reference is not just to the impact of Rousseff's removal from power in terms of the austerity measures quickly put in place by her successor, the deeply unpopular Michel Temer,[24] including a 20-year spending freeze. The measures constitute "the mother of all austerity plans", according to the *Washington Post* (2018) and they have been described by the UN special rapporteur on extreme poverty and human rights, Philip Alston, as the most socially regressive austerity package in the world (*Washington Post*, 2018).

2016 is also the year that never ends in the sense that Brazilians were left somewhat in limbo as they awaited elections in October 2018. And Rousseff's party, the Workers Party, continued to battle against odds that were unscrupulously stacked against it in that its initial presidential candidate, the still very popular two-time Brazilian president Lula, was hastily convicted of corruption on what look to many Brazilian and international observers as shaky grounds, begging the question to what extent his imprisonment is part of the same process of lawfare that ousted Rousseff.

Returning to the documentary, one might think that the lack of voiceover and minimal intertitles with explanations and names and roles of participants means that the film makes no concessions to those who have not been following Brazilian politics closely over the past few years. But in truth *O processo* is shot and edited with such skill that the political persuasion and importance of each individual portrayed

FIGURE 3.3 Promotional poster for *O processo*

(*The Trial*, Maria Augusta Ramos, 2018). Reproduced with permission of Maria Augusta Ramos

is made self-evident. Nevertheless it is perhaps worth singling out a couple of characters that appear in the film.[25] One of the first figures to appear in the documentary, for example, is Eduardo Cunha, then the leader of Congress and for many Dilma Rousseff's nemesis as the mastermind of impeachment. Cunha, within months of Rousseff's impeachment, was imprisoned on grounds of corruption and money-laundering, having been named in the Panama Papers and implicated and found guilty in the national grafting scandal involving the state petroleum company Petrobras. He is currently serving a 15-year sentence.

Then we have Janaína Pascoal, the high-profile evangelical Christian law professor and co-author of the impeachment submission who perhaps surprisingly granted the filmmaker access. While she might well come across as genuine, her undoubtedly eccentric performance[26] in front of the camera stands in contrast to Gleisi Hoffman, Workers Party president and remarkably calm, patient and self-assured under the circumstances, and who features extensively in the film. Thus with the exception of one or two key male Workers Party senators, it is the women, both to the left and the right, and in front of and behind the cameras, that stand out in *O processo*, in a political world otherwise occupied by unscrupulous, duplicitous and in many cases misogynistic men.

It is interesting to note that two other high-profile women filmmakers, Petra Costa and the aforementioned Anna Muylaert (the latter as producer) have been involved in their own documentation of the impeachment process. Petra Costa, together with her editor Jordana Berg, have been working on a documentary entitled *Impeachment* (expected 2019). In this they have received support from Sundance (documentary edit and story lab) and the Venice Film Festival. Lô Politi, along with Anna Muylaert as producer (with Cesar Charlone), are also working on a similar project, again without recourse to public or party funding.[27] The number of women filmmakers drawn to the subject of impeachment lends weight to the view that what happened to Rousseff, regardless of what one might think of her political ability, was regarded as an assault on all women in positions of power and influence, and was felt particularly strongly within increasingly well organised and politicised women's filmmaking circles.

Concluding remarks

In the current climate of on the one hand a rise in intolerance and open acts of violence and sexism as endorsed by representatives of far-right politics, and on the other of women-centred movements that challenge this intolerance, one can hope that stories told by women (both as directors and scriptwriters) about women will increase and find new audiences. But this is contingent on the right kind of institutional support, such as accessible methods of funding for the full range of audio-visual production, as well as dealing in a meaningful way with the age-old problem of film distribution. The growing wave of intolerance with regard to what are interpreted as leftist cultural representations and how they are funded (the misinformed reactions to the Rouanet Law as discussed in Chapter 1, for example) has already had an impact in terms of an increase in "male allies" showing their support for women working in the film industry.[28] And filmmakers and cultural commentators (female and male) are beginning to reflect on the unwritten codes that discourage women from taking on leadership roles in filmmaking (or elsewhere), speaking out against signs of prejudice and "spoil[ing] the party" (Knott, 2014), in the case of Kátia Lund in relation to *City of God*. And as films like *Que horas ela volta?* and Kleber Mendonça Filho's *Aquarius* (2016), as analysed in Chapter 10, ably demonstrate, there are both female and male filmmakers in Brazil sharing stories that find an audience about strong women who refuse to remain silent and not question their designated places in society.

Notes

1 Two other important texts in English are Marsh (2012) and Benamou and Marsh (2013). An important reference for these texts and many of the Brazil-focused chapters in Shaw and Martin's collection was the Mulheres da Retomada film festival and conference in Tulane in 2010, organised by Ana López: filmmakers Lúcia Murat, Sandra Kogut, Consuelo Lins and Petra Costa were all in attendance at the conference.

2 It was not until 2002 that a monograph dedicated to the work of Carmen Santos was finally published: Ana Pessoa, *Carmen Santos: o cinema dos anos 20*.

3 Included in Paulo Paranagua's essay on "pioneering" women filmmakers (*Framework* 1989). Gilda de Abreu is the focus of a monograph *Gilda, a paixao pela forma* (Miceli 2008).

4 See, for example, Mocarzel (2010).

5 Most academic studies that discuss *A hora da estrela* focus on the film as adaptation. Traci Roberts-Camps (2017) updates the analysis of Amaral's contribution to Brazilian filmmaking by reading *A hora da estrela* together with her more recent films.

6 Nowadays, with a marked shift towards intersectional approaches in academic research, Adélia Sampaio is being discussed, and she serves as an inspiration for a new generation of Afro-Brazilian women filmmakers starting to make a serious mark on the short-filmmaking landscape in Brazil and beyond (Sobrinho, 2017).

7 Unlike a number of other scholars, Nagib (2017: 32) defines the *retomada* or renaissance of filmmaking in Brazil from the mid-1990s, as lasting from 1994–1998.

8 *Variety* ran a feature on the large number of female producers from Brazil who had films at the Berlinale in 2018: Hopewell and Lang, 2018. It is worth acknowledging that a number of female producers work in partnership with their director husbands: these include Mariza Leão (wife of Sergio Rezende), and Emilie Lesclaux (wife of Kleber Mendonça Filho). Nagib (2017: 35) cites other such personal/professional partnerships in the film industry.

9 In interview with Knott (2018), Lund further lamented that at Cannes ahead of *City of God's* release "she already sensed that she was being treated by the press not as a director but as 'the woman who took care of the kids and was the tour guide of the favela'".

10 The theme of women looking after other people's offspring, leaving them unable to bring up their biological children, is also explored by Walter Salles and Daniela Thomas in their contribution (*Loin du 16e*) to the portmanteau film *Paris Je t'aime* (2006): Shaw (2017:131).

11 Some of these "conquests" were set in motion, albeit very tentatively, by the previous government of Fernando Henrique Cardoso. That said, the number of women in Higher Education more than doubled during PT governments (2002–2016).

12 The subject of cordiality, and other films that deal with the subject of maids and mistresses, will be dealt with in Chapter 10 in this volume.

13 The ability to reach a wide audience was facilitated in part by co-producer Globo Filmes: the film was featured twice on TV Globo's primetime show *Fantástico*, and within six months of its theatrical release, the film had screened on both cable and terrestrial TV (Telecine and TV Globo).

14 For further explorations of maid-mistress relations in Brazilian film, see the special issue of *Journal of Iberian and Latin American Studies* entitled "Intimacy and Cordiality in Contemporary Brazilian Culture" (2018).

15 The film's title in Portuguese – literally "What time will she be back?" – references this tradition of the *terciarização do cuidado* or outsourcing of care.

16 For example, the then Minister of Social Development, Tereza Campello, joined Muylaert at a screening in Porto Alegre in January 2016, and another in Recife in November 2015 screened to an invited audience of domestic workers.

17 Three weeks later Assis would be prevented by angry spectators from introducing his new film, *Big jato* (2015) at the Brasilia Film Festival. His leading man, Mateus Nachtergaele, replaced him on stage, with the audience's approval.

18 See Nogueira (2009).

19 Interestingly, the film deals with the experience of female singers in the hierarchical, chauvinist world of the *brega* music scene in Pernambuco. See Dantas et al. (2017).

20 Alessandra Nilo, Isabela Cribari, Lia Leticia, Liana Cisne Lins and Séphora Silva.

21 Natalia Vanderley details the social media storm and its impact in a Masters dissertation completed in 2016 entitled *O que porra é cinema de mulher?* Through fear of legal action, and perhaps fear of recriminations from within the ranks of the local film industry, Vanderlay at least superficially hides the identity of those involved in the post in her dissertation.

22 Cláudio Assis made this point in light of the Q & A controversy: "I had a very sexist (*machista*) upbringing. All north-easterners are sexist. Brazil is sexist. The world is sexist" (in Stivaletti 2015).

23 See Allen (2017) and Holmes (2018).

24 In an explosive review of the film, Jay Weissberg writing in *Variety* describes Temer as "a man who invites credible corruption allegations like rats attract fleas" (2018).

25 In fact Rousseff's participation in the behind-the-scenes filming is minimal: the only footage we see of her that is not public access footage is of a meeting with foreign correspondents. Writing about Rousseff in May 2016, *Guardian* correspondent Jonathan Watts commented "in the past month she may well have given more interviews to overseas journalists than in the previous six years".

26 Jay Weissberg (2018) describes Pascoal as "a ridiculous figure [...], a melodramatic shill whose flamboyant performances make one wonder if she's simply lying or truly delusional". We should acknowledge the veritable field-day that left-wing commentators have had at Pascoal's expense, which borders on misogyny in many instances.

27 The male filmmaker Adirley Queirós released in 2017 *Era uma vez Brasília*, enthusiastically received at the Locarno Film Festival, about the impact of impeachment proceedings on the lives of ordinary people in Brasilia and the satellite town Ceilândia. Another male director, Douglas Duarte, released *Excelentíssimos* in late 2018: the film, whose original remit was to depict the Brazilian legislature and executive in action, focuses on the time of impeachment and beyond.

28 See Shaw (2018).

References

Allen, A. L. 2017. *Shifting Horizons: Urban Space and Social Difference in Contemporary Brazilian Documentary and Photography*. Hoboken: Wiley.

Amadeu da Silveira, S., Machado, M. B. and Savazoni, R. T. 2013. "Backward march: the turn-around in public cultural policy in Brazil". *Media, Culture and Society*. 35: 5, pp. 549–564.

Ancine. 2018a. *Diversidade de gênero e raça nos longas-metragens brasileiros lançados em salas de exibição 2016*. https://oca.Ancine.gov.br/sites/default/files/repositorio/pdf/informe_diversidade_2016.pdf.

Ancine. 2018b. "Divulgado resultado preliminar do Concurso Produção para Cinema 2018". www.Ancine.gov.br/pt-br/sala-imprensa/noticias/divulgado-resultado-preliminar-do-concurso-produ-o-para-cinema-2018.

Benamou, C. and Marsh, L. L. 2013. "Women Filmmakers and citizenship in Brazil, from Bossa Nova to the retomada". In Nair, P. and Gutiérrez-Albilla, J. D. (eds) *Hispanic and Lusophone Women FIlmmakers, Theory, Practice and Difference*. Manchester: MUP, pp. 54–71.

Buarque de Holanda, Heloísa. 2017. "Prefácio". in Holanda, K. and Tedesco, M. C. (eds) *Feminino e plural: mulheres no cinema brasileiro*. Campinas: Papirus, pp. 7–8.

Diário de Pernambuco. "Coletivos e entidades manifestam apoio à punição aplicada a cineastas". 2015. *Diário de Pernambuco*. 3 September. www.diariodepernambuco.com.br/app/noticia/viver/2015/09/03/internas_viver,596221/coletivos-e-entidades-manifestam-apoio-a-punicao-aplicada-a-cineastas.shtml.

Dantas, D. F, Santos, I. and Nolasco, R. I F. 2017. "*Amor, plástico e barulho*: protagonismo e rivalidade feminina como elementos estéticos e narrativos no cinema pernambucano". In Holanda, K. and Tedesco, M. C. (eds), *Feminino e plural: mulheres no cinema brasileiro*. Campinas: Papirus, pp. 187–198.

Dennison, S. (ed). 2018. "Intimacy and Cordiality in Contemporary Brazilian Culture", special issue of *Journal of Iberian and Latin American Studies* 24:3.

Fagundez, I. and Mendonça, R. 2016. "Como primeira 'presidenta'. Dilma deixou algum legado para as mulheres?". *BBC Brasil*. 1 Setembro. www.bbc.com/portuguese/brasil-37226797.

Geledés, 2015. "*Que Horas Ela Volta?* silencia sobre racismo e os privilégios da branquitude". 30 November. www.geledes.org.br/que-horas-ela-volta-silencia-sobre- racismo-e-os-privilegios-da-branquitude/.

Globo. 2015. "Após confusão no Recife, Claudio Assis pede desculpas a Anna Muylaert". *Globo*. 1 September. https%3A%2F%2Foglobo.globo.com%2Fcultura%2Ffilmes%2Fapos-confusao-no-recife-claudio-assis-pede-desculpas-anna-muylaert-17371387.

Holanda, K. and Tedesco, M. C. (eds). 2017. *Feminino e plural: mulheres no cinema brasileiro*. Campinas: Papirus.

Holmes, T. 2018. "Capturing Brazilian Society in Movement: From Cordiality and Circulation and "Spaces In Between". In Maria Augusta Ramos's *Futuro Junho* (2015)", *Journal of Iberian and Latin American Studies* 24:3, pp. 367–389.

Hopewell, J. and Lang, J. 2018. "Brazilian Women Producers Make a Splash in Berlin". *Variety*. 15 February. https://variety.com/2018/film/festivals/brazilian-women-producers-make-a-splash-in-berlin-1202701700/.

Genestreti, G. 2018. "MinC lança editais para o audiovisual com cotas para minorias". *Folha de S. Paulo*. 6 February. www1.folha.uol.com.br/ilustrada/2018/02/minc-lanca-editais-para-o-audiovisual-com-cotas-para-minorias.shtml?fbclid=IwAR0Ol2v2r_GU0LHFkXZcSUVawn85rCQUny3M4URm4DXYAvPud95pJWjPwuM.

Knott, M. H. 2014. "Heroines of Cinema: Kátia Lund, the Director of *City of God* Who Never Was". *Indiewire*. 9 January. www.indiewire.com/2014/01/heroines-of-cinema-katia-lund-the-oscar-nominated-director-who-never-was-31586/.

Lima, J. D. 2018. "A lista da ANCINE que dá notas a diretores. E por que é criticada". *Nexo*. 21 August. www.nexojornal.com.br/expresso/2018/08/21/A-lista-da-Ancine-que-d%C3%A1-nota-a-diretores.-E-por-que-%C3%A9-criticada.

Marsh, L. L. 2012. *Brazilian Women's Filmmaking: From Dictatorship to Democracy*. Champaign: University of Illinois Press.

Miceli, S. 2008. *Gilda, a paixao pela forma*. Rio de Janeiro: Ouro Sobre Azul.

Mocarzel, Evaldo. 2010. *Ana Carolina: Coleção Aplauso*. São Paulo: Imprensa Oficial.

Mutch-Vidal, N. 2017. "'Sempre estamos lutando para nos firmar' Adélia Sampaio (2016). The absence of Afro-Brazilian women from the Brazilian Film Industry". Unpublished undergraduate research project, University of Leeds.

Nagib, L. 2017. "Beyond Difference: Female Participation in the Brazilian Film Revival of the 1990s". In Martin, D. and Shaw, D. (eds), Latin American Women Filmmakers: Production, Politics, Poetics. London: IB Tauris, pp. 31–47.

Nogueira, A. M. C. 2009. "O novo ciclo de cinema em Pernambuco: uma questão de estilo". Unpublished Masters dissertation. Federal University of Pernambuco.

Paranaguá, P. A. 1989. "Pioneers: Women Filmmakers in Latin America". *Framework* 37, pp. 129–138.

Pelli, R. 2015. "Acusados de machismo em debate, Claudio Assis e Lirio Ferreira dizem sofrer censura". *O globo*. 5 September. https://oglobo.globo.com/cultura/filmes/acusados-de-machismo-em-debate-claudio-assis-lirio-ferreira-dizem-sofrer-censura-17403739.

Pessoa, A. 2002. *Carmen Santos: o cinema dos anos 20*. Sao Paulo: Aeroplano.

"'Que horas ela volta?': Cláudio Assis polemiza sobre filme de Regina Casé". *G1* 1 September. http://g1.globo.com/pop-arte/cinema/noticia/2015/09/que-horas-ela-volta-claudio-assis-polemiza-sobre-filme-de-regina-case.html.

Rich, B R. 2017. "Preface: Performing the Impossible in Plain Sight". In Shaw, D. and Martin, D. (eds), *Latin American Women Filmmakers: Production, Politics, Poetics*. London: IB Tauris, pp. xv–xx.

Schwarz, R. 2005. "A Brazilian Breakthrough". *New Left Review* 36. https://newleftreview.org/II/36/roberto-schwarz-a-brazilian-breakthrough.

Shaw, D. and Martin, D. (eds), *Latin American Women Filmmakers: Production, Politics, Poetics*. London: IB Tauris.

Shaw, D. 2017. "Intimacy and Distance – Domestic Servants in Latin American Women's Cinema: La mujer sin cabeza and El niño pez / The Fish Child (Puenzo, 2009)". In Shaw, D. and Martin, D. (eds), *Latin American Women Filmmakers: Production, Politics, Poetics*. London: IB Tauris, pp. 123–148.

Shaw, D. 2018. "*Latin American Women Filmmakers: Production, Politics, Poetics*: Connections and Collaborations". Keynote delivered at Latin American Women's Filmmaking symposium. Senate House, London 18 September.

Sobrinho, Gilberto Alexandre. 2017. "Identidade, resistência e poder: mulheres negras e a realização de documentários". In Holanda, K. and Tedesco, M. C. (eds). 2017. *Feminino e plural: mulheres no cinema brasileiro*. Campinas: Papirus, pp. 163–174.

Stivaletti, T. 2015. "Claudio Assis comenta vaias em Brasília". 21 September. *FilmeB* . www.filmeb.com.br/noticias/nacional-producao/claudio-assis-comenta-vaias-em-brasilia.

Veras, L. 2018. "*O processo*: 2016, o ano que não tem fim". *Revista continente*. 22 May. https://revistacontinente.com.br/secoes/entrevista/-o-processo---2016--ano-que-nao-tem-fim.

Wanderley, N. L. 2016. "O que porra é cinema de mulher? A mostra Cinema de Mulher e o desvelar do machismo do audiovisual pernambucano". Unpublished Masters Thesis, Federal University of Pernambuco.

Washington Post, "Brazil passes the mother of all austerity measures". 2016. *Washington Post*. www.washingtonpost.com/gdpr-consent/?destination=%2fnews%2fworldviews%2fwp %2f2016%2f12%2f16%2fbrazil-passes-the-mother-of-all-austerity-plans%2f%3f&utm_ term=.0c2c445c7865.

Watts, J. 2016. "A Warrior to the End: Dilma Rousseff a Sinner and Saint in Impeachment Fight". *Guardian*. 12 May. www.theguardian.com/world/2016/may/09/dilma-rousseff- brazil-impeachment-fight-congress-vote.

Weissberg, J. 2018. "Berlin Film Review: *The Trial*". *Variety*. 14 March. https://variety.com/ 2018/film/reviews/the-trial-review-1202725767/.

Xavier, M. 2015. "The Campaigners Challenging Misogyny and Sexism in Brazil". *Guardian*. 3 December. www.theguardian.com/global-development-professionals-network/2015/ dec/03/sexism-misogyny-campaigners-brazil-social-media.

Ximenes, L. n/d. "Entrevista: Renata Pinheiro, primeira mulher a dirigir um longa de ficção em Pernambuco". http://observatoriofeminino.com.br/entrevista-com-renata- pinheiro-diretora-de-amor-plastico-e-barulho/.

4

BRAZIL'S LGBTQ COMMUNITIES AND FILM CULTURE

In 2004 the federal government in Brazil embarked on an ambitious programme designed to combat homophobia (Brasil Sem Homofobia or Brazil without homophobia), in a clear signal that the recently elected Workers Party government intended to embrace the diversity agenda and in particular the promotion of rights of erstwhile marginalised individuals and groups, with a range of planned initiatives from education, civil marriage, to targeted support for members of the trans community. In this, the Workers Party was building on very cautious moves by previous governments post-dictatorship and a number of key institutional shifts, such as the Federal Medical Council's ceasing to interpret homosexuality as a deviance or disease in 1985, nine years before a similar declaration was made by the World Health Organization. But above all the 2004 programme was a reaction to a series of terrifying statistics regarding gay, lesbian and trans experiences, whereby Brazil had clocked up one of the worst records for homophobic hate crimes and murders of members of the LGBTQ community anywhere on earth. Such statistics were and have continued to reveal the deeply negative flipside to the picture-postcard image of Brazil as a tolerant and sexually liberal nation. Such images of Brazil as seen from abroad (see Chapter Eight), and of the mega-cities of Rio de Janeiro and São Paulo as seen from more provincial places within the nation itself, stem in part from a superficial awareness of cultural celebrations such as Carnival, understood by many to be exemplars of a kind of free-flowing, experimental approach to love and sexuality: admired by many as a sign of social progress and liberal sexual politics, and condemned in equal measure by more conservative groups as symbolic of permissiveness and perversion. More recently initiatives such as São Paulo's internationally renowned annual Pride, one of the world's largest; federal civil partnership legislation dating from 2013;[1] the recognition of "social names" for trans people, and national health service (SUS) support for gender reassignment, have given the distinct impression of progress, but despite the increased visibility of Brazil's LGBTQ communities, and despite the good intentions of the Workers Party government (2003–2016) and a number of high-profile attempts at educating the wider public, the terrifying statistics of violence against the LGBTQ community have in fact worsened. And with the ousting of Dilma Rousseff from the presidency in 2016, and the resounding defeat of São Paulo's LGBTQ-friendly mayor Fernando Haddad in elections in the same year, progress in legalising gay and trans rights has come to a standstill. Brazil's LGBTQ movement celebrated 40 years of existence in 2018 while not one single proposal promoting gay and trans rights was made into law (Fernandes 2018), and with the victory of an openly homophobic candidate in the presidential elections of November 2018, Brazil's sizeable LGBTQ community fears it has little to celebrate. The current climate is ably summed up by Linn da Quebrada (Caparica 2016), trans artivist and the subject of a documentary discussed later in this chapter:

> I'm a constant target of aggression and violence. From all sides. And not just me. Many people like me are the target of this kind of violence. A violence that comes from inside the home, from TV, from the church, the street, schools, and even from among our own friends. Sometimes it's camuflaged and sometimes it has no shame in revealing itself. It's even allowed by law to an extent and encouraged by those in power. And hate disguised as opinion is as much to blame as those who kill.

What this chapter seeks to do is to reflect upon the interaction between film culture and both the LGBTQ communities and society at large in the twenty-first century, an interaction (and film production) that has increased exponentially during the period under examination, in large measure as a result of the diversity agenda referred to above, along with a wider range of and broader access to film funding, as discussed in Chapter One. As we will see, in Brazil in the second decade of the twenty-first century it is difficult to separate discussions about diversity, both in terms of film production and its representation on screens, from ongoing debates on what has been confusingly dubbed "gender ideology", a misnomer by which conservative elements claim that accepting gender as a social construct, as Judith Butler (2006) has argued we should, results in brainwashing children and young people in particular into going against the natural, biological or biblical order of things, whereby girls are girls and boys are boys, and it therefore puts at risk the "Brazilian family".[2]

The scant history of LGBTQ film culture in Brazil

LGBTQ film culture has very shallow roots in Brazil. Not only is there a scarcity of films dealing with the broad subject, but there is an equally thin historical bibliography, with Antonio Moreno's A *personagem homosexual no cinema brasileiro* (2001) and David William Foster's *Gender and Society in Brazilian cinema* (1999) still serving as the main academic references in Portuguese and English respectively. Like much

World Cinema in the period of the 1940s to the 1980s, popular comedy films in Brazil, such as the chanchadas, *pornochanchadas* and the hugely popular Trapalhões series of films (see Chapter 2) were speckled with camp characters whose sexuality was more often than not reduced to cheeky one-liners and a source of humorous derision. More serious representations had to deal with the prevailing censorship and thus were frequently skewed in their representation. For example, cultural products dealing with non-hetero-normative relations were severely repressed during the dictatorship (1964–1984). It is likely to be no coincidence that the three most striking films to deal with gay and lesbian desire from the dictatorship period all presented the well-worn idea of homosexuality itself being put on trial. In *O menino e o vento* (*The Boy and the Wind*, Carlos Hugo Christensen, 1967) regarded as the first Brazilian film to deal with homosexual desire, José Roberto (Enio Gonçalves) returns from holiday to discover that he is falsely implicated in the alleged murder of a young man he had befriended on his trip and who had subsequently disappeared. In *O beijo no asfalto* (*The Kiss*, 1981), noteworthy in as much as it was a box-office smash and provoked considerable discussion at the time of its release,[3] straight Arandir (Ney Latorraca) fulfils the wish of a dying man he comes across in the street and gives him a kiss on the mouth. Arandir's trial in this case is by the sensationalist media and his conservative father-in-law (Tarcísio Meira) who is revealed in the end as the homosexual of the tale, when he shoots Arandir in an act of passion and declares his love for him.[4] The third key film from this period is *Amor maldito* (1984), significant above all for being the first, and until 2017 the only Brazilian feature film to be directed (and co-written and produced) by a black woman, Adélia Sampaio.[5] In the film Fernanda (Monique Lafond) stands accused of killing her lover Sueli (Wilma Dias), who had committed suicide as a result of intense pressure from her ultra-conservative and homophobic family.

The first memorable trans performance on screen is Milton Goncalves in the title role of *Rainha Diaba* (*Devil Queen*, Antonio Carlos da Fontoura, 1974), a film defined by the director as a black, gay, pop thriller (Murat 2008: 75). *Rainha Diaba* was made partly under the inspiration of the director's time spent in New York in the early 70s, where he would hang out with the city's colourful Puerto Rican trans community. The *rainha* of the film is an unlikely drug lord with violent tendencies and a loyal army of trans followers (the *diabetes*). The character was said to have been based on Madame Satã (Madam Satan), a larger-than-life, violent character of Rio de Janeiro's bohemian neighbourhood Lapa who in the 1930s moonlighted as a cabaret drag artist. The story of Madame Satã was revived for the cinema to critical acclaim in 2004 by Karim Ainouz (*Madame Satã*), starring Lázaro Ramos.

For Lufe Steffen (in Toller 2018), the first authentically portrayed trans character in Brazilian fiction cinema was Lilica in Hector Babenco's critical and commercial hit *Pixote: a lei do mais fraco* (*Pixote*, 1981).[6] Babenco went on to adapt the Argentine Manuel Puig's novel *O beijo da mulher aranha* (*Kiss of the Spider Woman*, 1985), the US-Brazilian co-production for which William Hurt won an Oscar for his role as the transgender Luis Molina. And Babenco's prison drama *Carandiru* (2003) includes a stand-out performance by Rodrigo Santoro as the trans prisoner Lady

Di. What is striking about the three trans characters portrayed in Babenco's films is that they are incarcerated (Molina and Lady Di appear exclusively in prison and the teenage Lilica spends time in a FEBEM or youth reform centre). Babenco's films thus portray the characters' trans positioning as a struggle against both State control of their bodies, and as an expression of transgression, delinquency and/or deserving to be punished. Likewise, Sérgio Toledo's *Vera* (1987), relates the experiences of trans poet Anderson Herzer who was brought up in a FEBEM and committed suicide at the age of 20.[7]

The times they are a-changing: Anna Muylaert's *Mãe só há uma* (2016)

Throughout the twenty-first century there has been a steady production of both short and feature-length documentaries that have screened at film festivals and on cable television channels at home and abroad which provide a historical overview of the LGBTQ experience in Brazil, such as *Dzi Croquettes* (Tatiana Issa and Raphael Alvarez, 2009), which documents the influential countercultural theatre troupe of the same name of the 1970s, and *Lampião da esquina* (Livia Perez, 2016) which similarly makes creative use of found footage and interviews with key players in the eponymous seminal magazine aimed at gay men which was published between 1978 and 1981. In *Meu amigo Claudia* (2009) Dacio Pinheiro recounts the story of one of São Paulo's quasi-mythical *travestis* of the 1980s. As well as this all-important gap-filling historical perspective in films,[8] there has also been an expressive number of films that document the shifts in experience of Brazil's LGBTQ communities over the course of the new millennium, such as *Vestidas de noiva* (Fabia Fuzeti and Gabi Torrezani, 2015) in which the two female directors discuss and document their own civil wedding plans. In Caio Cavechini and Carlos Juliano Barros's 2016 film *Entre os homens de bem* (*The Stranger in the House*) we follow, over the course of three years, the experiences of LGBTQ and Human Rights activist Jean Wyllys, one of a very small number of openly gay members of Congress. Wyllys rose to fame in 2005 when he became the first gay participant to win the popular series Big Brother Brasil.

One such feature-length fiction film to document these shifts is Anna Muylaert's *Mãe só há uma* (*Don't Call Me Son*, 2016), the follow-up to her box-office hit *Que horas ela volta?* discussed in Chapter 3. *Mãe só há uma*, which literally means there is only one mother, is another feature film by Muylaert that reflects on changing times. The film was greeted warmly by critics and played to packed houses on the festival circuit, although it has not repeated the popular success at home of *Que horas ela volta?*.

In *Mãe só há uma* Muylaert drew inspiration from the true story of a baby that was stolen from a maternity hospital in Brazil, only for his mother to be jailed and for him to be forcibly returned to his biological family when he was a teenager. In her film Pierre, like Jessica in *Que horas ela volta?*, pushes against social mores, convention and a supposedly progressive new family: his refusal to settle into his new home and family is expressed through his deliberately provocative cross-dressing (he chooses a bright red dress on one occasion to wear to a family gathering).[9] Thus, while generational clashes are presented in both of Muylaert's films, the focus here is more intently on questions around sexual identity and biology. In this film Muylaert pulls no punches, with no pussyfooting around a potential conservative viewing public with what is in many ways a joyful celebration of gender fluidity.

The Brazilian film poster for *Mãe só há uma*, of the character Pierre on a bicycle raising his middle finger (complete with nail polish) and staring at the camera, is a likely gesture of defiance on the part of the filmmaker against the growing wave of criticism of gender ideology.[10] When Muylaert made the film Judith Butler had already visited Brazil in 2015 and she had been heckled by a small group of conservatives. The incident received, as is often the case, more indignation and therefore more coverage on social media than it perhaps merited. In October 2017 an online petition acquired over 360,000 signatures in an attempt to prevent Butler from taking part in a conference in São Paulo. Unlikely as it is that 360,000 Brazilians are both familiar with the work of Judith Butler and prepared to lobby online against it, it is worth pointing out that on that occasion her talk was not on gender, identity or performance, by rather on her recent work on democracy. The protests, while still relatively insignificant in size, were larger than before, and provoked strong reactions, given in particular the burning of an effigy of Butler by a member of the protesting crowd.

Muylaert commented in interview that for her the film is an exploration of a new dynamic that she witnessed post-2014: "nowadays people are more uninhibited, free from labels, less concerned with what box to put their worries in" (in Moraes 2016). By aligning the "true story" of a teenager obliged to rethink his identity after being returned to his biological parents, with one of exploration of gender and sexuality, Muylaert was staking a claim for understanding sexuality as fluid and gender as a social construct.

Exhibiting the LGBTQ experience

Like many minority groups, LGBTQ communities in Brazil, both filmmakers and viewers, rely on the enthusiasm and commitment of individuals, a number of community-focused film festivals and occasional sources of dedicated funding support for the production and dissemination of LGBTQ-themed films. A key individual in the current exhibition landscape is Lufe Steffen. A self-defined "cultural agitator", he directed, among other films, *São Paulo em Hi-Fi* (*Sao Paulo in HiFi*, 2013), a documentary exploration of São Paulo's gay nightlife in the 60s, 70s and 80s, and he regularly runs LGBTQ film courses in the state of Sao Paulo.[11] Steffen was also responsible for a ground-breaking 10-part series entitled *Cinema Diversidade* (Diversity Cinema) screened on cable channel Prime Box Brasil in 2017–2018, and for one of relatively few books on LGBTQ filmmaking in Brazil in the twenty-first century: *O cinema que ousa dizer seu nome* (the cinema that dares to speak its name, 2016).

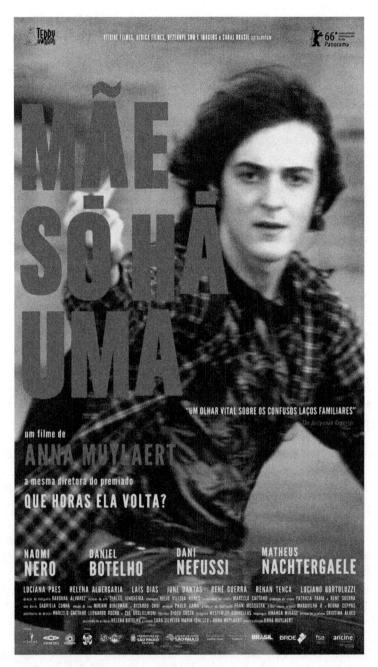

FIGURE 4.1 Promotional poster for *Mãe só há uma*

(*Don't Call Me Son*, Anna Muylaert, 2016). Reproduced with permission of Anna Muylaert

Brazil's foremost film and arts festival celebrating diversity is Festival Mix Brasil, which dates from 1993 and includes screenings in the state of São Paulo and Rio de Janeiro. The festival took its inspiration from the New York Gay and Lesbian Experimental Film Festival. When it first began, according to Steffen, as the only gay film festival in Brazil at the time it encouraged the production of gay-themed films, starting with short films and eventually moving into feature-film production. The festival's website makes clear the role it assumes in consciousness-raising and challenging the growing wave of intolerance in contemporary Brazil, as well as in exhibiting LGBTQ films. The 2017 edition of the festival screened 32 Brazilian films from five different regions of the country, "a clear demonstration of the energy and vitality of Brazilian LGBTQ audio-visual production which is both challenging and continues to grow".

Festival Mix Brasil has benefitted from both government support (State and municipal governments in São Paulo and the Ministry of Culture) and the institutional support from Itaú Cultural, SESC São Paulo and Spcine,[12] organisations that have been happy to have their names associated with a diversity agenda. The 2017 edition of the festival included a short-film selection entitled "Growing up with Diversity" (Crescendo com a Diversidade), aimed at young people and, according to the festival website, emerging as a result of a desire "to build a more just and tolerant society". The films were screened on the Spcine cinema circuit attached to public schools in São Paulo, and the selection included a workshop aimed at 8–15 year olds on making diversity-friendly films. Again, the festival website is quick to justify the workshops, perhaps sensing the potential for criticism from conservative circles: "the best way for a society to become more tolerant and open to plurality is by understanding and living from early on with difference". The 2018 edition of the festival has announced, at the time of writing, that gaming will feature in the programme, and that LGBTQ rights post-2018 elections will be debated as part of a larger conference, and a remarkable 20 feature-length and 39 short films by Brazilian filmmakers will be screened.

While the films screened at Mix Brasil and other specialist festivals undoubtedly play a key role in community support, their circulation is limited. As it happens, however, the most talked about LGBTQ-themed film in the world of the last few years is Brazilian: the arthouse smash film of 2018 *Call Me By Your Name* (Luca Guadagnino), which portrays the love affair between two men (one 17 and one 28). As it is co-produced by the ubiquitous Brazilian Rodrigo Teixeira, discussed in Chapter 2, it qualifies as a Brazilian film. It raised surprisingly few eyebrows in Brazil, despite the high-profile critique of the film in the US by actor James Woods, who accused it of being an apologia for paedophilia. Woods was roundly condemned on social media for his judgement and himself accused of hypocrisy, given his track record of relationships with much younger women. The only significant murmurings in Brazil regarding the film came from evangelical Christian websites, and were in reaction to Oscar presenter Jimmy Kimmel's comments that the purpose of homosexual content in films is primarily to annoy Christians.[13]

Homophobia, hashtags and *Praia do Futuro*

Perhaps the most controversial recent gay-themed Brazilian film is *Praia do Futuro* (*Future Beach*, Karim Ainouz, 2014), partly set in the beach of the same name in Fortaleza, capital of the northeastern state of Ceará. In the film a German tourist drowns on the beach, and the lifeguard, Donato (Wagner Moura), inconsolable because he was unable to save him, begins an intense relationship with the dead man's friend, Konrad (Clemens Schick), which takes him to Berlin. The relationship between the two men, then, is the focus of the film.

In response to complaints from some cinema-goers in the northeast of Brazil who were reportedly shocked by the sex scenes contained in the film, a number of cinemas began verbally advising customers that the film contained scenes of homosexual intimacy, and a film theatre in the northeastern state of Paraíba allegedly stamped film tickets to indicate that customers had been "advised". One such stamped ticket was soon circulating on social media and causing outrage from those who saw it as a form of censorship. The cinema chain involved later denied that the stamp had anything to do with such warnings, and was instead an indication that ID had been provided in order to pay a half-price entrance ticket. No denials of verbal warnings about the sex scenes were made, however.

Regarding the controversy surrounding the exhibition of the film, director Ainouz commented:

> We're saddened by this type of reaction because intolerance and prejudice are wretched manifestations of the human soul – and like fascism and racism, they are usually the result of ignorance. But it's great that our film can help advance this debate, and who knows, promote greater tolerance and respect for difference.
>
> *(Figueira 2014)*

To counter the homophobic reactions to the film, producers launched the hashtag #homofobianaoeanossapraia (homophobia isn't our beach).[14] And fans of the film started a protest on Tumblr by superimposing on the film posters of Hollywood blockbusters, amongst others, the stamp AVISADO, and providing comical warnings written in incorrect grammar (to emphasise the perceived intellectual weaknesses of those who both provided and agreed with the original warnings on *Praia do Futuro*).[15]

The fact that any kind of polemic emerged around *Praia do Futuro* indicates that the film found an audience beyond the usual art-house and festival circuit, possibly as a result of the high profile of lead actor Wagner Moura. A number of social media users commented specifically on their discomfort at the shift in representation of masculinity as portrayed by Moura, from the crusading and for many, heroic and hyper-masculine Captain and then Coronel Nascimento in the *Elite Squad* films, as discussed in Chapter 7, to gay lifeguard.[16]

Gay director Karim Ainouz had already explored non-heteronormative relationships using an established heterosexual actor in the forementioned *Madame*

FIGURE 4.2 Wagner Moura as lifeguard in a still from the trailer for *Praia do Futuro* (*Futuro Beach*, Karim Ainouz, 2014)

Satã, his breakthrough film based on the real-life adventures of a notorious *malandro* and some-time drag artist from 1930s Rio's underworld. But *Madame Satã* provoked little reaction from conservative viewers, perhaps given its more limited exhib-ition, and the fact that both title and poster of the film made the subject matter clear. In Ceará beach-front lifeguards are part of the military firefighting corps, the Corpo de Bombeiros Militar, and the Brazilian poster for *Praia do Futuro* hints only at Moura's character's lifeguarding, and thus a possible filmic continuation of his successful military defence roles on screen. Thus, one might extrapolate that for a film with a gay or trans lead to offend, it needs to be released in commercial cinemas, depict non-hetero sex *and* intersect with strongly gendered and in par-ticular hyper-masculine institutions such as the armed forces.

Where films portray homosexuality and the trans experience as marginalised or focused on the performative, which is ideally camp, comical, or both, and thus not perceived as a threat to mainstream culture and society, they tend to escape without negative comment from the public. Consider, for example, the troubled character Dunga (Matheus Nachtergaele) in *Amarelo manga* (*Mango Yellow*, Claudio Assis, 2002) and the theatre troupe in *Tatuagem* (*Tattoo*, Hilton Lacerda, 2013), with its army and dictatorship subplot. And consider also the most widely viewed gay-themed Brazilian film to date to screen at cinemas: *Cazuza: o tempo não para* (*Cazuza: Time Doesn't Stop*, Walter Carvalho and Sandra Werneck, 2004), a bio-pic of the much-loved pop star Cazuza who died of an AIDS-related illness in 1990. A Globo Filmes co-production, it attracted over three million spectators to cinemas.

Praia do Futuro may have troubled audiences as a result of the action taking place in the northeast of Brazil, frequently regarded as being more openly homophobic than the centre-south region, where Rio de Janeiro and Sao Paulo are found. This does not mean, however, that contemporary art-house/festival films (i.e. those that tend not to reach a sizeable portion of the general public) focus only on the centre-south region. While *Corpo elétrico* (*Body Electric*, Marcelo Caetano, 2017) is set in

São Paulo, its main character, Elias (Kelner Macedo) is a Northeastern man (from the state of Paraíba), a factory worker who plays hard on the city's gay scene. In *Boi neon* (*Neon Bull*, 2015), director Gabriel Mascaro challenges the perceived limits of northeastern masculinity in the world of travelling rodeos. Lufe Steffen also points to the importance of the Surto e Deslumbramento collective in Pernambuco as making a distinctive contribution to LGBTQ filmmaking in the northeast in recent years (in Toller 2018).

In the same year that *Praia do Futuro* was released, Brazil put forward for consideration for the best foreign film Oscar *Hoje eu quero voltar sozinho* (*The Way He Looks*, Daniel Ribeiro, 2014), a sensitively portrayed coming-of-age drama about a blind teenager Léo (Ghilherme Lobo) and his budding relationship with a school friend Gabriel (Fábio Audi). Like *Praia do Futuro*, *Hoje eu quero voltar sozinho* played well at the Berlin Film Festival, where it was awarded a Teddy, the annual awards for films with LGBTQ content. Brazilian films have fared particularly well in this awards category at Berlin, to the point where one could argue that outside of Brazil it is one of the recognised strengths of Brazilian film culture. The list of other films to be awarded Teddies includes the aforementioned *Mãe só há uma*, *Tinta bruta* (*Hard Paint,* Felipe Matzembacher and Marcio Reolon, 2018) and *Bixa Travesty* (*Tranny Fag*, Kiko Goifman and Claudia Priscila, 2018), discussed below.[17]

MC Linn da Quebrada, Trans Pride and *Bixa Travesty*

Despite the exponential increase in sensitive portrayals of Brazilian trans individuals on screens at home and abroad, there are only a small number of trans working behind the cameras.[18] The non-binary trans film editor Calí dos Anjos made headlines in 2015 when they were awarded funding from Riofilme in 2015 to direct their first film: the 10-minute short film *Tailor* (2017), part documentary and part animation about a trans cartoonist. Trans artist, activist and consultant Ariel Nobre transformed his on-going art project *Preciso dizer que te amo* into a documentary short of the same name in 2018. Taking as its subject trans experiences and the fight against suicide, it screened in competition at the Festival do Rio in 2018.

MC Linn da Quebrada, a trans funk artist from the poor suburbs of São Paulo, is credited as co-scriptwriter on *Bixa Travesty*, one of the most striking LGBTQ films to have emerged on the World Cinema festival circuit in recent years. The documentary premiered in the Panorama section of the Berlin Film Festival 2018, where the directors Goifman and Priscila read out a statement post-screening, first refusing to recognise Michel Temer's government, and then calling for a discussion about violence against black and LGBTQ people. As well as being well-received in Berlin, the film was given a standing ovation at the Brasilia film festival in 2018, where it won four awards, including the audience prize. It also screened at Mix Brasil 2018, where Linn da Quebrada performed at the closing party.[19]

An experienced performer both on stage and screen, Linn da Quebrada has played trans characters in two fictional films: *Corpo elétrico*, in which she plays Simplesmente Pantera, and Tata Amaral's *Sequestro relâmpago* (2018), in which she appears as the character Marilda. The title of the film *Bixa travesty* is the moniker Linn came up with to describe her gender identity: *bixa* and *travesty* being playful misspellings of the words *bicha* (queer) and *travesti* (trans).[20]

The film blends images of Linn da Quebrada performing on stage, chatting with her girlfriends, in hospital recovering from testicular cancer and philosophising straight to camera on sexual and identity politics. It contains a range of contrasting registers, varying from the at times aggressive lyrics of her funk songs, which challenge the "alpha-male" content of so much funk music, to the at times vacuous and high-camp conversations with fellow trans performer and friend Jup do Bairro, to discussions of sexual identity politics that use an almost academic register. Linn is seemingly given free rein to express her views: some are articulately expressed while others appear less well-formulated. The effect of this is to interpret Linn's world as one in which she has not set out to be a political activist, but where her very existence is political. As she states, "it is a political duty [for me] to be happy".

The film also contrasts highly stylised sequences of performance with mundane, almost kitsch moments, such as a scene in the kitchen of her small flat where she chats to her domestic worker mother while she makes dinner.[21] Her mother is clearly respectful of her daughter's gender identity, even if she struggles to use the right pronouns to describe her. In the conversation Linn threatens to tattoo the word *ela* (she/her) on her forehead: towards the end of the film we see her at a tattoo studio making good on her threat. All of these contrasting elements work to give a rounded depiction of Linn as star (she clearly loves the camera and states that she is her own biggest fan) and woman, but without resorting to a conventional behind-the-scenes portrait or star-at-home clichés. For example, we see old footage a friend had recorded of her in hospital. What begins conventionally with an image of her hair falling out as a result of the cancer treatment, continues with her wrapping tape round her head with the words *cuidado, frágil* (take care: fragile) and ends with her sucking a large white dildo, romping naked about the en-suite bathroom and brazenly revealing close-ups of her penis, foreskin and anus.

The literal inscription of femininity onto Linn's body by way of the tattoo is significant, given the importance placed on Linn's body and skin[22] throughout the film: her genitalia that visually "belie" her status as female, and her black skin, her "cloak of courage" that is a source of pride and resistance. The fact that she frequently appears on camera in a state of undress, showering (alone and with others), without make-up (showing her pock-marked complexion) and without "concealing the evidence" of her male genitalia and lack of breasts,[23] serves as a gesture of empowerment and as a challenge to the common understanding of trans women as relying on invasive surgery and the temporary transformative power of makeup and clothes to claim femininity.[24]

A link is forged in the film with Ney Matogrosso, a gay recording artist and political activist who rose to fame at the height of the dictatorship (the early 1970s) with highly stylised, androgynous stage performances. Linn had been given a glove used by Matogrosso on stage, which she treated as a kind of lucky charm. The glove is made somehow more aggressive, sexual and therefore transgressive in the

FIGURE 4.3 Promotional poster for *Bixa Travesty*

(*Tranny Fag*, Kiko Goifman and Claudia Priscilla, 2018). Reproduced with permission of Kiko Goifman

hands of Linn da Quebrada. There is thus a harmony between the overtly sexual and the political, which provides the film's main site of resistance. The film ends with the credits rolling over what appears to be Linn and Matogrosso meeting for the first time (they exchange a meaningful embrace),[25] perhaps drawing a comparison between the past and present in terms of both conservative back-lash and non-heteronormative oppression, and culture and performance as sites of resistance.

Concluding remarks

In September 2017 an art exhibition in the southern city of Porto Alegre entitled *Queermuseu: Cartografias da Diferença na Arte Brasileira* (Queermuseum: Cartographies of Difference in Brazilian Art) was closed down ahead of schedule, following a social-media campaign by right-wing protestors led by the Movimento Brasil Livre (MBL – see Chapter 9), who claimed that it had made use of public money (the Rouanet Law) to promote paedophilia, zoophilia and blasphemy (Carneiro 2018). Rio de Janeiro's evangelical mayor Marcelo Crivella then joined in the collective indignation, refusing to allow the exhibition to be held at Rio's new art museum (MAR). The exhibition did, however, continue its journey to Rio, thanks to a record-breaking crowd-funding campaign instigated by the Director of the Visual Art School of the Lage Park in Rio, Fabio Szwarcwald, who despite bringing much-needed financial support and interest to the School, nearly lost his job over the exhibition.

The Queermuseum case highlights a number of issues and challenges in the current climate in Brazil faced by LGBTQ cultural production, of which film is an increasingly expressive part. First, homophobia is perhaps much more entrenched in Brazilian society than the liberal legislation and increase in LGBTQ cultural production in the twenty-first century might suggest. According to a 2014 poll, for example, only 45% of Brazilians supported same-sex marriage, while 48% did not (Lipka 2015). The fact that the Escola Sem Homofobia (Schools Without Homophobia) initiative to prevent bullying of LGBTQ students had to be all but abandoned by 2012 attests to the widespread, deep-seated prejudice in Brazil, and arguably to the Workers Party's failure to communicate its diversity agenda effect-ively to its conservative and unenlightened population. This dissenting population is easily manipulated by fake news and decontextualised information relating to Brazil's LGBTQ culture. This was amply demonstrated during the 2018 elections, when right-wing candidate Jair Bolsonaro during his election campaign was able to convince so many of his supporters that the Workers Party had distributed gay con-version kits to schools. A video was widely circulated online and viewed millions of times of a bottle teat in the form of a penis, supposedly distributed by Workers Party presidential candidate Fernando Haddad to Brazilian schools and creches when he was Minister of Education, as part of the Brazil Without Homophobia campaign. With its 15 million subscribers, the YouTube satirical channel Porta dos Fundos captured the extent to which LGBTQ culture had been misrepresented and used in anti-PT propaganda, in one of its most hard-hitting videos, aptly entitled "Fake News" (2018).

With regard to traditional film formats, popular audiences continue to lap up stereotypical camp performances and think nothing of pejorative comments aimed at gay characters in films: consider, for example, the runaway success *Minha mãe é uma peça*, as discussed in Chapter 2. Audiences are frequently reported to react negatively in cinema halls to displays of non-heteronormative affection, and while booing scenes of Freddie Mercury (Rami Malik) kissing another man in the smash hit *Bohemian Rhapsody* (2018) might seem innocuous to some, such reactions need to be understood in a context in which holding hands with one's gay partner in public in the supposedly open-minded city of São Paulo in 2019 can result in death.[26]

Notes

1 *União estável*, literally stable union, a form of civil partnership, has existed in Brazil since 2004.
2 Social media commentators have been quick to draw analogies between this insistence on family and Christian values and events on the run-up to the military takeover of 1964. For an overview of "gender ideology" in relation to Brazil, see Correa 2017.
3 Based on the 1961 play of the same name by controversial playwright Nelson Rodrigues, it was first adapted for the screen in 1964 by Flavio Tambellini and most recently by Murilo Benício (2018). In the latest version, Arandir is played by black actor Lázaro Ramos. Other films based on Nelson Rodrigues's work that have gay characters include Arnaldo Jabor's *Toda nudez será castigada* (*All Nudity Shall Be Punished*, 1972) and *O casamento* (*The Wedding*, 1975).
4 For detailed readings of the film, see Foster (1999: 129–138) and Dennison (2005: 125–134).
5 Sampaio was also notably a gay filmmaker. The film received a limited release and was marketed as *pornochanchada* or soft-core porn.
6 Film Scholar B Ruby Rich (2013: 151) took issue with the portrayal of trans culture (and homosexuality more broadly) in the film. She writes: "*Pixote* can't be held up as an example of how gay desire can be depicted, given its sensationalistic and sordid treatment of gay sex as accommodation, substitution and punishment, but again, its very registering of the subject matter was unusual for its time and arguably helped to open future spaces for gay desire on Brazilian screens".
7 The film was well received at the Berlin Film Festival. Herzer wrote a best-selling auto-biography published posthumously in 1983 entitled *A queda para o alto* (Falling Upwards).
8 Also worthy of mention is the video initiative at the Museu da Diversidade Sexual (Museum of Sexual Diversity) in São Paulo, which seeks to document everyday stories of LGBTQ individuals.
9 The choice of outfit is reminiscent of a gay student of ITA (Aeronautical Technology Institute) who wore a red dress and high heels to his graduation ceremony in 2016 in order to protest against homophobia in the armed forces.
10 Another possible reaction being referenced in the film poster is a gesture of defiance against the impeachment process of president Dilma Rousseff already under way at the time of the release of the film. My reasoning here is that many of Dilma's supporters would add the word Mãe or mother as an affectionate suffix to her name, thus forming Dilmãe. "Mãe só há uma": in other words there is only one mother: Dilma.
11 For example at SESC Ribeirao Preto in 2018.
12 A cultural institute attached to Itaú bank, the São Paulo branch of a commercial associ-ation (and one of the largest funders of the arts in Brazil) and São Paulo's film commission respectively.

13 See, for example, the site *Gospel Mais* (Chagas 2018).

14 The expression "it isn't my beach" is a commonly used one in Brazil, roughly meaning "not my cup of tea".

15 One such meme provides the warning that the film *Home Alone* contains scenes of child abandonment.

16 See for example the Sergeant in the Fire-fighting Corps captured sounding off on video (TV Bol 2014).

17 Also in Berlin in 2018 Greek director Evangelia Kranioti premiered *Obscuro barroco*, a film about trans women in Rio de Janeiro, and Marcelo Martinessi launched *Las herederas* (*The Heiresses*, 2018), a Brazilian co-prodution about a well-to-do lesbian couple.

18 Even in front of the cameras: as well as Rodrigo Santoro's aforementioned performance in *Carandiru*, there is Flavio Tambellini's *A Gloria e a graca*, in which the protagonist, a trans woman, is not played by a trans actress.

19 Linn da Quebrada also performed after a screening at Sheffdocs 2018 in the UK.

20 The English-language title *Tranny Fag* is a fitting rendering of the Portuguese.

21 By way of example of this kitsch register, Linn informs us that her mother makes the best stroganoff.

22 A number of films take such an intersectional approach to portraying the trans body/black skin: see for example the short film *Pele* (*Skin*, Adam Golub and Liana Nigri, 2017), featuring Dandara Zainabo, a 19-year-old trans woman, and Alice Riff's *Meu corpo é político* (*My Body is Political*, 2017), a documentary featuring a group of trans women including Linn da Quebrada.

23 The film includes interesting reflections on the invasive nature of gender reassignment surgery, and the reasons why Linn has avoided such surgery to date.

24 The usual images of a trans woman "getting ready" are replaced here with an overtly political scene where Linn puts on lipstick using the wing mirror of a police car.

25 Ney Matogrosso regularly appears in LGBTQ documentaries, serving as a kind of spokesperson for an older generation of non-cis performers on screen, even if he always refused to be considered a spokesperson for the gay community at large.

26 Here I am referring to Plínio Henrique de Almeida Lima, who was stabbed to death in a homophobic attack while walking in central Sao Paulo with his husband in December 2018. See *Huffpost* 2018.

References

Butler, J. 2006. *Gender Trouble: Feminism and the Subversion of Identity*. London and New York: Routledge Classics.

Caparica, M. 2016. "MC Linn da Quebrada: 'o ódio disfarçado de opinião é tão culpado quanto quem mata'". *Lado BI*. 26 May. www.ladobi.com.br/2016/05/mc-linn- quebrada-enviadecer/.

Carneiro, J. D. 2018. 'Queermuseu', a exposição mais debatida e menos vista dos últimos tempos, reabre no Rio". 16 August https://www.bbc.com/portuguese/brasil-45191250.

Chagas, T. 2018. "Oscar premia filme que relativiza valores e exalta relação homossexual entre um adolescente e um adulto". *Gospel Mais*. 6 March. https://noticias.gospelmais.com.br/oscar-filme-homosexual-adolescente-adulto-95827.html.

Correa, S. 2017. "Gender Ideology: Tracking its Origins and meanings in Current Gender Politics". *LSE Engenderings*. 11 December. https://blogs.lse.ac.uk/gender/2017/12/11/gender-ideology-tracking-its-origins-and-meanings-in-current-gender-politics/.

Fernandes, M. 2018. "Os 13 projetos de lei que estão parados no congresso". *Huffington Post Brasil*. 7 June. www.huffpostbrasil.com/2018/06/06/os-13-projetos-de-lei-prioritarios-sobre-direitos-LGBTQ-que-estao-parados-no-congresso_a_23450721/?ncid=other_huffpostre_pqylmel2bk8&utm_campaign=related_article.

Figueira, J.V. 2014. "Internautas ironizam alerta sobre sexo gay em *Praia do Futuro* e produção lança campanha anti-homofobia". *Adoro Cinema*. 24 May. www.adorocinema.com/slideshows/filmes/slideshow-107613/.

Foster, D. W. 1999. *Gender and Society in Contemporary Brazilian cinema*. Austin: University of Texas Press.

Herzer, A. 1983. *A queda para o alto*. São Paulo:Vozes.

Huffpost. 2018. "O que se sabe sobre o assassinato de um cabeleireiro na Av. Paulista". *Huffington Post Brasil*. 23 December. www.huffpostbrasil.com/2018/12/23/o-que-se-sabe-sobre-o-assassinato-de-um-cabeleireiro-na-av-paulista_a_23625911/.

Lipka. 2015. "Same-sex marriage makes some legal gains in Latin America". *Pew Research Centre*. Feb 28. www.pewresearch.org/fact-tank/.

Moraes, F. 2016. "Anna Muylaert fala sobre *Mãe Só Há Uma* e inspiração no caso Pedrinho". *Metropoles*. 20 July. www.metropoles.com/entretenimento/cinema/anna-muylaert-fala-sobre-mae-so-ha-uma-e-inspiracao-no-caso-pedrinho.

Moreno, A. 2001. *A personagem homosexual no cinema brasileiro*. Rio de Janeiro: Funarte.

Murat, R. 2008. *Antônio Carlos da Fontoura: Espelho da alma*. São Paulo: Imprensa Nacional.

Rich, B. R. 2013. *New Queer Cinema: The Director's Cut*. Durham and London: Duke.

Steffen, L. 2016. *O cinema que ousa dizer seu nome*. São Paulo: Giostri.

Toller, A. F. 2018. "Vivendo a retrospectiva: panorama histórico do cinema LGTB brasileiro". *Cinematorio*. 7 September. www.cinematorio.com.br/2018/09/vivendo-a-retrospectiva-panorama-historico-do-cinema-LGBTQ-brasileiro/.

TV UOL 2014. "Sargento dos bombeiros faz vídeo indignado com filme 'Praia do Futuro'".12 December. http://tvuol.uol.com.br/video/sargento-dos-bombeiros-faz-video-indignado-com-filme-praia-do-futuro-04024E993260C4995326.

5

AFRO-BRAZILIAN FILMMAKING IN THE TWENTY-FIRST CENTURY

When Luiz Ignacio Lula da Silva (Lula) came to power in 2003, one of his first cabinet appointments was Gilberto Gil as Minister of Culture. Gil, an Afro-Brazilian singer-songwriter and huge star in Brazil, was born in Salvador in Bahia and has always been closely associated with Afro-Brazilian culture: with its 80% non-white population, Bahia is the Brazilian state with the highest concentration of people of Afro-Brazilian descent. Along with high-profile (white) counter-cultural singer-songwriters such as Caetano Veloso and Chico Buarque, Gil earlier in his career had suffered censorship, and particularly post-1968 and the so-called "coup within the coup" which ushered in a period of intense political repression. Like Lula, Gil had been imprisoned during the dictatorship, and together with fellow Bahian singer-songwriter Caetano Veloso, he spent two years in exile in London.

Gil, who had served as Culture Secretary in his home state of Bahia, joined the ranks of a remarkably small number of black lawmakers, which included Benedita da Silva, Brazil's first black senator who would go on to briefly serve as governor of the state of Rio de Janeiro (2002–2003) and minister in Lula's government with Gil (2003–2007), and Joaquim Barbosa, appointed by Lula to the Supreme Court (2003–2014) and the court's future president.[1] Unlike the appointment of ex-footballer Pele, the most famous black man on earth and notoriously apolitical, as "extraordinary" Minister of Sport in Fernando Henrique Cardoso's government (1995–1998), Lula's choice of "black celebrity" Gil as head of the Ministry of Culture was not simply an honorary role, nor a token gesture towards a more racially representative or popular form of leadership. Between 2003 and 2008 Gil worked with the remit given him by Lula (to "democratise culture") and introduced a series of important measures, such as the introduction of *pontos de cultura* (funded cultural hotspots) which contributed to: i) broadening the definition of culture and cultural producers, and ii) shifting the financial support for culture partially away from the Rio/São Paulo axis. Other initiatives sought to increase access of erstwhile marginalised groups to more mainstream cultural productions. While Gil's policies and leadership style may have displeased many working within the cultural industries,[2] there is no disputing that his term in office[3] marked a bold shift towards both a more diverse and inclusive cultural agenda, and a greater prominence for culture within government: between 2003 and 2007 the Ministry's investment in culture increased from 706.2 million to 1.6 billion reals (Gil 2008).

As we will explore later in this chapter, these culturally inflected democratising initiatives, along with a raft of educational and social schemes increased or introduced during Lula's two terms of office, such as affirmative action and the *Bolsa Família* family welfare packages, impacted positively on the lives of the country's poorest and most vulnerable citizens, the overwhelming majority of whom are Afro-Brazilian.

The structuring absence of Afro-Brazilians in audio-visual culture

Within the cultural industries in Brazil popular music has long been the area with the most significant presence of black performers and composers (and even producers, if not record company bosses). In contrast, cinema, and audio-visual culture more broadly, has always been marked by a "structuring absence" of Afro-Brazilians, whether in front of the cameras or behind them. This absence was captured by Joel Zito Araújo in *A negação do Brasil* (*The Denial of Brazil*), a PhD project that analysed the presence/absence of non-whites in Brazilian soap operas from the 1960s to the 1990s which was transformed into both a book (2000)[4] and a widely discussed feature-length documentary of the same name directed by Araújo (2000). In film terms, this absence is observed in the negligible number of black or mixed-race actors in key roles historically, while the presence is keenly felt in the stereotypical representation of Afro-Brazilians' place in society on screen: for example as maids, servants, and other "background subalterns", as sexually available, and as perpetrators of violence and therefore a threat to the white middle-class family.

One genre of film that has been marked by the presence of high-profile Afro-Brazilian actors (although their numbers remain negligible) is popular comedies, particularly from the 1940s onwards.[5] For example, during the chanchada era (see Chapter 2), the diminutive Afro-Brazilian actor known as Grande Otelo (literally Big Othello) featured in a large number of films, often as part of a duo with the white actor Oscarito. What is striking about these performances is that the humour at the level of plot is rarely predicated on Grande Otelo's race and/or colour: such jokes consist mostly of the occasional quickfire racist gag.[6] Greater emphasis is placed within the film narrative on the pair's lowly social status, and their ability to get themselves into comic situations relating much more to class than race. Likewise, Afro-Brazilian Mussum, a member of the Trapalhões comedy team who dominated box-offices in the 1970s and 80s, played the part of one of a group of four hapless men trying to trick fate and get an advantage in life.

This reduction of the black experience to one of class is also witnessed in the otherwise well-intentioned series of *Cinema Novo* films dealing with Afro-Brazilian themes that starred important black actors such as Antonio Pitanga, Milton Gonçalves, Léa Garcia and Zózimo Bulbul. These include Glauber Rocha's *Barravento* (*The Turning Wind*, 1962), the multi-directed *Cinco vezes favela* (*Favela x 5*, 1962*)* and Carlos Diegues's *Ganga Zumba* (1963). In fact the prolific (white) filmmaker Diegues made a number of feature films portraying aspects of Afro-Brazilian culture, many of which were big-budget, popular hits: from the box-office smash *Xica da Silva (*1975), starring black actress Zezé Motta and based on the true story of a slave who rose to a position of power and influence in seventeenth-century Brazil, to *Quilombo* (1984), another historical drama, about a runaway slave community, with a soundtrack written and performed by none other than Gilberto Gil, and *Orfeu* (1999), a remake of Marcel Camus's Oscar-winning 1958 Franco-Brazilian co-production (see Chapter 8). While the representation of black culture in Diegues's films has been challenged by some critics and academics,[7] his ability to produce at least notionally progressive films that find an audience means that he has contributed more to increasing the visibility of Afro-Brazilian actors and Afro-Brazilian culture and history than most other white film directors (Xexéo 2018).

It is perhaps ironic, then, that Diegues was one of the most vocal critics of Gilberto Gil's policies of inclusion, at least when it came to cinema, which stood to benefit Afro-Brazilian communities, among others. In reaction to State-run companies being encouraged to fund cultural projects (through incentive schemes as discussed in Chapter 1) that worked with "social counterparts", Diegues claimed that the government was "imposing ideological and political perspectives on films in a way that not even the military dictatorship had dared to do" (Johnson 2005: 29). Marcelo Ikeda (2015: 105–106) argues that while it is obvious that the changes in funding calls were not made in order to dictate the themes of audio-visual works, as a result of pressure from some industry quarters, and from the public, the government was forced to rethink the social counterpart strategy. This left important initiatives such as including poor and marginalised communities in employment and cultural production opportunities when filmmaking in such communities to the inclination of individual filmmakers and NGOs.[8]

While Carlos Diegues arguably cornered the market in terms of producing Afro-Brazilian-themed films favoured by the public, the less well known work of a number of black filmmakers has proved extremely influential among a new generation of Afro-Brazilian directors. A key reference is the work of actor, director and activist Zózimo Bulbul (1937–2013). Bulbul's experimental short film *Alma no Olho* (*Soul in the Eye*, 1973) which he wrote, directed, produced and starred in, continues to be quoted by many contemporary Afro-Brazilian filmmakers and digital opinion-formers as a source of inspiration. *Alma no olho* was made with leftover film stock from the feature film *Compasso de espera* (*Standstill*, Antunes Filho, 1973), itself an interesting critique of race relations in Brazil in which Bulbul had just starred. *Alma no olho*, which was inspired by black panther Eldridge Cleaver's book *Soul on Ice*, is dedicated to Afro-American jazz artist John Coltrane, and features his music. With no words spoken and shot with a static camera in a studio, Bulbul uses facial expressions, movement, and focus on different parts of his body (sweating armpit hair, torso, buttocks, and so on) to convey in eight minutes 500 years of colonial and post-colonial black history, which tellingly ends with a both a literal and symbolic breaking of shackles. Bulbul, who made other short films on Afro-Brazilian topics and the important feature-length documentary, *Abolição*, released on the 100th anniversary of the abolition of slavery in Brazil, is regarded as the first filmmaker to use the phrase *cinema negro* (black cinema).

In 2000 the young and dynamic film studies graduate Jefferson De, together with other black filmmakers, took advantage of a slot in a short film festival in São Paulo to launch a film manifesto dubbed *Dogma Feijoada*, in reference both to the Danish Dogma 95 manifesto, and Brazil's national dish, black bean stew, with its slave origins. The *Feijoada* manifesto picks up on the idea of *cinema negro* and offers a timely definition of it, while calling for greater representation of Afro-Brazilians behind the camera and a more considered representation of the black experience on screens. The manifesto encouraged the production of films in which both director and protagonist were black. Film storylines must be related to black culture and focus on ordinary people, and stereotypical representations were to be avoided at all costs (Heise 2012: 133; Carvalho and Domingues 2018: 4).

Although the *Feijoada* group as such was relatively short-lived, dissipating around 2005, Noel dos Santos Carvalho and Petronio Domingues (2018: 15) highlight the importance of the group as the first collective and unified action in the public sphere by black directors.[9] They point to a series of other films (particularly documentaries), including Carvalho's own work, which were made under the influence of the manifesto (2018: 8), such as De's *Distraída para a morte* (Distracted to Death, 2001) which represented Brazil at the most important African film festival on the

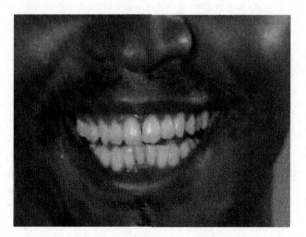

FIGURE 5.1 Zózimo Bulbul in close-up. Still from *Alma no olho*

(*Soul in the Eye*, Zózimo Bulbul, 1973)

circuit, Fespaco in Burkina Faso (2018: 19). Tatiana Heise (2012: 134) demonstrates how De's short films adhered to the *Feijoada* manifesto but with his first feature fiction film, *Broder* (2011), De failed to follow his own dogma by including a white protagonist, played by Globo actor Caio Blatt. Carvalho and Domingues (2018: 11), however, argue that Blatt plays one of three leads, the others being black, and the Blatt character's inclusion is justified, given that much of the storyline is predicated on his character's humble background and his subsequent problematic desire to act and be black.

Challenging the myth of racial democracy

The late arrival of black movements within Brazilian cinema needs to be understood in the context of a culture which has long promoted the myth of racial democracy. This myth, which is still to this day vigorously defended in many sectors of Brazilian society, given its central place in the national narrative, holds that Brazil is a racial paradise: a "tropical mulatto republic" (Reiter and Mitchell 2010: 4). The myth took hold particularly after the publication of sociologist Gilberto Freyre's seminal text *Casa-grande & senzala* (*The Masters and the Slaves*, 1933), discussed in the context of the promotion of racial and class intimacy in Chapter 10 of this volume. In a nutshell, the myth that developed, which was especially promoted by populist president Getúlio Vargas (1930–1945), claims that, as a result of Brazil's history of miscegenation, itself the result of the Portuguese colonisers' penchant for dark, exotic women, there is no real tradition of racism in Brazil, only social prejudice. As Tatiana Heise (2012: 30–31) rightly observes, "[b]y dismissing racial conflict as a legitimate problem in national life, Freyre stymied discussions of the subject and refuted the need for black resistance in a society ruled by whites".

> After the 1930s, asserting one's blackness was transformed into an act of civic upheaval and antipatriotism and little by little, as the Vargas regime made sure that its version of the truth was accepted, asserting ethnic difference became an act of political incorrectness not only aimed against the state, but against mainstream society.
>
> *(Reiter and Mitchell 2010: 4)*

Hence the fierce criticism and complete lack of appreciation of the need for black-only carnival groups in Bahia, for example, such as Ilê Aiyê, which was founded in 1974, and hence the sustained questioning of the need for a government division to promote racial equality. In 2003 Lula created the Secretaria de Políticas de Promoção da Igualdade Racial, a racial equality secretariat with ministerial powers and a remit focused on the Afro-Brazilian population. In 2015 the Secretariat was subsumed into the Ministry for Women by Dilma Rousseff, in a drive to reduce the number of government ministries, and it was disbanded altogether by Michel Temer in 2016.

This denial of racial prejudice in Brazil also explains the resistance to the introduction of higher education affirmative action measures on the basis of colour/race/ethnicity. In 1997, in a country with just under half of the population self-declaring as *preto* or *pardo* (black or mixed-race) in the census, a mere 1.8% of *pretos* and 2.2% of *pardos* aged between 18 e 24 had a university education (Carvalho 2014). Rio de Janeiro was the first state to attempt to address this historical shortfall, by adopting so-called *cotas* or quotas in 2000, whereby 45% of places in State Universities were to be set aside for students coming through the state school system, with race/colour being added as a criterium the following year. The University of Brasilia adopted a similar system around the same time, with 20% of places being reserved for black and indigenous students. However it was not until 2012 that a federal law was introduced (Law 12, 711, known as the Quota Law) that obliged all federal universities to reserve half of their places for state school students, with part of that quota being specifically reserved based on racial criteria, according to the racial profile of each State.

University quotas based on race have been as widely contested as they have been supported, with the need for such quotas being dismissed even by otherwise liberal-minded intellectuals such as sociologist Roberto da Matta, and the aforementioned counter-cultural singer-songwriter and friend of Gilberto Gil, Caetano Veloso. Oliveira Lima et al. (2014: 154–158) summarise the views of a group of white students regarding quotas that echo the concerns put forward by such intellectuals: that racial quotas trouble rather than uphold the principle of equality; that classifying colour in Brazil is a complicated process, that the real solution lies in investing in the state school system and that Afro-Brazilians would find the experience of higher education difficult and alienating. It is little wonder, then, that attempts to establish quotas for black actors and actresses in film, TV and publicity amounted to nothing: the final version of the Statute of Racial Equality, promulgated in 2010, had such a clause written out as it passed through Congress.

Between the years 2000 and 2017 the number of Afro-Brazilians graduating from university quadrupled. While both the rolling out of quotas and the expansion of the public university system during Workers Party rule can therefore be said to have made a substantial difference in access to education in Brazil, the sobering fact is that, even with a fourfold increase, the figures were still only 9.3% of the total Afro-Brazilian population in 2017. The number of white Brazilians with university degrees also increased during this period: it doubled, to 22% in 2017 (Brito 2018).

Beyond *City of God*

If Lula and Gilberto Gil's policies represented a political sea change a few years into the twenty-first century, then Fernando Meirelles and Kátia Lund's *Cidade de Deus* (*City of God*, 2002) arguably pointed to a similar sea-change in filmic terms. A huge hit in Brazil and around the world and nominated for four Oscars, a record for a Brazilian film, *City of God* was for many the first film to attempt to capture on screen an "authentic" version of favela life. It also marked a move away from both the Globo soap opera and traditional theatrical style of acting that had dominated big-screen performances, through its use of non-professional actors who contributed to the dialogues, in an attempt at a more naturalistic representation. But above all, the film marked a sea-change in that it presented for the first time in a big-budget home-grown production a cast made up almost entirely of Afro-Brazilian actors.[10] Two hundred actors were selected to work on the film project, most of whom were teenagers and young black men who lived in favelas and had no previous contact with cinema. The group would form the basis of *Nós do cinema*, an acting co-operative of sorts set up in conjunction with Fernando Meirelles's 02 Productions that, now under the name *Cinema Nosso* continues to be a significant producer of black audio-visual talent.

Lula wholeheartedly embraced *City of God*, interpreting it as a demand for attention to be drawn to the plight of favela inhabitants (2005: 115–116). He incorporated references to the film into his successful presidential campaign of 2002. Film director Walter Salles (2005: 4) stated "I still don't know how Meirelles and Lund managed to achieve such a sense of realism"; academic and film critic Lúcia Nagib (2005:34) also had high praise for the realist aspects of the film, and the highly regarded film critic Ely Azeredo (2005: 93–94) wrote that "City of God is the first Brazilian fictional film with the look from the other side of the 'divided city'".

Not everyone was as enthusiastic about the representation of this "other side", however. Joel Zito Araújo described the film as "an update on the stereotype of the black man as a criminal" (in Fontes 2007: 134). For a number of critics such as Ivana Bentes (2002), the violence in *Cidade de Deus* appears to be spontaneously generated, having no relation to Economics or social injustice. Furthermore, Tatiana Heise describes the spin-off film *Cidade dos homens* (*City of Men*, Paulo Morelli, 2007)) as being populated by young black men with bare torsos, gold necklaces, using "bandit slang", and carrying automatic weapons over their shoulders. The favela in these films is reduced to "the consumable spectacle of poor people killing each other" (Bentes 2002).

Likewise, Cidade de Deus inhabitants were reportedly unhappy with how their community was portrayed in the film, whereby practically all residents were depicted as drug dealers. Black hip hop artist and Cidade de Deus resident MV Bill was especially vocal in his complaints about the film, criticising in particular the lack of respect shown to favela communities by the filmmakers (Bill 2005: 121) What those who praised *City of God* failed to appreciate was the risk that prejudice against young marginalised black men would actually increase as a result of how they were portrayed in the film, an issue discussed in Chapter 7 in relation to *Tropa de Elite* (*Elite Squad*, José Padilha, 2007).

A parallel can be drawn between the spectacularisation of black bodies in *City of God* and *City of Men*, and *Besouro* (*The Assailant*, 2009), João Daniel Tikhomiroff's big-budget (8.81 million reais) tale of a Brazilian capoeirista (capoeira fighter) Besouro Manganga, but here the black lead's outbursts of violence are arguably made more palatable by placing them in the past and in the context of Besouro's struggle against racial discrimination and oppression in the early twentieth century. The film, which reached over 600,000 spectators at cinemas on its release, and which has since been viewed over one million times on YouTube, was the first Brazilian film to use CGI extensively, and the fighting scenes were choreographed by Huen Chiu Ku, who had worked on *Kill Bill* (Quentin Tarantino, 2003). While the tale and the acting might be very formulaic, the film is worthy of note for depicting a black "superhero" in an expensive mainstream film, nine years before *Black Panther*.[11]

In 2006 Tata Amaral worked with a predominantly black cast to make *Antonia*, a fictional portrait of an all-female hip-hop group set in the Vila Brasilandia favela in Sao Paulo. The cast was made up of singers linked to the bourgeoning hip-hop, R&B and funk scene in the periphery of Sao Paulo with little or no acting experience. At the same time that the film was released, a Globo co-produced spin-off prime-time mini-series with the same lead actresses was aired to relative acclaim.

Antonia the film and TV series, which like *Besouro* were overtly commercial products with rather conventional storylines, nonetheless made important contributions to the "favela movie" phenomenon in contemporary Brazilian audio-visual culture, in that they provided an antidote to the habitual representation of the favela as a masculine space with little or no room for female agency.[12] Likewise, *Sou feia mas tô na moda* (*I'm Ugly but I'm Trendy*, 2005), Denise Garcia's low-budget portrait of female funk singers in Rio de Janeiro, highlights the female contribution to a musical genre conventionally read as male-dominated and sexist in outlook. The film's title refers to a big funk hit of the same name by City of God resident Tati Quebra Barraca, a larger-than-life character whose self-reflexive funk lyrics, looks and performance all challenge the stereotypes of the typical muse of male *funkeiros*, as well as the female dancers that frequently perform with them on stage and in videos. The title could equally refer to the City of God favela as it appears in the film: less visually stylish than in *City of God* the film, and less sanitised than the São Paulo favela that features in *Antônia*, but exuding creativity. But perhaps the most striking, and exciting, aspect of Garcia's film is the extent to which the (black female) funk artists who are featured "radically resist traditional gender norms" (Marsh 2012: 176). For example, in one scene early on in the film *funkeira* Denise da Injeção speaks to camera while walking with a group of male *funkeiros* through the favela's streets, confidently discussing the history of funk, ensuring she physically stays in the centre of the frame and talking over the top of the camera-shy men who accompany her, and therefore demonstrating that she is "as much an owner of the history of funk as any of her male colleagues" (Marsh 2012:179).

While *Cidade de Deus*, *Cidade dos homens*, *Besouro*, *Antonia* and *Sou feia mas tô na moda* all contributed in one way or another to the broadening of the representation of Afro-Brazilians on the big screen, they were all directed by white filmmakers. Two key films directed by Afro-Brazilians provided some much-needed nuance to discussions arising from the legacy of *City of God*. The first of these is a feature-length fictional film that revisits the Cinema Novo classic *Cinco Vezes favela* (*Favela x 5*), the self-explanatory *5 x favela, agora por nós mesmos* (*5 x Favela, Now By Ourselves*,

2010). Produced by Carlos Diegues, who had contributed an episode to the original 1962 film, and Globofilmes, it mirrors the original *Cinco vezes favela* in that it draws together five self-contained stories about favela life. *5 x favela, agora por nós mesmos* was a film venture supported by a number of favela-based social action organisations, including CUFA (Central Única das Favelas), based in Cidade de Deus, Nós do Morro in Vidigal, Observatório de Favelas in Complexo da Maré and Afroreggae, based in Parada de Lucas. The five stories included in the final film were conceived, workshopped and acted by young people from the different communities involved, along with a number of high-profile actors (Zózimo Bulbul and *Porta dos Fundos* comedian Gregorio Duvivier, for example) and contributors to the soundtrack (such as MV Bill). The stories set out to avoid the filmic clichés of the favela, with an inter-title at the beginning of the film declaring that viewers were already familiar with the favela of criminals and the police: now it was time to see the favela of those who live there:

> As a counterpart to *Five Times Favela* of 1962 […], the 2010 version can be read as a critical revision of the leftist ideal of using art to raise the consciousness of the masses. The focus now is on the masses raising the consciousness of the arts.
>
> *(Fraga 2010)*

A number of the stories, for example, are refreshingly candid about the porous borders between legality and illegality in the favela. Like Viviane Ferreira's short film *O dia de Jerusa* (*Jerusa's Day*, 2014), and Anna Muylaert's *Que horas ela volta?* (*The Second Mother*, 2015) discussed in Chapter 3, "Fonte de Renda" ("Source of Income", Manaira Carneiro) makes reference to the impact of university quotas on low-income families. In the case of "Fonte de Renda", the focus is on the harsh reality of surviving university study with no money to buy books and pay bus fares, rather than the euphoria of winning a place at a good university. Like the black character Matias (André Ramiro) in *Tropa de Elite*, Maycon (Silvio Guindane) is the only black student on his law course, but unlike Matias he briefly dabbles in petty drug dealing among his prejudiced white class-mates to make ends meet, without being judged or overtly punished within the diegesis for his actions. As Ivana Bentes (2013: 11) puts it, "[t]he favela is still seen as a place of deprivation and negativity, of individuals who are fragmented and atomised within their social universe who, whilst strongly marked by collectivism, rely on personal and particular resolutions in order to cope with everyday life".

The second key filmic response to *City of God* is *Cidade de Deus: dez anos depois* (*City of God: Ten Years Later*, 2013), a documentary film that reflects directly on the impact of the film *City of God* on the lives of the non-professional cast, and which was directed by Cavi Borges and Afro-Brazilian and Nós do cinema graduate Luciano Vidigal, who also co-wrote the film. Vidigal also directed the episode "Concerto para violino" in *5 x favela: agora por nos mesmos*. Borges and Vidigal interviewed members of the cast of *City of God* and crowd-funded to raise money

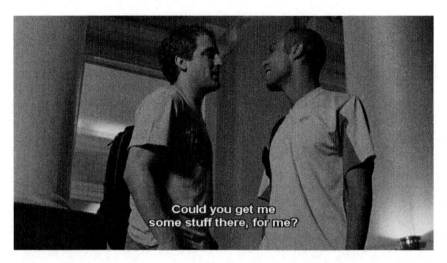

FIGURE 5.2 Edu (Gregório Duvivier) asks his one black classmate Maicon (Sílvio Guindane) to get him drugs. A still from *5 x favela, agora por nós mesmos*

(*Favela x 5, Now By Ourselves*, Mainara Coveiro, Wagner Novais et al., 2010)

to ensure that each was paid 90 dollars for their work. Eighteen responses were included in the completed film. The curiosity to know more about the lives of the cast, who had become celebrities overnight in 2002–2003 when *City of God* was released, is demonstrated in the fact that the documentary played well on the national and international film festival circuit.

The film notably places greater emphasis on reflections on the City of God community, and on race relations and racial prejudice, than *City of God* the fictional film. It also arguably offered greater agency to the participants to share their stories (and be paid for their participation), given that the news and social media has seemingly never tired of reporting on various members of the cast falling on hard times or simply eking out an existence beyond the cameras. The most sought-after cast member in this regard is Rubens Sabino da Silva (who played Neguinho), an erstwhile street kid who was arrested in 2003 for snatching a handbag and later "discovered" by TV journalists living in *cracolândia*, a controversial area of Sao Paulo that houses drug (especially crack cocaine) users. Even those actors who found work after *City of God* have struggled to make ends meet: Alexandre Rodrigues, *City of God*'s narrator Rocket, posed for an awkward selfie with a white red-headed female passenger while driving an UBER in São Paulo in 2018: the selfie soon went viral on social media in Brazil.

Documenting blackness

As explored in preceding chapters, the increase in film funding, particularly for smaller film projects via *editais* or funding calls, has encouraged the emergence of screen stories that are indicative of a more inclusive and diversity-led cultural agenda. These include short, medium and feature-length documentaries dealing with Afro-Brazilian themes. As with the LGBTQ films discussed in the previous chapter, many of these films document hidden or overlooked histories, including a substantial number that focus on *quilombos* or communities of slave descendants, which had been given greater visibility and recognition of their cultural importance by both Gilberto Gil and Lula during their time in office but which, with the swift turn to the right in Brazilian politics of late, and particularly post-impeachment, are, increasingly under threat.[13] Afro-Brazilian brother and sister Daniel and Lilian Sola Santiago produced and directed *Família Alcântara (Alcântara Family* 2005) which documents an extended black family from the southeastern state of Minas Gerais who use theatre, choral singing and *congada*, an Afro-Brazilian cultural and religious manifestation that references the King of the Congo, to express their complex history and identity. Claudio Farias's *Quilombos maranhenses: cultura e política* (Quilombos in Maranhão: Culture and Politics, 2007) reveals the experiences of Afro-Brazilians residing in Maranhão, the state with the largest number of *quilombos*. As Tatiana Heise (2012: 146) argues, "the documentary reinforces a sense of difference and division among Brazil's racial groups". More recently Josias Pires released *Quilombo Rio dos Macacos, o filme* (*The Maroon Community of Rio dos Macacos* 2017) which portrays the daily struggles and demands of *quilombo* residents in Salvador, Bahia in their battle to keep their land.[14]

Joel Zito Araújo featured a *quilombola* or *quilombo* resident Miuda dos Santos as part of his monumental *Raça* (Race, 2013), a documentary co-directed with Megan Maylan that followed three Afro-Brazilians over the course of five years. It now serves as an important reflection on the black experience in the twenty-first century under the Workers Party government. The other participants were Paulo Paim, a Workers Party Senator (currently the only black member of the Brazilian Senate) and author of the Statute for Racial Equality, and hip-hop artist Netinho de Paula who set up in 2005 Brazil's first black-focused TV channel (TV da Gente).

Given the extent of the historical silencing of the Afro-Brazilian population (Sobrinho 2018: 171), there is still evidently a need for the traditional style of documentary with black "talking heads" occupying the frame and addressing the viewer, with the political intention of territorialising a space that is traditionally denied them (171). A good illustration of this is *Mulheres negras: projetos de mundo* (Day Rodrigues and Lucas Ogasawara, 2016), in which we hear from nine forthright and dynamic Afro-Brazilian women. The subtitle is significant as it points to a supranational racial identity of the kind referenced in Bulbul's *Alma no olho*, for example. A similar preoccupation is evident in the more experimental *Kbela* (Yasmin Thayna, 2015) with its closing intertitle dedicating the film to "all the black women in the world".

Thayná's short film *Kbela*, based on her own short story "Mc Kbela", features Afro-Brazilian women who free themselves from unattainable European beauty standards by affirming the beauty of their natural Afro hair. An intertitle informs viewers that the film was financed via the internet by 117 people, which raised a

FIGURE 5.3 Jerusa (Léa Garcia). A still from the trailer for *O dia de Jerusa*

(*Jerusa's Day*, Viviane Ferreira, 2014)

total of 5,000 reals to cover production costs. Despite the film's lack of funding from formal sources, it was part of the official selection of the 2017 editions of both the Rotterdam film festival and Fespaco. In *Kbela* the director breaks with the talking heads tradition and taking her inspiration from Bulbul's *Alma no olho*, she opts instead for corporeal performance and rhythmic and sonorous constructions to create images and sounds that capture the condition of black women (Sobrinho 2018: 172). *Kbela* is available free to view on a number of platforms, including Afroflix, set up by Thayná and based on Kweli TV, an international online streaming network showing films entirely made by or featuring, black people.

Viviane Ferreira's short fictional film *O dia de Jerusa*, discussed in more detail in Chapter 3, was similarly self-produced and similarly went on to make a mark on the European film festival circuit (it played at the Short Film Corner at Cannes in 2014). *O dia de Jerusa* was shot in Bixiga, a historically important neighbourhood in São Paulo for Afro-Brazilians, given that it was the site of a *quilombo*, before being "settled" by Italian immigrants. Likewise the critically acclaimed *Elekô*, a short film made by the Mulheres de Pedra collective which also screened at Rotterdam, was partly filmed in the Cais do Valongo, an area of downtown Rio where slaves were once brought and sold. Like *Kbela*, both films are available to view for free online.

Afro-Brazilians doing it for themselves: black audio-visual organisations and the debate around "place of speech"

Cinema Nosso, Afroflix, and the Mulheres de Pedra collective mentioned above are three examples of a raft of audio-visual initiatives that have emerged in the twenty-first century that are led by Afro-Brazilians. In 2007, Zózimo Bulbul established the *Afro Carioca de Cinema*, an organisation uniting Afro-Brazilian filmmakers that runs workshops and film screenings. Bulbul also set up Brazil's largest black film festival, the *Encontro de Cinema Negro Zózimo Bulbul Brasil Africa Caribe e Outras*

Diasporas (Zozimo Bulbul Black Film Meeting: Brasil, Africa, Caribbean and Other Diasporas) which has been running since 2008. As the name makes clear, the festival seeks to encourage a strong relationship between Afro-Brazilian and African and Afro-descendent filmmakers. Likewise, the Forum Itinerante do Cinema Negro (FICINE, Itinerant Forum for Black Cinema), set up by black filmmaker and activist Janaina Oliveira, focuses on building links between black Brazilian cinema and African cinemas, with special focus on Cape Verde. FICINE founding member Aline Lourena also heads up Thelirios, an audio-visual content company which employs mostly black women and works with black and indigenous women's stories, while in 2016 filmmaker Viviane Ferreira founded APAN – Associação dos Profissionais do Audiovisual Negro (the Association of Black Audio-Visual Professionals), whose goals include the increase in black narratives on screen.

All of these initiatives speak to the need to not only increase and nuance Afro-Brazilian representation on screen, but also for Afro-Brazilian creatives to gain training and then assert agency in relation to production, exhibition and distribution. This focus on agency has led to a series of debates around the issue of the locus of enunciation, or the *lugar de fala* (place of speech) in relation to Afro-Brazilian culture: who has the right to speak to Afro-Brazilian concerns? By way of example taken from television, comedian Marcelo Adnet, known for his work on TV and film, produced the short video for his regular spot on Globo's *Tá no Ar* in 2017 entitled "Branco no Brasil" which translates as Whites in Brazil, and is a play on words on Banco do Brasil, the national bank. In the video, a stylish recreation of so many advertisements for banks offering exclusive, preferential treatment to its clients, a number of white Brazilians look straight to camera, including Adnet, and confirm the advantages they enjoy, using phrases such as "I have access to the best jobs, the best opportunities, and of course, I always earn the best salary". Barely visible in the background, uniformed black staff serve coffee, work as bank security guards, and so on. The tagline of the mock advert is "Branco no Brasil: há 500 anos levando vantagem" (Brazilian whites: holding an advantage for 500 years).

Adnet's sketch quickly went viral and generated considerable discussion, which, like most internet discussions in the second decade of the twenty-first century, fell quickly into call-and-response style accusations between those on the Left, who praised Adnet's candour and critique of white privilege, and those on the Right, who accused Adnet and his fans of overplaying the victim (*mimimi*) and claiming that Brazil should be understood along meritocratic lines. But a number of Afro-Brazilian observers critiqued the Left's celebration of the sketch by drawing attention to the entirely white writing team behind it, and to the almost complete lack of black personnel in *Tá no ar*'s production, as well as in the Globo organisation more broadly.[15]

The debate around the *lugar de fala* intensified with the screening of Daniela Thomas's Globo Filmes co-produced *Vazante* (2017) at the Brasília Film Festival. Set in the early nineteenth century on a slave plantation, the film caused controversy with its focus on the daily suffering, not of the slaves, but of members of the white slave-holding family. Given that the film was billed as denouncing the violence of slavery, it was criticised for not developing the subjectivities and viewpoints of black characters and instead for reiterating the dominant discourse surrounding slavery, which has silenced black voices (Serelle and Sena 2018). Further controversy ensued as a result of Thomas's handling of the post-screening debate in Brasília: feeling under attack and unable to respond objectively to questions relating to the representation of the black Brazilian experience, Thomas capitulated, only to seek to defend herself shortly afterwards from the safe vantage point of an open letter published in the *Revista Piauí*. In the Letter Thomas commented on a scathing critique of the film published in *Cinética* by Juliano Gomes. Given a right to reply by the *Revista Piauí*, Gomes claimed that Thomas's reaction to the reception of her film in Brasília amounted to a display of "white fragility", as conceptualised by Robin D'Angelo, whereby whites become exaggeratedly stressed when removed from their racial comfort zone.

According to Inácio Araújo, "[Vazante] was the trigger for a kind of delayed-effect bomb that polarised opinion about the representation of black men and women in the history of Brazilian cinema". Carlos Diegues weighed in on the debate, in an opinion piece published in the *Globo* newspaper in December 2017. In reaction to criticism from Afro-Brazilian commentators on the representation of slavery in the film, he wrote: "The restrictive invention of the term 'place of speech' is nothing more than university nonsense, which can only serve to restrict our freedom of expression". In the light of Diegues's claim, black filmmaker Day Rodrigues (2018) asked "Does this mean I'm trapped in a juvenile utopia whenever I demand black protagonism and when I racialise plots, scripts and direction?"

Concluding remarks

In 2018 a record number of films directed or co-directed by Afro-Brazilians screened at the Brasília Film Festival, with André Novais Oliveira's *Temporada* (Long Way Home) picking up five of the twelve official competition prizes, including for best film, best actress (Grace Passô, in the role of the protagonist, Juliana) and best supporting actor (Russão). The same year the festival inaugurated a new prize, the Prêmio Zózimo Bulbul, for black filmmaking, in partnership with APAN. Meanwhile in Rotterdam in early 2019, one of the largest-scale retrospectives of Afro-Brazilian films was held, entitled "Soul in the Eye", with guest curation by the aforementioned FICINE founder Janaína Oliveira. Thus, for those with access to these two festivals, there was a large number of stimulating films to view made by Afro-Brazilian filmmakers from the 1970s onwards, and coverage in the broadsheets and specialist sites underscoring the current success of Afro-Brazilian filmmakers. For everyone else, the perennial issue of access to films continues to be challenge, despite the excellent distribution initiatives in place, such as Afroflix, and despite a number of key filmmakers' willingness to make their work available online for free.

The difficulties in accessing Afro-Brazilian films were highlighted in 2018 when a group of students pooled resources and organised their own black Brazilian film festival (Mostra de Cinema Negro Brasileiro) in the southern and predominantly white city of Curitiba. The students in question had organised a very impressive programme of screenings as a result of their frustration at not having the opportunity to study the work of any black filmmakers on their film studies programmes (Hypeness 2018). Therefore, the event also highlighted the extent to which the Brazilian curriculum remains overwhelmingly white, despite initiatives such as the federal law introduced in 2003 making it compulsory to teach of African and Afro-Brazilian history in schools.

Despite an awareness of the under-representation of black and mixed-race groups in audio-visual culture, it was only in 2017 that Ancine set up a Gender, Race and Diversity Commission. The commission reported that in 2016 a total of 75.4% of films released that year had been directed by white men (Ancine 2018). Thus, eighteen years on from Joel Zito Araújo's ground-breaking work on the lack of visibility of Brazil's black and mixed-race population in audio-visual culture, the underrepresentation of non-white Brazilians working behind the cameras continues to be a major issue. With the reorganisation and reformulation of cultural drivers taking place within Ancine as a result of the election of Jair Bolsonaro to the presidency, and of shifts away from a diversity and inclusion agenda elsewhere in government, it remains to be seen whether the tentative but nonetheless important strides taken in the direction of a more racially representative audio-visual industry can be sustained.

Notes

1 Other notable non-white lawmakers from the time include Marina Silva, Senator (1995–2011) and Minister for the Environment (2003–2008) and Nilma Lino Gomes, Minister in the Ministry of Women, Racial Equality and Human Rights (2015–2016).
2 See Johnson 2005: 28–32.
3 Marcelo Ikeda (2015: 99), in his analysis of the impact of Gil's term of office on audio-visual policy, refers to it as the Gil-Juca years, in reference to the important role played by fellow Bahian Juca Ferreira as executive secretary in the Ministry. Ferreira would go on to be Minister of Culture when Gil resigned in 2008.
4 As with women and LGBTQ communities in Brazilian film culture, there is a dearth of academic work on Afro-Brazilian film, with two Brazilian monographs and one American from the turn of the twenty-first century still serving as the principle references for appreciating the representation of black and mixed-race Brazilians in audio-visual culture: the aforementioned *A negação do Brasil* by Joel Zito Araújo; *O negro brasileiro e o cinema* by João Carlos Rodrigues (2001) and Robert Stam's *Tropical Multiculturalism: A Comparative History of Race in Brazilian Cinema and Culture* (1997). Carvalho and Petrônio (2018) list a number of important recent articles on black filmmaking in Brazil.
5 Dennison and Shaw (2004: 14–15) discuss the clowning tradition in Brazilian popular culture and in particular the black singing clowns who would go on to star in a number of early films.
6 Shaw and Dennison (2007: 133–140) in their analysis of Grande Otelo's film career, point out that as well as being the butt of racist one-liners, he always played second fiddle (and second billing) to Oscarito in these films, despite his arguably higher star profile.
7 See, for example, the critical reaction to *Xica da Silva* as discussed by Adamatti (2016).

8 Here I am thinking of initiatives such as Nós do Cinema/Cinema Nosso, mentioned later in this chapter in relation to *City of God*, and "legacy" initiatives such as those put in place by Vic Muniz and the producers of *Waste Land* (see Chapter 9). Diegues appears to have taken issue with the perceived dirigisme, rather than the broad idea of the democratisation of culture: as we will see, he would co-produce in 2010 an important film with the Cinema Nosso initiative.

9 Likewise, the "Manifesto do Recife" (2001), launched at a film festival in the northeastern capital of Pernambuco, demanded greater opportunities for Afro-Brazilian actors, presenters and journalists (Carvalho and Domingues 2018: 7).

10 On a smaller but still significant scale, Carlos Diegues's *Orfeu* (1999) is also set in a modern favela and has a mostly black cast.

11 In August 2018 Globo announced that it was working with Tikhomiroff on developing a TV series based on the film (Vianna 2018).

12 Lúcia Sá (2013: 167) argues that Antonia needs to be read as a response to *City of God*, given the complete lack of drugs in the favela.

13 This threat extends to other groups involved in historical land disputes such as indigenous communities and the MST or landless people's movement. Using language that deliberately evoked slave-holding times, Jair Bolsonaro on the run-up to his presidential election campaign in 2018 notoriously dismissed *quilombo* residents as being overweight, indolent and not even capable of procreating.

14 For a list of films portraying *quilombos*, see Cruz (2016).

15 See for example Luka (2017).

References

Adamatti, M. M. 2016. "Crítica de cinema e patrulha ideológica: o caso Xica da Silva de Carlos Diegues". *Revista famecos: mídia, cultura e tecnologia*. 23:3. http://revistaseletronicas. pucrs.br/ojs/index.php/revistafamecos/article/view/23120/14605

Araújo, J. Z. 2000. *A negação do Brasil: o negro na telenovela brasileira*. São Paulo: Senac.

Azeredo, E. 2005. "The Looks in *City of God*". In Vieira, E. (ed) *City of God in Several Voices: Brazilian Social Cinema as Action*. Nottingham: CCC Press, pp. 93–96. Trans. C. Anchor.

Bentes, I. 2002. "Cidade de Deus promove turismo no inferno". *O Estado de Sao Paulo*. 31 August.

Bentes, I. 2013. "Film of the Year: *5 x Favela, Now By Ourselves/ 5 x favela, agora por nós mesmos*". In Bayman, L. and Pinazza, N. (eds) *Directory of World Cinema: Brazil* Bristol and Chicago: Intellect, pp. 10–13. Trans. N. Pinazza.

Bill, M.V. 2005. "Cidade de Deus: History's Silent Protagonist". In Vieira, E. (ed) *City of God in Several Voices: Brazilian Social Cinema as Action*. Nottingham: CCC Press, pp. 121–126. Trans. E. Martins Lopes.

Brito, D. 2018. "Cotas foram revolução silenciosa no Brasil, afirma especialista". *Agência Brasil*. 27 May. http://agenciabrasil.ebc.com.br/educacao/noticia/2018-05/cotas-foram-revolucao-silenciosa-no-brasil-afirma-especialista.

Carvalho, I. 2014. "Dez anos de cotas nas universidades: o que mudou?". *Revista forum*. 14 March. www.revistaforum.com.br/digital/138/sistema-de-cotas-completa-dez-anos-nas-universidades-brasileiras/.

Carvalho, N. and Domingues, P. 2018. "Dogma Feijoada: a invenção do cinema negro brasileiro". *Revista brasileira de ciências sociais*. 33: 96, pp. 1–18.

Cruz, D. 2016. "Histórias quilombolas: filmografia e bibliografia básicas". PSTU website. www.pstu.org.br/historias-quilombolas-filmografia-e-bibliografia-basicas/.

Fontes, E. R. 2007. "Corpo negro e cultura brasileira em cinco filmes nacionais: uma leitura de *Cidade de Deus, Orfeu negro, Orfeu, Madame Satã* e *Ônibus 174*". *Opsis* 7: 8, pp. 125–138.

Fraga, P. 2010. "*5 x Favela – Agora Por Nós Mesmos* é arte engajada sem ser política". Geledés. 25 August. www.geledes.org.br/5-x-favela-agora-por-nos-mesmos-e-arte-engajada-sem-ser-politica/.

Freyre, G. n/d. *Casa-grande & senzala*. Lisbon: Livros do Brasil.

Fundação cultural de Curitiba. 2018. "Cinema Negro Brasileiro em Mostra na Cinemateca". Fundação Cultural de Curitiba website. 24 July. www.fundacaoculturaldecuritiba.com. br/cinema/noticias/cinema-negro-brasileiro-em-mostra-na-cinemateca.

Gil, G. 2008. "O presidente pediu, eu fico". *Revista época*. 25 January. http://revistaepoca. globo.com/Revista/Epoca/0,,EDG81327-9556-506,00.html.

Heise, T. 2012. *Remaking Brazil: Contested National Identities in Contemporary Brazilian Cinema*. Melksham: University of Wales Press.

Hypeness. 2018. "Estudantes de Curitiba fazem vaquinha para criar Mostra de Cinema Negro". *R7*. 20 July. https://meuestilo.r7.com/hypeness/estudantes-de-curitiba-fazem-vaquinha-para-criar-mostra-de-cinema-negro-20072018.

Ikeda, M. 2015. *Cinema brasileiro a partir da retomada: aspectos econômcios e politicos*. São Paulo: Summus Editorial.

Johnson, R. 2005. "TV Globo, the MPA and Contemporary Brazilian Cinema". In Shaw, L. and Dennison, S. (eds), *Latin American Cinema: Essays on Modernity, Gender and National Identity*. Jefferson (NC): MacFarland, pp. 11–38.

Luka. 2017. "A limitação de Branco no Brasil". *Operamundi*. 19 January. https://blogs. operamundi.uol.com.br/bide/branco-do-brasil-adnet/.

Marsh, L. L. 2012. *Brazilian Women's Filmmaking: From Dictatorship to Democracy*. Champaign: University of Illinois Press.

Nagib, L. 2005. "Talking Bullets: The Language of Violence in *City of God*". In Vieira, E. (ed) *City of God in Several Voices: Brazilian Social Cinema as Action*. Nottingham: CCC Press, pp. 32–43. Trans. L. Shaw.

Oliveira Lima, M. E., Costa Neves, P. S. and Silva, P. B. 2014. "A implantação de cotas na universidade: paternalismo e ameaça à posição dos grupos dominantes". *Revistas brasileira de educação*. 19:56 (Jan-Mar).

Reiter, B. and Mitchell, G. 2010. *Brazil's New Racial Politics. Boulder, Co.:* Lynne Rienner.

Rodrigues, D. 2018. "A diretora negra e os lugares de fala". *Operamundi*. 1 September. https:// operamundi.uol.com.br/sociedade/49913/a-diretora-negra-e-os-lugares-de-fala.

Rodrigues, J. C. 2001. *O negro brasileiro e o cinema*. São Paulo: Pallas.

Sá, L. 2013. "Filming Favelas: Space, Gender and Everyday Life in Cidade de Deus and Antonia". In Kantaris, J. and O'Bryen, R. (eds) *Latin American Popular Culture: Politics, Media, Affect*. Woodbridge: Tamesis, pp. 167–186.

Salles, W. 2005. "A Traumatised Chicken in Crossfire". In Vieira, E. (ed) *City of God in Several Voices: Brazilian Social Cinema as Action*. Nottingham: CCC Press, pp. 3–4.

Stam, R. 1997. *Tropical Multiculturalism: A Comparative History of Race in Brazilian Cinema and Culture*. Durham and London: Duke.

Vianna, K. 2018 "Besouro: Rede globo desenvolve serie com super-heroi negro". *Adoro Cinema*. 29 August. www.adorocinema.com/noticias/series/noticia-142862/.

Xexéo, A. 2018. "Caca Diegues: um cineasta imortal". *O globo*. 2 September. https://oglobo. globo.com/cultura/caca-diegues-um-cineasta-imortal-23031381.

6

SCREENING THE INDIGENOUS EXPERIENCE IN BRAZIL

Perhaps one of the most striking features of Brazilian film culture over the course of the late twentieth and twenty-first centuries thus far is the shift in representation of indigenous peoples on screen. This is partly as a result of the highly regarded initiative Vídeo nas Aldeias (Video in the Villages), to be explored in more detail below, and partly because of greater public awareness and interest in the complex case of indigenous peoples in Brazil and their relation to "the nation". But the most significant reason for this shift is the growth in grassroots activist movements within indigenous communities themselves from the 1990s onwards (Gleghorn 2017: 169),[1] and the extent to which film has been incorporated into their activist repertoire. Taking advantage in 2000 of the problematic discourse around the "celebration" of Brazil's 500-year anniversary, high-profile indigenous mobilisations and protests in Brasilia and elsewhere sought to draw attention to the need to retrace indigenous history, and bring indigenous issues to the centre of political debate. But despite these protests the dominant discourse in the audio-visual sphere, in terms of what images and messages are reaching a wide public, continues to be one of a history of harmonious encounter between Brazilian "Indians" and "non-Indians".[2]

The myth of this harmonious encounter can be traced back as far as 1500, when the Portuguese "discoverer" Pedro Alvares Cabral was blown off course to India and reached the Brazilian coast. Travelling with Cabral's fleet was Pero Vaz de Caminha, whose letter to the Portuguese King Manuel I dated 1 May 1500 and describing first contact with the land and peoples in Porto Seguro, Bahia, is regarded as the nation's foundational text. The letter emphasised the friendly, almost intimate curiosity of both the sailors and the natives towards each other. It focused in great detail on the physical appearance (and in particular the nudity) and gentle, innocent disposition of the natives, their lack of faith and therefore their likely predisposition to be converted to Christianity, and the wide range of raw materials contained in the land. Perhaps the most celebrated filmic representation of Caminha's first contact text is Humberto Mauro's 1930 silent classic *Descobrimento do Brasil* (*The Discovery of Brasil*).[3] In an iconic scene Mauro recreated, at great cost and in a celebratory, patriotic tone, Brazil's First Mass, demonstrating that harmonious contact relied on a reading of Brazilian history that pushed towards assimilation as a naturally occurring phenomenon for the benefit of all.[4] Thus the huge reduction in number of the estimated five million people who lived in Brazil at the time of first contact is given a positive twist (spontaneous assimilation), in sharp contrast to the revisionist reading of cultural destruction and genocide.

While Pero Vaz de Caminha's letter continues to be studied rather unproblematically in schools and continues to influence much mainstream audio-visual production,[5] the reports of other early explorers have all but been forgotten. Take for example the German explorer Hans Staaden (1529–1576), responsible for disseminating the belief that Brazilian Indians were violent cannibals, after being captured by and writing about his experiences living among the Tupinambá.[6] European and Brazilian-born Jesuits, highly influential in Brazil until their expulsion in 1759, also painted a much less flattering portrait of the different indigenous cultures they encountered, with tales of sorcery and barbaric acts perhaps inevitably dominating a discourse designed in part to justify their "civilising" mission and spread of the Christian faith.

Most fictional films produced in Brazil since *Descobrimento do Brasil* have displayed a similar preference for depicting "first contact Indians" through the centuries (that is, unproblematically indigenous and their attire and lifestyle demonstrate this). This is likely as a result of the "dumb intellectual inertia of Eurocentric trap concepts such as 'authenticity', 'tradition/modernity' and 'real Indians'" (Stam et al. 2015: 35). The most-watched film of the turn of the millennium/five hundredth anniversary of the "Discovery" of Brazil was Guel Arraes's light-hearted *Caramuru: a invenção do Brasil*, based on the real-life encounter between a seventeenth-century Portuguese explorer, Diogo Alvares, renamed Caramuru, and a Tupinambá princess, Paraguaçu. The film was "cut" from a very popular TV series on Globo (*A Invenção do Brasil*, 2000), and screened as part of the TV channel's five hundredth anniversary celebrations.[7] Robert Stam et al. (2015: 257) acknowledge the efforts of the scriptwriters (director Arraes together with Jorge Furtado, both known for their quirky sense of humour) to offer a "polyperspectival narration" by depicting the moment of discovery from both the perspective of the Portuguese and the local inhabitants, but ultimately, the indigenous people portrayed in *Caramuru* are picturesque, ambiguous and comical (Araújo de Souza 2016) and the film's humour is largely predicated on their laziness and promiscuity. As Mabel Araújo de Souza (2016) argues, "films that deal with exploitation in a gentle and carnivalesque way erase the history of genocide of the indigenous population that continues to this day. Both the film [Caramuru] and the five hundredth anniversary celebrations of "discovery" omitted to mention the violence that indigenous peoples experienced, as well as the various forms of resistance bound up with their contemporary identity".

Like *Caramuru*, other mainstream fictional films that attempt a rounder, less romanticised portrait of indigenous history tend to feature "white saviours" in leading roles. Noteworthy in this regard is *Xingu* (Cao Hamburger, 2011), about the Villas-Boas brothers, explorers in the 1950s and 60s who were largely responsible for negotiating the creation of the Xingu Park indigenous reserve in the Amazon region. The film reached millions of viewers in Brazil, once again as a result of its transmedial relationship with Globo TV: it was reedited as a miniseries and screened on Globo at primetime. *O Rio da Dúvida* (*The River of Doubt*, Joel Pizzini, 2018), a feature-length documentary which mixes found footage and fictional recreations of events surrounding the 1913–1914 scientific expedition of Brazilian Marshall Cândido Rondon and US ex-president Theodore Roosevelt, portrays the contribution of Rondon, the founder of the Indian Protection Service (Serviço de Proteção ao Índio), in an unproblematic way.[8] The film notably had the full support of the Rondon family and it received funding from the state government of Rondonia, the Brazilian state that bears the marshall's name. Thus, despite making an acclaimed documentary *500 almas* (*500 Souls*) about the Guató Indians, Pizzini's latest film is unlikely to challenge any prevailing myths about Rondon and indigenous culture. The feature-length fictional film *Rondon o desbravador* (*Rondon The Pioneer*, Marcelo Santiago, 2016) traces a similar hagiographic path. Having once again a guaranteed interest in the subject matter emerging out of a Globo miniseries *Rondon, o grande chefe* (Rondon, the Great Leader, Marcelo Santiago, 2015), director Santiago, who has garnered a reputation for making flattering biopics of the "great men" of Brazilian history, quickly produced a feature-length version of his mini-series.

Before embarking on a discussion of recent films that debunk the harmonious encounter and white saviour myths, it is worth drawing attention to the small but very significant number of memorable filmic interventions that were made in Brazil prior to 2000 which fiercely challenged these prevailing myths, and in particular three key films from the last decades of the twentieth century. The most memorable and discussed of these films is *Iracema: uma transa amazônica* (*Iracema*, Jorge Bodansky and Orlando Senna, 1974), a scathing antidote to the many representations of the romantic myth of Iracema, the Indian beauty of José de Alencar's foundational novel of the same name (1865), in which Iracema is recast as a prostitute working along the controversial Trans-Amazonian Highway.[9] Deeply sceptical of the progress promised by opening up the Amazon, and critical of both the destruction of the environment and of the abandonment of the indigenous cause that such progress provoked, the film was banned in Brazil by the military dictatorship until 1981, despite garnering critical praise at Cannes in 1976. Then in 1983 Sergio Bianchi released *Mato eles?* (*Shall I kill them?*) to acclaim at the key Brazilian film festivals of Gramado and Brasilia. Bianchi's short film is a darkly humorous satirical mockumentary that overtly criticises FUNAI, the National Indigenous Foundation whose function is supposedly to protect the interests of indigenous peoples in Brazil, going as far as to suggest that the organisation profits from their labour. The title hints at both the eventual extermination of Brazil's indigenous populations, and at collusion and indifference in the face of extermination. The extermination theme is picked up by Sílvio Back's *Yndio do Brasil* (*Our Indians*, 1995) in which the filmmaker pieces together the distorted history of Brazil's indigenous populations as seen in filmic representations (both national and international), superimposed with his own poems denouncing their annihilation (Stam 2003: 223). The film notably takes the usually glorified Marshall Rondon to task for his push towards integration, described by Back in interview as the equivalent of genocide (in Couto 1995).[10] Back's film draws attention to the vast pictorial and filmic iconography of the "Brazilian Indian" (the early photographic and filmmaking adventures in the Amazon of documentarian Silvino Santos;[11] the romanticised fiction features mentioned above; foreign blockbuster incursions into the Amazon, and so on) and by laying extracts of these films "end to end without apparent rhyme or reason" (Stam 2003: 223) the result is a damning critique of this filmic representation, which offers no clear or accurate vision of either indigenous history or of the customs and traditions of indigenous peoples. Thus, in *Yndio do Brasil* film culture in the twentieth century is dismissed as contributing nothing positive to the indigenous cause, and in particular with regard to the issue of giving voice to the indigenous peoples themselves.

Vídeo nas Aldeias

Vídeo nas Aldeias developed as early as 1986 out of an existing NGO, the Centro do Trabalho Indigenista (Centre for Indigenous Work). In 2000 it gained its own identity as an NGO and began to receive financial support from Brazil's Culture Ministry as part of the Programa Cultura Viva or Living Culture Programme.[12] While it is most closely associated with Franco-Brazilian Vincent Carelli, a social scientist who trained at the University of São Paulo and who continues to head up the organisation, two women were instrumental in shaping the NGO in terms of bringing memorial, participatory and training elements to the centre of the organisation's work: the anthropologist and Carelli's wife Virginia Valadão (1952–1998), and visual anthropologist Mari Correa (Aufderheide 2008: 31 quoted in Gleghorn 2016: 176). There are currently 88 films documented on the Video nas Aldeias online catalogue. According to Gleghorn, "Films are produced for internal consumption, as a way to promote the transmission of knowledge from generation to generation, but many also have an intercultural persuasion, commonly used to broker dialogue with nearby groups and the dominant society" (176).[13] A number of the short films, as well as the feature-length documentaries *As hiper mulheres*, (*The Hyper Women*, Takumã Kuikuro, Leonardo Sette and Carlos Fausto, 2011), *O mestre e o divino* (*Master and Divino*, Tiago Campos Torres 2013) and *Martírio* (*Martyrdom*, Vincent Carelli, Tatiana Almeida and Ernesto de Carvalho, 2016) can be viewed online via the NGO's VOD platform, and didactic material, such as the teachers' guide *Cineastas indígenas: um outro olhar* (Indigenous Filmmakers: Another View), has been produced with a view to introducing school-age children both within indigenous communities and elsewhere, to the indigenous filmmaking experience in Brazil. The catalogue of films listed on the Vídeo Nas Aldeias website often cites the "nação" (literally nation) or ethnicity of the filmmaker/subject (Xavante, for example), rather than a named director, in what is an important gesture in terms of pointing to the collective nature of indigenous cultural practices, in accurately documenting indigenous history, and of countering indigenous representations that have all too often ignored ethnic distinctions.

Two Vídeo nas Aldeias films released in 2008 notably refashion the foundational first-contact myth. In *Ma ê dami xina – já me transformei em imagem* (*I've Already Become an Image*, Zezinho Yube, 2008) the Huni Kui filmmaker films tribal leaders re-enacting first contact from their perspective, and then captures the reactions of community members to a screening of the re-enactment (Stam et al. 2015: 40). In *Mokoi Petuá Petei Jeguatá* (*Two Villages, One Path*), the Mbya-Guarani filmmakers Germano Beñites, Ariel Duarte Ortega, Jorge Ramos Morinico portray two contrasting interpretations of history: the view of the "official" white tour guides at the ruins of the São Miguel Jesuit Missions in Rio Grande do Sul, Brazil's southern-most state, and those of the Guarani who are reduced to selling handmade souvenirs at the tourist site in order to survive (Stam et al. 2015: 257).

Martírio

Gleghorn's claim that Vídeo nas Aldeias films are made by indigenous filmmakers for internal consumption is nowadays only partially true. With Carelli's own film *Martírio* one senses a shift to focusing on the pressing issue of land and indigenous interaction with Brazil's powerful agribusiness interests and the need to reach a supportive audience to aid in lobbying for the indigenous cause. *Martírio* is Carelli's monumental attempt, over the course of almost three hours, to recount Brazilian history from an indigenous perspective (Carelli, quoted in Merten 2016). This award-winning ethnographic documentary[14] is to date the most widely disseminated film of the Vídeo nas Aldeias NGO, with 1,200 copies being made available at the time of its release, and further opportunities for viewing online, including a three-month window of free viewing which was widely advertised on social media. The film blends footage originally shot by Carelli in 1988 and then abandoned (we are informed that many of the interviews with the Guarani-Kaiowá remained untrans-lated until the making of *Martírio*) with more recent interviews (with centre-stage given over to testimony of Guarani elders), old films of the Rondon period, for example, newspaper and TV news reports and footage of an armed attack filmed by the Guarani-Kaiowá themselves during the making of the film. Martírio forms part of a trilogy which began with *Corumbiara* (*Corumbiara: They Shoot Indians, Don't They?* 2009), a feature-length documentary in which Carelli charts the 1995 massacre of the same name, and it ends with *Adeus, Capitão* (Farewell Captain, in production at time of writing).

Carelli ironically punctuates *Martírio* with subheadings such as "O índio civilizado" ("The Civilised Indian", dating from the time of the Serviço de Proteção ao Indio or Indian Protection Service in the early twentieth century, when indigenous peoples learned Portuguese and were put to work) and "O índio emancipado" ("The Emancipated Indian", with its references to the populist dicta-torship of Getúlio Vargas [1937–1945] and the creation of a series of rather hollow initiatives such as the national "Day of the Indian"). The subheadings remind us of canonical historiography that focuses on indigenous relationships with "Brazilians", whereby chronological advances are regarded as altruistic and in the interests of the indigenous population and they are invariably predicated on the population's ability to map culturally onto a centrally defined set of national characteristics. When these are seen to be at odds with national policy, the indigenous experience is frequently omitted from historical accounts, such as The Paraguayan War (1864–1870) or Vargas's "marcha para o oeste" or push to open up the western interior. *Martírio* revises such nationally celebrated historical moments by focusing on the impact on indigenous peoples (once again removed from their land, and often put to work at the service of the State in order to expel other indigenous groups).

In order to explain the origin of the Guarani-Kaiowá's current struggle with agribusiness (with soya cultivation now taking over from growing yerba mate and cattle farming) it is to the "little-known"[15] Paraguayan War that the Guarani return to tell their history. It was as a result of Brazil's victory in the war, a victory celebrated in Brazilian historiography, despite the huge loss of life and damage to Paraguay that it caused (the country lost 40% of its land to the Triple Alliance of Brazil, Argentina and Uruguay), that ownership of much of the Guarani Indians' lands shifted to Brazil, with 25% of the state of Mato Grosso do Sul, home to the Guarani-Kaiowá, being made up of former Paraguayan territory.

The multimillionaire business interests behind much of the beef and soya belt in Brazil rarely feature in such films, unless captured in debates in Congress. Instead, as in *Martírio*, it is the gruff, rather inarticulate, provincial and always white smaller-scale landowners whose voices are heard locally in defence of agribusiness and the dispossession of indigenous groups. They are frequently caricatured and edited in such a way to reduce their presence to the performative and thus disregard their views. In *Martírio* the angle at which one landowner is shot, for example, which emphasises his slovenly, man-spreading posture and unbuttoned shirt as he dismisses the Guarani-Kaiowá as "not even Indians", as Paraguayan interlopers encouraged by unscrupulous anthropologists, makes it difficult to take his views seriously. This is a world occupied by fans of the kitsch Brazilian rodeo imported directly from the US, with its parade of white "promo girls", of the much maligned *música sertaneja* (a watered down version of both a Brazilian and US country music tradition) and of agricultural shows and charity fundraisers for thinly disguised white supremacist groups.

One voice representing business interests that is taken seriously in *Martírio*, and which Carelli endeavours to challenge rather than dismiss, is that of Kátia Abreu, Minister of Agriculture in Dilma Rousseff's second term of office (2014–2016). Rousseff's decision to appoint Abreu in 2014 proved very controversial, particularly among environmentalists, who dubbed her "A Rainha da Motoserra" (The Chainsaw Queen) and "Miss Desmatamento" (Miss Deforestation) for her outspoken support of agribusiness interests.[16] So her presence on screens post-impeachment comes as a bleak reminder of the lack of support for the indigenous cause of the PT (Workers Party) governments and in particular Rousseff's second term of office. Of all the pressing social issues that the PT governments tackled during the twenty-first century, the indigenous issue (and in particular, the urgent need for a lasting settlement regarding the permanent demarcation of indigenous lands) was one of the most overlooked and the PT government's failure to act, and its seeming privileging of views of the *bancada ruralista* or rural lobby in congress and the senate and agribusiness in general over the needs of indigenous populations, was a source of considerable criticism.

Abreu's voice punctuates *Martírio*: in the opening sequence she asks in a polit-ical rally when will men and women have "peace to work", with the subsequent sound of indigenous chanting highlighting the extreme irony of such a question. Later she speaks of the indigenous occupation of land as *invasões* or invasions, thus drawing analogies with the other great "enemy" of landed interests: the MST (the Landless Peoples Movement). Her articulate and impassioned words are shown in the context of the views of other less guarded *ruralista* politicians, including footage of the then leader of the *bancada ruralista* in Congress, Luiz Carlos Heinze making his now infamous claims that Dilma Rousseff's government was full of ex-slaves, Indians, gays and lesbians, "tudo que não presta" (only the worthless). We also see an example of the kind of performative excess that has become a staple in both the (televised) congress and senate, in which a lawmaker "breaks down" and weeps in front of the cameras at the thought of the three policemen killed in the line of duty as a result of tensions between an indigenous group and landed interests.[17]

While *Martírio* highlights many of the journeys made to Congress and the Senate by activist indigenous groups over the last twenty or so years, it also includes footage of a rare visit to a site of indigenous tension made by a political figure: the visit to the region occupied by the Guarani-Kaiowá made by Aristides Junqueira, then Attorney General. This serves as a reminder that historically erstwhile uncom-mitted public figures who have taken the time to visit the region have often been moved by the indigenous "problem". This problem is both legal and moral: as Junqueira describes it on camera, FUNAI awards land to indigenous groups and the landowners appeal to the Courts, with the result of limbo and tension on both sides. The moral problem is summed up by Junqueira succinctly: in those days and in those lands, cattle were worth more than people (cabeça de gado vale mais do que gente).

While Carelli's film can feel overwhelming and historically disorientating at times, it does successfully get across the massive dimensions of the contemporary "indigenous problem" and the extent to which history has conspired against the Guarani Kaiowá. It also puts forward a less fatalistic (but perhaps simplistic) argument than many other documentaries of its kind: Carelli sees the indigenous problem as a "false problem": "Tem lugar para os índios e tem lugar para o agronegócio. Uma coisa não impede a outra. Os índios não estão pedindo nenhum absurdo." (There is space for indigenous groups and space for agribusiness. One thing doesn't impede the other. Indigenous peoples aren't asking for the moon." (Carelli, quoted in Merten 2017).

FIGURE 6.1 Guarani marching to demand land rights. A still from the trailer for *Martírio*

(Vincent Carelli, Ernesto de Carvalho, Tatiana Almeida, 2017)

Terra Vermelha **and** *A Nação que não Esperou por Deus*

In order to capture a full sense of the representation of indigenous peoples in twenty-first-century Brazilian film culture it is also important to consider films being made with indigenous groups but without the support of agencies such as Vídeo nas Aldeias and from within a more mainstream tradition. Both filmmakers discussed in the next section, Marco Bechis and Lúcia Murat, have established reputations working in fiction film, as well as documentary, and both films, *Terra vermelha* (*Birdwatchers*, 2008) and *A Nação que não esperou por Deus* (*The Nation that Didn't Wait for God*, 2015) are international co-productions (with Italy and Portugal respectively). Both films deal with the life experiences of indigenous peoples from the Mato Grosso do Sul region in the Brazilian mid-west: the Guarani-Kaiowá and Kadiwéu peoples respectively.

What is striking in the case of these films is the question of agency in relation to the representation of the indigenous experience in Brazil in the twenty-first century, both in terms of the role of indigenous peoples in constructing the narrative contained within the respective films, and what we might extrapolate from those narratives regarding the place of indigenous peoples in contemporary Brazilian culture.

Terra vermelha is a fiction film relating the difficulties facing the Guarani-Kaiowá which was jointly developed with the indigenous population and casts them in the principal roles of the film. The Guarani-Kaiowá are acknowledged as co-authors of the film and they in instances play themselves and recreate scenes based on real experiences: clashes with white ranchers, struggles to reclaim their land and deal with a hostile state, alcoholism, depression, suicide, the impact of consumerism on the younger generations, and so on. The film was co-scripted by Luis Bolognesi of the travelling cinema initiative Tela Brasil (see Chapter 1), himself a trained anthropologist and successful filmmaker (*Ex-Pajé/Ex-Shaman*, 2018). *Terra vermelha* is almost entirely spoken in Guarani (with Portuguese subtitles). It premiered at the Venice Film Festival in 2008 in the presence of a number of the indigenous stars. Ademilson Concianza, who plays the teenager Irineu, went on to train at the Instituto Brasileiro de Audiovisual (IBEV)/Escola de Cinema Darcy Ribeiro in Rio de Janeiro (in photography and film). Ademilson is currently both a videomaker and a spiritual leader in his village.[18]

In what is by far the most striking and remarked upon scene from the film (the opening sequence that prefaces the film credits) a group of tourists seen in a stunning overhead shot, are travelling silently along a rainforest river by boat when their guide points out a group of "Indians" with bows on a riverbank. They shoot arrows into the sky and the tourist group beats a hasty retreat. The indigenous group, looking indifferent, then leave the riverbank and head back to the truck which brought them, changing into their western clothes and accepting payment for their "performance". When the performance ends, the diegetic sound of birdsong is replaced by a soaring baroque religious chorus,[19] making a bridge both between the "fake" first-contact experience offered by twenty-first-century "Indians" and their colonial counterparts, and between early European and religious interests and new-age explorers (including, inevitably, the Italian-Chilean filmmaker (Bechis) and technical crew, and by implication, the film audience). Our first glimpse of indigenous people in the film, then, likens them to rare, exotic birds, an object of curiosity and aesthetic beauty for outsiders (both foreign and Brazilian tourists). The rest of *Terra vermelha* deftly challenges such a representation, in a story that includes hard-hitting images of teenage suicide victims hanging from trees, dire poverty, as the group is reduced to camping on a roadside, exploitation of labour and assassination. There is a real sense as we watch the story in the film unfold, that the Guarani-Kaiowá are left with no alternative but to eke out an existence whatever way they can, meaning that what might be dismissed as simplistically presented dichotomies, for example, between tradition and modernity (evil landowners and suffering indigenous people) are in fact a genuine feature of their lives. That said, in terms of the representation of women and sexuality, the indigenous voice arguably shouts louder than the standard denunciatory press pieces that dominate reports on Indians in the UK media, for example.[20] The character Lia, played wonderfully by the non-professional indigenous actress Alicélia Batista Cabreira, surprises in her demonstration of agency in relation to the sexual advances of the ranchers' security guard. A kind of anti-Iracema, Lia is neither the loving nation-building mother figure of the original Iracema foundational text and its filmic adaptations, nor the irresistible Indian of the *pornochanchadas*, nor the exploited prostitute of *Iracema, uma transa amazônica*.

The documentary *A nação que não esperou por Deus* revisits the Kadiwéu people who featured in Lúcia Murat's historical revisionist fiction film *Brava gente brasileira*

FIGURE 6.2 Amateur actors play a dispossessed group of Guarani confronting white landowners. A still from *Terra vermelha*

(*Birdwatchers*, Marco Bechis, 2008)

of 2000, which she shot on location in the late 1990s. The original script for *Brava gente brasileira* had been adapted to incorporate inspiration gathered from the Kadiwéu themselves. The Hi-8 footage of the pre-filming of *Brava gente brasileira* on location features in the new documentary (hence the acknowledgement of Rodrigo Hinrichsen as co-director) alongside sequences from the 2000 film itself, the contemporary Kadiwéus watching a screening of the film on their reserve, and interviews with those who featured in the original fiction film.

Revisiting the Kadiwéu enabled Murat to reflect on the rapid change taking place even in demarcated indigenous lands, thus debunking the myth that indigenous groups settled in State-demarcated reserves live some kind of idyllic existence away from modernity and the other "evils" associated with displaced groups, such as threats from agribusiness. In fact the very issue of being reduced to a demarcated "reservation" is highlighted as problematic for the Kadiwéu. The title of the film is a reference, explained in voiceover by one of their leaders, to the fact that when God created them, they did not wait to be given sustenance, but instead became hunter-gatherers (and therefore by nature at odds with the principle of being housed in a relatively small, enclosed space). When Murat revisited the Kadiwéu (in 2014) they were embroiled in a battle with local ranchers over access to land, after a judge had awarded in the Kadiwéu's favour. We witness a meeting between representatives of the ranchers and the Kadiweu. The discourse of both sides is almost identical to that captured by Vincent Carelli in *Martirio*, with indigenous voices reminding those present that European discovery is a myth and thus that land is a birthright of indigenous peoples. In a shift away from what are arguably quite Manichean representations of Brazilian landowners in the more politically engaged audio-visual sphere, it is a young, articulate female landowner who calmly and patiently listens to the Kadiwéu and then airs her views. Her arguments (that she is barely eking an existence on the land as it is, that she just wants to be able to get on with her work)[21] echo the more strongly worded sentiments of the likes of Kátia Abreu as seen in *Martírio*. The meeting ends on a seemingly positive note, with both parties agreeing to work together, but the hope of resolution is soon quashed when an appeal judge votes against the Kadiwéu. While this is not documented in the film, the implication is that co-operation is nothing more than a necessary expedient when judgements do not work in the favour of the ranchers, and hostilities quickly resume.

If Lúcia Murat can be praised for avoiding a more stereotypical portrayal of the representatives of agribusiness, her seeming tolerance of the presence of evangelical Christian movements on Kadiwéu land did evoke criticism.[22] As discussed in Chapter 1, for many observers, the growth of the evangelical movement, and particularly its growing strength within politics, with the formation of an increasingly influential parliamentary lobby (the *bancada evangélica*) presents as much of an impediment to social justice as does the *bancada ruralista*. Films have in fact been slow to pick up on and discuss the steady growth in presence of evangelical churches on indigenous land, with the notable exception of *Ex-Pajé* (*Ex-Shaman*), Luis Bolognesi's critically acclaimed "docu-fiction hybrid" (Weissberg 2018) that premiered at the Berlin Film festival in 2018 and which laments the presence of evangelicals among the Pater Surui of Western Brazil, an uncontacted group until as recently as 1969.[23]

Evangelical Christianity infiltrated the Kadiwéu lands by offering schooling and medical care quite early on in the reserve's history, in the absence of such support from FUNAI. *A Nação que não esperou por Deus* offers a rather sympathetic portrayal

FIGURE 6.3 An evangelical pastor and member of the Kadiwéu community preaching in a still from the trailer for *A nação que não esperou por Deus*

(*The Nation That Didn't Wait For God*, Lúcia Murat and Rodrigo Hinrichsen, 2015)

of an indigenous evangelical pastor whose style of support for his congregation (and in particular, his use of native language for communication in religious cere- monies)[24] arguably point to the possibility of an interesting syncretic relationship with Christianity, despite the Brazilian evangelical church movement's poor record when it comes to demonstrating tolerance of other religious and cultural practices. In a post-screening debate when the film was first released, Murat restricted her comments on the issue of evangelisation to the hope that it would not result in the Kadiwéu stopping thinking for themselves. She cited the fact that when she visited the Kadiwéu and organised the screening of *Brava gente brasileira* the church had expressed concerns about women appearing naked. Her team feared women would stay away from screening as a result, but they did not, and the film screened to a delighted full house.

Concluding remarks

As witnessed in Vincent Carelli's presentation in *Martírio* of "bottom-up" history conveyed through popular memory, film can play a key role in legitimising oral history by "inscribing" it on the screen (Stam et al. 2015: 40), thus potentially con- tributing to the on-going battle for justice for indigenous groups in Brazil. If we move away from the traditional long and short-film format we find many examples of indigenous filmmaking, such as those promoted by the Celulares Indígenas (Indigenous Mobile Phones) (2009) programme, which put mobile phones and their cameras at the disposal of the indigenous communities to record rights violations or other significant events and then share the resultant *celumetragens* (mobile phone "shorts") online (Pitman 2018). Indigenous film and video production is only one part of a growing movement of indigenous engagement with digital technology that serves the important purposes of community building, consciousness-raising and self-protection among indigenous groups.[25] And animated short film produc- tion, either by or about indigenous groups, is flourishing: take, for example, *A festa dos encantados* (Feast of the Enchanted, Masanori Ohashy, 2015), a film screened in a number of festivals in Brazil and abroad and based on a Guajajara legend. Consider also the remarkable work of educator Daniele Rodrigues, who since 2012 has worked with school children in the Rio suburbs and made six animated short features that tackle the issue of stereotypes surrounding indigenous peoples (Fernandes 2018). Rodrigues reports that the need to make the films emerged as a reaction to the dearth of good classroom material on the indigenous experience, despite the law introduced in 2008 making it compulsory to teach indigenous his- tory and culture in schools.

In a Q and A that took place at the Odeon cinema in Rio de Janeiro after a screening of *A nação que não esperou por Deus*, director Lúcia Murat referenced the Parque das Nações Indígenas in Campo Grande, capital of the state of Mato Grosso do Sul and, as we have seen, home to a large number of indigenous groups. The park is one of the largest in the world and it is adorned with statues commemor- ating the contribution of indigenous peoples to the Brazilian nation. Despite this "official" recognition, Murat observed during filming that the public reaction to indigenous peoples in Mato Grosso was more often than not one of open racism.[26] Murat sought to make the point that while an open-minded and empathetic film audience in the centre-south (i.e. Rio and São Paulo, for example) might defend indigenous rights, there were very few voices being raised in Mato Grosso to defend indigenous interests. As we have seen, it is the uncritical readings of indigenous culture, such as *Caramuru*,[27] which reach a wide public, while the indigenous-produced short films of Vídeo nas Aldeias, for example, make it no further than specialist film festivals[28] (Heise 2012:142) and VOD platforms, where they risk preaching to the already converted.

Film critic and blogger Inácio Araújo is critical of *Martírio* for its "determination to show everything, instead of editing, cutting, concentrating […] in my view, love for a cause at times can be so great that it ends up ruining a film. I think that was the case here" (2017). In Araújo's view a (veteran) filmmaker such as the late Andrea Tonacci, who made the festival and critics' favourite *Serras da desordem* (*Hills of Disorder* 2006) about the massacre of the Awá–Guajá in the 1970s,[29] demonstrates how to make stunning films "about Indians, with Indians and among the Indians" (2017). Araújo's critique is ultimately predicated on the advent of digital technology and what he sees as an inability to edit images, given that most that are captured digitally are of good quality. While Araújo may have a point with regard to technology and its impact on how filmmakers relate to the images they capture digitally, his statement suggests that even the work of ethnographic documentary filmmakers, when it enters the film exhibition circuit, is to be judged by some critics by the aesthetic standards expected of traditional arthouse production.

As witnessed in films such as *A nação que não esperou por Deus*, *Martírio* and *Birdwatchers*, the extreme hardship experienced by indigenous groups in twenty-first-century Brazil is exacerbated when it intersects with agribusiness interests. Under the Michel Temer government (2016–2018), supported by the agribusiness lobby, funding to FUNAI was slashed and conditions had become so desperate for the Guarani Kaiowá that leader Ladio Veron toured Europe in 2017 seeking international support for indigenous territorial claims. But frustrated claims, violence and desperation have been the order of the day throughout the twenty-first century, and not just post-impeachment. A total of 390 Guarani-Kaiowá leaders were reportedly killed between 2003 and 2014 (Woods 2017). Currently 690 territories, 453,000 square miles or 13% of Brazil's land mass (mostly in the Amazon region) occupied by 0.4% of the population have been designated indigenous land in Brazil. While the full demarcation of indigenous lands was guaranteed under Brazil's 1988 constitution, this project has never come close to being completed. Given the political direction of travel at the time of writing, this constitutional guarantee will at best continue to be ignored, and at worst it will be formally rescinded. As Vicente Carelli poignantly observed in voiceover in *Martírio*, "It is in the treatment of the indigenous population that Brazilian society is revealed".

Notes

1 Charlotte Gleghorn (2017: 169) refers to a series of "masterfully executed public protests – notably the televised demonstration orchestrated by the Kayapó and pro-indigenous allies against the Altamira hydroelectric plant in northern Brazil in 1989" as adding potency to the indigenous film movement.

2 The misnomer Indian to denote the indigenous peoples of the Americas is no longer widely used in the English-language academy (one notable exception being the work of Robert Stam). However, the equivalent term índio continues to be widely used in Brazil, partly as a result of the fact that the adjective Indian (from or of India) is distinctively rendered as *indiano* in Portuguese.

3 For an interesting reading of the film and its links to Caminha's text, see Richard A Gordon (2005).

4 Another such reading of history can be found in Brazilian post-independence novels which sought to contribute to the nation-building project: they were often full of tales of white men and women falling in love and procreating with indigenous people. See Doris Sommer (1991). Both of the nineteenth-century Brazilian Indianist novels Sommer discusses (*O guarani* and *Iracema*) have been adapted for cinema screens many times over, from as early as 1917 and including forays into soft-core porn (the commercially successful *pornochanchadas*), such as *Iracema: a virgem dos lábios de mel* (*Iracema, the honey-lipped virgin,* Carlos Coimbra, 1979).

5 For example, indigenous characters and scenarios regularly feature in successful soap operas and miniseries on TV in Brazil, and in these their representation is almost always stereotypical. Interestingly, however, the first wide-reaching mainstream TV series to document the life of indigenous peoples was critically acclaimed: *Xingu: a terra mágica* (*Xingu: The Magic Land*), which first aired on the now extinct TV Manchete in 1985, managed to avoid many of the clichés associated with indigenous representation. Manchete was perhaps unusual in the Brazilian context in that it regularly gave producers free rein to make more creative, challenging programmes. Brothers Walter and João Moreira Salles cut their documentary-making teeth in collaboration with Manchete with a series of fascinating explorations of China and the USA, for example.

6 A notable exception is the *retomada* film *Hans Staaden* (Luis Alberto Pereira, 1999). See Nagib 2007: 74–80. Nelson Pereira dos Santos's 1971 late *cinema novo* film *Como era gostoso o meu francês* (*How Tasty Was My Little Frenchman*) also deals with the *tupinambá* and the subject of cannibalism, but here the issue is tackled critically: in a subtle critique of the prevailing dictatorship, the film suggests that cultural cannibalism (i.e. incorporating the strengths of one's enemies) is a more prudent strategy than assimilation. For an interesting reading of the film and its relationship to history, see Martin-Jones (2018: 124–134).

7 For a discussion of the Globo miniseries, see Stam 2003: 206–208.

8 Here it is worth acknowledging that Rondon himself was mixed-race (white and indigenous), but brought up within a typically white, military tradition in the nineteenth century. Rondon travelled with his own cinematographer, Major Luiz Thomaz Reis, and there is therefore a relative wealth of footage of his expeditions that dates from a time when very little filmed material has survived. For more information on early cinema in Brazil, including the work of Reis, see Conde (2018) and Martins (2013).

9 For useful readings of the film see Stam (2003: 217–219); Furtado (2013).

10 Silvio Back made the much less discussed and distributed documentary *República Guarani* in 1981, in which he was more overtly critical of the policy of integration promoted by Marshall Rondon. On this issue it is worth stating that Joel Pizzini's previously mentioned documentary *O Rio da Dúvida* does at least acknowledge the problematic

nature of this policy: one of Rondon's granddaughters who is interviewed in the film reflects that her grandfather would likely take a different view on the matter, were he alive today (Duchiade 2018).

11 See Martins (2013).

12 According to their website, the organisation receives sponsorship from UNESCO, Petrobras and the Embassy of Norway.

13 For brief discussions of Vídeo nas Aldeias and some of the short films the organisation has produced, see Heise (2012: 137–140), Stam et al. (2015: 40, 257) and Gleghorn (2017: 176–177).

14 According to Paul Henley's definition of anthropological filmmaking practices: see Henley and Flores (2009).

15 *Economist* (2012).

16 Abreu was the running mate to left-leaning Ciro Gomes (PDT) in his unsuccessful presidential election campaign in 2018. By contrast presidential candidate Guilherme Boulos (PSOL) chose as his running mate the high-profile indigenous activist Sônia Guajajara.

17 Carelli's voiceover at this point in the film is quick to remind viewers of the incomparable number of indigenous lives lost as a result of current tensions.

18 Two other budding Kaiowá filmmakers attended at the same time. All three received scholarships awarded by the School, which was set up as an NGO in 2002 and offers both fee-paying and means-tested scholarship opportunities for shorter and therefore more accessible courses relating to film and video-making. The School has been supported by Petrobras since 2007 and its mission statement emphasises its goal to democratise access to audiovisual training and jobs. See www.escoladarcyribeiro.org.br/indigenas-do-ms-vao-cursar-direcao-roteiro-e-montagem-na-escola-de-cinema-darcy-ribeiro/

19 The inspired choice of music is "Sacris Solemnis" by Domenico Zipoli (1688–1726), an Italian baroque composer and Jesuit missionary who worked in South America among the Guarani.

20 See, for example, Vidal 2016.

21 The recurrence of references to working the land is more than coincidence and serves to demonstrate that the land is being used constructively. It is therefore distinctive from the large, unproductive holdings that continue to exist and which prompted in part the creation of the MST or Landless Peoples Movement.

22 See for example Janot 2015.

23 *At Play in the Fields of the Lord*, Hector Babenco's critically acclaimed US/Brazilian co-production from 1991, is critical of modern-day evangelising in the Amazon. The policy of no contact, supported by FUNAI, has also arguably influenced critics in their suspicion of any form of evangelisation. There are around 100 uncontacted indigenous groups living in the Amazon region, the largest number of anywhere on earth (Survival International n/d).

24 It is worth noting in this regard that many of the Kadiwéu who were filmed in 1999 in their youth only spoke Kadiwéu, but now speak Portuguese. The evangelical church ceremonies therefore inadvertently serve the purpose of maintaining the use of the native language within the group's everyday cultural practices.

25 See, for example, the Indios Online web portal (www.indiosonline.net), set up in 2004 as an ethnojournalism project to encourage indigenous communities to report on abusive incidents, as well as document their cultural practices and provide material to challenge mainstream preconceptions about indigenous people (Pitman 2018).

26 The international pressure group Survival International describes the racism against indigenous peoples in Brazil as "endemic" (Survival International n/d).

27 Given its impressive box-office returns, it is worth mentioning the adventure film series aimed at children, *Tainá: uma aventura na Amazônia* (*Tainá: An Amazon Adventure*, Tânia Lamarca and Sérgio Bloch, 2000; *Tainá II: a aventura continua* (*Tainá II: New Amazon Adventure*, Mauro Lima, 2004) and *Tainá III: a origem* (*Tainá III: The Origin*, Rosane Svartman, 2011). Like the US hit feature animation films *Rio* and *Rio II*, directed by Brazilian Carlos Saldanha, the focus of these films is the protection of the environment, and only as a somewhat distant corollary, the survival of indigenous peoples. An animation series based on the Tainá character is currently screening on the Nickelodeon channel on Brazilian television.

28 It is worth observing, despite the bleak outlook, that the number of festivals and retrospectives in Brazil screening a wide range of indigenous-produced films, and critical films about the indigenous experience, has increased significantly over the course of the twenty-first century. Worthy of mention is an indigenous retrospective in 2016 at the thirty-second São Paulo Bienal art exhibition, curated by the high-profile indigenous leader Ailton Krenak.

29 For an interesting analysis of this film, see Margulies 2011.

References

Araújo de Souza, M. F. 2016. *História, cinema e representações sobre indígenas: uma análise de Caramuru, a invenção do Brasil (1995–2005)*. Unpublished Masters Dissertation, State University of Feira de Santana.

Araújo, I. 2017. "Desventuras do digital". *Canto do Ignacio*. 24 April. https://cantodoinacio.wordpress.com/2017/04/24/desventuras-do-digital/.

Conde, M. 2018. *Foundational Films: Early Cinema and Modernity in Brazil*. Oakland: University of California Press.

Couto, J.G. 1995. "*Yndio do Brasil* faz a crítica do racismo". *Folha de São Paulo*. 17 November. www1.folha.uol.com.br/fsp/1995/11/17/ilustrada/27.html.

Duchiade, A. 2018. "Correntes da dúvida: novo filme de Joel Pizzini conjuga ficção e documentário". *Jornal do Brasil*. 23 July. www.jb.com.br/index.php?id=/acervo/materia.php&cd_matia=932464&dinamico=1&preview=1.

Economist. 2012. "The Never-Ending War: Paraguay's Awful History". *Economist*. 22 December. www.economist.com/christmas-specials/2012/12/22/the-never-ending- war.

Fernandes, F. 2018. "Animações retratam história e cultura de diferentes povos indígenas". *Portal Multirio*. 16 April. www.multirio.rj.gov.br/index.php/leia/reportagens-artigos/reportagens/13766-anima%C3%A7%C3%B5es-retratam-hist%C3%B3ria-e-cultura-de-diferentes-povos-ind%C3%ADgenas.

Furtado, G. P. 2013. "The Borders of Sense: Revisiting *Iracema, uma Transa Amazônica* 1974". *Journal of Latin American Cultural Studies* 22: 4, pp. 399–415.

Gleghorn, C. 2017. "Indigenous Filmmaking in Latin America". In Delgado, M. M., Hart, S. M. and Johnson, R. (eds) *A Companion to Latin American Cinema*. Chichester: Wiley Blackwell, pp. 167–186.

Gordon, R. A. 2005. "Recreating Caminha: The Earnest Adaptation of Brazil's Letter of Discovery in Humberto Mauro's "Descobrimento do Brasil" (1937)". *MLN* 120: 2, pp. 408–436.

Heise, Tatiana Signorelli. 2012. *Remaking Brazil: Contested National Identities in Contemporary Brazilian Cinema*. University of Wales Press.

Henley, P. and Flores, C. Y. 2009. "Interview: Reflections of an Ethnographic Filmmaker-Maker: An Interview with Paul Henley, Director of the Granada Centre for Visual Anthropology, University of Manchester". *American Anthropologist* 111: 1, pp. 93–99.

Margulies, I. 2011. "Reenactment and A-filiation in Andrea Tonacci's *Serra da Desordem*". *Cinephile* 7: 2, pp. 5–14.

Martin-Jones, D. 2018. *Cinema Against Doublethink*. London and New York: Routledge.

Martins, L. 2013. *Photography and Documentary Film in the Making of Modern Brazil*. Manchester: MUP.

Merten, L. C. 2017. "Em 'Martírio', Vincent Carelli faz relato da luta dos guaranis-caiovás pela retomada de suas terras". *O estado de São Paulo*. *13 April*. https://cultura.estadao.com.br/noticias/cinema,em-martirio-vincent-carelli-faz-relato-da-luta-dos-guaranis-caiovas-pela-retomada-de-suas-terras,70001736797.

Nagib, L. 2007. *Brazil on Screen: Cinema Novo, New Cinema, Utopia*. London and New York: IB Tauris.

Pitman, T. 2018. "Warriors and Weavers: The Poetics and Politics of Indigenous Appropriations of New Media Technologies in Latin America". *Modern Languages Open*, 1, pp. 1–31.

Sommer, D. 1991. *Foundational Fictions: The National Romances of Latin America*. Berkley: University of California Press.

Stam, R. 2003. "Cabral and the Indians: Filmic Representation of Brazil's 55 Years". In Nagib, L. (ed) *The New Brazilian Cinema* London and New York: IB Tauris, pp. 205–228.

Stam, R., Porton, R. and Goldsmith, L. 2015. *Keywords in Subversive Film/Media Aesthetics*. Chichester: Wiley-Blackwell.

Survival International. n/d. Survival International Website. www.survivalinternational.org/tribes/brazilian.

Vidal, J. 2016. "Brazil's Guarani Indians killing themselves over loss of ancestral land". *Guardian*. 18 May. www.theguardian.com/environment/2016/may/18/brazils-guarani-indians-killing-themselves-over-loss-of-ancestral-land.

Weissberg, J. 2018. "Berlin Film Review: Ex-Shaman". *Variety*. 14 March. https://variety.com/2018/film/reviews/ex-shaman-review-1202724925/.

Woods, L. E. J. 2017. "Brazilian Tribal Leader Tours Europe to Plead for Help to Stop Killings and land Grabs". *Guardian*. 8 June. www.theguardian.com/environment/2017/jun/08/brazilian-tribal-leader-tours-europe-to-plead-for-help-to-stop-killings-and-land-grabs.

PART II

7

CINEMA AND PUBLIC SECURITY

The *Elite Squad* phenomenon (2007–2010)

Brazil's public security dilemma

Safety and security for citizens to go about their daily lives is one of the greatest challenges facing Brazil in the post-dictatorship period, and second only to economic motives for both voting decisions and for fuelling emigration. The meagre resources made available at state and municipal level for public security in Brazil are channelled much less into protecting vulnerable groups such as children, women, the LGBTQ community and those living in deprived areas, and more on combatting armed gangs who are involved in drug trafficking. So much so that, despite referencing homicide, feminicide, violence against women and the security of the nation's borders in its national public security policy,[1] public security in Brazil to all intents and purposes means waging an "internal war" against organised and heavily armed gangs who deal in drugs. The battlefield on which this war is waged is more often than not the favelas and poor neighbourhoods of Brazil's large cities, to the point that for many, especially those living outside of these poor neighbourhoods, the enemy within is synonymous with both the favela and the *favelado* (the favela resident). The language and images disseminated to the greater public are of civil war, and as we will explore in this chapter, along with TV and increasingly social media, films have played a key role in shaping the public's perception of this internal war in the twenty-first century. No two films have had more of an impact on the public's understanding of and relationship to public security than José Padilha's box-office smash hits *Tropa de elite* (*Elite Squad*, 2007) and *Tropa de elite: O inimigo agora é outro* (*Elite Squad: The Enemy Within*, 2010)

The pay and conditions of Brazil's state-level administered *Polícia Militar* and *Polícia Civil* are notoriously poor: police officers are more likely to be killed in the line of duty in Brazil than in any other country, and like many low-level state employees, their wages rarely keep up with inflation and they are frequently paid late. Such conditions led to a strike by police officers in Vitória, capital of the state of Espírito Santo in February 2017 which lasted for three weeks and resulted in 215 deaths (Dalvi, 2017). What began as a protest by eight wives of military policemen soon escalated into a state of siege, with many schools and businesses shutting down and citizens locking themselves in their homes. The looting, muggings and reports of murders that ensued were broadcast throughout Brazil and reinforced widely held views, bolstered by the media which seems intent on whipping up fear and distrust, regarding the ineffectuality of the State in combatting crime and violence, and the need for ordinary, upstanding citizens (*pessoas de bem*) to be armed in order to protect themselves and their property.

The dreadful conditions in which Brazil's civil and military police work have left many of them both susceptible to bribery and corruption and made them likely to extort money from members of the public and even join militias that run protection rackets in favelas and poor suburbs. This, coupled with their notorious heavy-handedness in dealing with favela residents, their seeming immunity from prosecution, the extremely low rates of crime-solving[2] and the country's painfully slow judicial system, means that citizens have traditionally held the police in contempt, and many crimes go unreported as a result.

As the police strike in Vitória demonstrated, Brazil's public security woes are not restricted to the megacities of São Paulo and Rio de Janeiro, despite the much higher profile these cities enjoy in the national and international media. Brazil holds the ignominious record for having the largest number (17) in the list of the world's 50 most dangerous cities, with Natal, Fortaleza and Belém, all in the northeast, making the top ten. Porto Alegre, capital of Brazil's southern-most state Rio Grande do Sul, is the only city outside of the north and northeast to make the list. Brazil's traditionally high number of homicides has increased exponentially, from 48,000 in 2005 to 63,888 in 2017. But it is the northern states such as Acre that are currently experiencing the highest increase in murder rates, partly as a result of organised crime gangs such as the PCC (Primeiro Comando da Capital) and CV (Comando Vermelho) shifting their areas of operation northwards and clashing with local crime gangs. Violent deaths in the state of São Paulo are currently at a record low, with both the security forces and organised crime gangs claiming responsibility for this drop in numbers.[3] While homicides have also declined dramatically in the state of Rio de Janeiro over the last 30 years, with an all-time low registered in 2012, a recent pique (2017: the highest in eight years), along with dramatic increases in carjacking, kidnappings and petty theft, resulted in the federal army occupying the state of Rio de Janeiro in 2018, ostensibly in an attempt to regain order.[4]

Brazil's prison service is also notorious: prisons are overcrowded and the conditions regularly attract the attention of both local and international human rights groups. Inmate numbers have more than doubled since 2000. In June 2016 40% of people in Brazilian prisons were there awaiting trial (Min. Justiça, 2016). Poorly paid prison guards are as corruptible as police officers, enabling incarcerated drug lords to continue to direct their business from inside. Gang culture is widespread and this, together with the subhuman conditions in which ordinary inmates live often provoke rebellions and inter-gang warfare, such as those in prisons in the north and northeast of Brazil in January 2017 in which 130 inmates were killed.

Politicians and political groups who have no interest in investing in welfare and educational programmes in poor communities and prisons, given that results can take more than the four years of a political mandate to bear fruit, focus entirely on combatting the "enemy within": those involved in the production, movement and sale of drugs. The negative impact of the police's heavy-handed manoeuvres (death of innocents from stray bullets or cases of mistaken identity; summary justice applied to low-level criminals and coercion of potential informants, who are almost exclusively young black men) are dismissed by some as collateral damage, and protested by others as human rights abuses.

Given Brazil's history of quite extreme cases of human rights abuses, even in times of democracy, such as the 1992 Carandiru prison revolt in São Paulo, in which 111 inmates were killed by police,[5] the Candelária massacre of 1993 in which off-duty police officers shot dead eight homeless people, including six teenagers, sleeping rough outside a cathedral in downtown Rio, and the 1993 Vigário Geral massacre, in which a "death squad" (hooded off-duty policemen) opened fire indiscriminately in a favela in Rio de Janeiro and killed 21 people, a large number of Brazilian and international NGOs emerged in the late twentieth and twenty-first centuries whose focus is the impact of security policies on the lives of ordinary citizens living in some of Brazil's most deprived urban areas. Brazil is the country where citizens are most likely to die at the hands of the police (Amâncio, 2017). At the same time many working in the security forces, and a rapidly growing proportion of the public, see human rights as impacting negatively on the effectiveness of public security policies. Human rights activists, like many other activists in Brazil and elsewhere, have suffered in particular from a perhaps deliberately cultivated lack of awareness on the part of the greater public of what their role entails and who they are seeking to protect, and increasingly they are victims of fake and distorted news. An illustration of this lack of awareness is the well-worn phrase "Direitos Humanos para Humanos Direitos" (literally Human Rights for Upstanding Humans), which implies that Human Rights activism serves exclusively to protect the undeserving (meaning those who have committed crimes). In a recent national poll, over half the respondents agreed with another well-worn phrase, and one closely associated with Jair Bolsonaro before and during his presidential campaign: "bandido bom é bandido morto" (a good criminal is a dead criminal) (Jardim, 2018).

Those who defend human rights that intersect in any way with combatting this "enemy within" are at serious risk of suffering violence and even death. Two recent examples of this are Patricia Acioli, a Rio judge shot dead in 2014 after convicting police officers for their role in organised crime, and the assassination in 2018 of Rio assembly member Marielle Franco, known for her work supporting victims of police abuse. Franco was shot dead, together with her driver, causing a national and international outcry, yet by year's end their murders were still unsolved. Franco is believed to have been investigating organised crime at the time of her assassination.

The enemy within on screen

In the broader context of audio-visual culture in Brazil in the post-dictatorship period (TV, films and material on social media), representations of the underworld of drugs and violence make up one of the four key themes that Brazilians can be guaranteed to tune into in their millions.[6] In the days before social media, it was sensationalist newspapers such as *O dia* in Rio de Janeiro and popular investigative reporting on TV that set the tone of representations of urban security issues, and the latter, witnessed in TV shows such as *Cidade alerta* (TV Record) and *Brasil urgente* (TV Bandeirantes), continue to be very popular. These shows are often criticised for their insensitive treatment of, for example, prisoners before they go to trial, and for their propensity to shock regarding what they are prepared to show on screen: mutilated corpses, graphic footage of murders, and so on. In cinematic terms, grizzly "true crime" films have always been popular: they were a staple in the early years of Brazilian cinema, and even during the censorship-heavy 1960s, 70s and up to the mid-80s, when films tended to avoid being openly critical of the security forces, a number of box-office hits graphically depicted true-crime tales of violence and deviance, focusing on and to an extent glorifying the perpetrators of crimes. *O bandido da luz vermelha* (*Red Light Bandit*, Rogério Sganzerla, 1968), *Lúcio Flávio, o passageiro da agonia* (*Lúcio Flávio*, Hector Babenco, 1976) and *O homem da capa preta* (*The Man in the Black Cape*, Sérgio Rezende, 1986) drew large numbers to cinemas and were based on tales of real-life criminals João Acácio Pereira da Costa and Lúcio Flávio, and the violent, gun-toting politician Tenório Cavalcanti respectively. What they have in common with the *Tropa de elite* films is a certain glorification of hyper-masculine (white) characters operating outside the law.

The late twentieth and early twenty-first-century representational shift in location of urban violence to criminal and criminalised spaces, for example prisons and favelas, is ably illustrated by three films. First, João Moreira Salles and Kátia Lund's documentary *Notícias de uma guerra particular* (*News of a Private War*, 1999), the first to interview members of BOPE, the special operations police unit in Rio that is the focus of the *Tropa de elite* films. Then two hugely successful fictional films from 2002–2003: the favela-set *Cidade de Deus* (*City of God*, Fernando Meirelles and Kátia Lund, 2002) and Hector Babenco's fictionalised account of the aforementioned Carandiru prison massacre (*Carandiru*). The extent to which the international hit *Cidade de Deus* has influenced the representation not only of violence but of Brazilian society more broadly, can be seen in the countless references to the film made by academics, foreign correspondents in their reports on Brazil, and in the number of documentaries, many containing more graphic violence than even the 18-certificate feature films referred to above, made by curious foreign film directors. Released the same year as *Tropa de elite*, the critically acclaimed *Manda bala* (*Send a Bullet*, Jason Kohn, 2007), a US-Brazil co-production, sews together a number of different storylines that deal with violence, personal security in urban spaces and political corruption, with focus on hostage victims in São Paulo whose family members have been sent their loved ones' ears as a demand for ransom payments, and the plastic surgeon whose specialisation is reconstructing the victims' ears. The UK feature-length documentary *Dancing With the Devil* (Jon Blair, 2009), co-produced by *Guardian* correspondent Tom Phillips and based on years of investigative journalism, is one of the best examples of the "foreign view" of Brazil's internal war. It distinguishes itself from other films on this broad topic in that it seeks to treat, along with the drug lords and the police, the role of evangelical churches in poor neighbourhoods, and the growing links between these churches and the drug lords.

All of the twenty-first-century films referred to above are characterised by references to, and often by the explicit depiction of, overwhelming and otherwise unimaginable cruelty and complete lack of morality on the part of criminals, and frequently of the police too: they equally display a sense of no easy solution or resolution in sight. These are almost exclusively male cinematic spaces in which barefoot kids carry heavy weaponry and masked drug dealers mutilate and murder at will. When women appear they are usually the playthings of the hyper-masculine characters, sensual dancers at funk balls,[7] and occasionally grieving mothers. In the entertainment-driven fictional worlds, most of which claim a high level of veracity,[8] it is rare that one of the main characters is not tortured, raped and/or gruesomely murdered. Together with the documentaries, they share with the Colombian so-called *pornomiseria* films,[9] a combination of images of and storylines depicting extreme deprivation and depravity.

Genesis of *Tropa de Elite*

The idea for the original *Tropa de Elite* film emerged in part from filmmaker José Padilha's experience of co-directing, with Felipe Lacerda, the remarkable documentary *Ônibus 174* (*Bus 174*, 2002). The film pieces together both the hijacking of a bus in Rio de Janeiro in 2000 and the police's disastrous attempt to negotiate safe passage for the hostages, using real-life footage of the hold-up and interviews with survivors, together with an exploration of what led the young hijacker, Sandro do Nascimento to a life of crime which ended so tragically. Alerted by a passenger that an armed robber was aboard the number 174 bus in the well-off Southern Zone of Rio, the military police intercepted the bus, provoking a hostage situation. The police's failure to cordon off the area resulted in members of the public, and TV crews, having a ring-side view of the hold-up, and realising this, the disturbed hijacker, whom it emerged later had witnessed both his mother being shot dead in front of him, and the Candelária massacre of 1993 when he was a young street kid, began to "perform" to the cameras. One of the hostages claimed that she did not believe Sandro intended to kill anyone. As he left the bus with another female hostage, a BOPE marksman fired a shot and accidentally hit the hostage, provoking Sandro to pull the trigger of his own gun, killing the young woman. These images, as well as the resulting images of Sandro being bundled into the back of a police van and beaten up, were beamed live across Brazil. Sandro died of asphyxiation in the back of the police van: no police officer was convicted over his death.[10]

FIGURE 7.1 Sandro Nascimento performs to the cameras in a still from *Ônibus 174*

(*Bus 174*, José Padilha and Felipe Lacerda, 2002)

In their meticulously researched film, Padilha and Lacerda interviewed everyone apart from the BOPE marksman because, according to Padilha, they wanted to make a film that "institutionalised the error" (Bellos, 2004). The film, then, provides a sympathetic portrayal of the criminal Sandro, and at first sight it appears highly critical of the police, and BOPE in particular. On further scrutiny, however, there are indications in the film that the view of the filmmakers is that BOPE is unable to fulfil its potential, as a result of constraints imposed upon it by politicians and the interests they represent. This idea is pursued in detail in *Elite Squad: The Enemy Within*.

In his research Padilha contacted Rodrigo Pimentel, a former captain of the BOPE and one who had featured in Moreira Salles's *Notícias de uma guerra particular*. With the release of Pimentel's controversial co-authored book *Elite da tropa* (2006) on the BOPE, Padilha had originally planned to use it as the basis for a documentary portraying the internal war from the perspective of the police.[11] Upon realising the animosity felt towards filmmakers by the police and BOPE, it was clear that Padilha would have to tell the story in the fictional mode. Thus, with the assistance of *City of God* scriptwriter Bráulio Mantovani, and Rodrigo Pimentel himself, Padilha set about transforming the book into a big-budget, action-packed feature film.

Briefly, the first *Tropa de Elite* film (herewith *Tropa I*) is set in 1997 shortly before a papal visit to Rio. In order to make the pope's visit safe, BOPE under Captain Roberto Nascimento (Wagner Moura) is charged with clearing drug dealers out of a favela that surrounds the Archbishop of Rio's official residence. While carrying out this duty, Nascimento, who desperately wants out of the BOPE to spend time with his new family, tasks himself with choosing a successor among two talented new recruits: friends Matias (André Ramiro) and Neto (Caio Junqueira). By the end of the film, the favela is cleared, Neto has been killed in the favela by drug dealers and Matias, hardened by the loss of his good friend and what he has witnessed as both a trainee BOPE agent and as a put-upon law student, has demonstrated himself to be ruthless enough to take on Nascimento's mantle.

In *Tropa de elite: o inimigo agora é outro* (*Elite Squad: The Enemy Within*), herewith *Tropa II*, Nascimento is now a Lieutenant Colonel in BOPE and Matias is a Captain. After a prison rebellion goes wrong and Matias shoots dead a prisoner mid-negotiation, public opinion, unconcerned by the potential human rights violation of BOPE's shoot-to-kill tactics, encourages the state governor to promote Nascimento to Under-secretary of Intelligence within the Public Security Division of Rio's city council, while Matias is made an example of and demoted to a desk job in the Military Police. Nascimento is now divorced and his wife Rosane (Maria Ribeiro) is living with a human rights advocate and local politician Diogo Fraga (Irandhir Santos). While the two men clash frequently in the film, Nascimento, working on a tip-off from Fraga via his son Rafael (Pedro Van Held), secures vital evidence proving that militias, formed by "moonlighting" police officers, with the blessing of corrupt politicians, are behind organised crime in many of Rio's favelas. Fraga forces a public enquiry, at which Nascimento gives evidence and helps to put a number of politicians and police officers behind bars. Rafael is mistakenly shot by disgruntled police officers instead of Fraga, and Nascimento survives an attempt on his own life when his fellow BOPE agents come to his rescue. The film ends with Rafael in hospital, emerging from his coma.

The personal selection process depicted in the first film forms a very effective and engaging way of structuring the story, as we gain insights into Nascimento's world-view and motivations, and we get to observe two different types of officer, how the BOPE special forces recruitment process works and how they handle the job at hand: clearing a favela of criminal factions in order to ensure the security of the Pope. Nascimento's voiceover, directed at the film viewer, is maintained throughout both films. It forms a kind of unfiltered confessional designed to inform spectators of all the aspects of both his job and the world in which he operates that make him angry. He is less concerned with drug dealing than with the presence of weapons in favelas. He has no time for NGOs and rich university students who like to help poor kids. And, at least in *Tropa I*, he despises recreational drug users: he holds them responsible for the escalating drug-related violence in the city. He asks: "How many children do we have to lose to drug trafficking in order for a rich kid to smoke some dope?"

But interestingly, Nascimento particularly loathes corrupt cops, of which Rio's 30,000-strong military police force seems to be almost entirely made up in both films. Voiceover and image combine in *Tropa I* to offer a portrait of the everyday moral and legal crimes committed by police officers that have nothing to do with public security: the physical abuse and financial exploitation of vulnerable people and small business owners in favelas, lack of camaraderie that results in the abuse and exploitation even of fellow police officers, and lack of productivity, inertia, indifference and sense of powerlessness to do anything about their corrupt and unproductive profession. The extent to which the officers are underpaid, under-resourced and caught up in vast webs of deceit and corruption that stretch to the highest echelons of public security management is also made clear. In a key sequence in *Tropa I*, we are informed by Nascimento that crime goes unpunished because everything is part of a system, and "the system functions merely to resolve the problems of the system". This idea is explored further in the film sequel, and later in Padilha's Netflix series *O mecanismo* (*The Mechanism*, 2018).

Nascimento might hold the standard Military Police in Rio in contempt, but he draws a clear distinction between them and his own special operations unit, the 100 members of BOPE. In *Tropa I* we are informed that BOPE is called in to handle situations that ordinary police officers cannot deal with. We see their physically and emotionally brutal recruitment and training regime. Their tactical skills, physical strength, distinctive black uniforms and the skull, dagger and handguns emblazoned on their logo,[12] shown frequently in close-up, set them apart from the world of inertia and corruption as witnessed in the images of the military police. The sense of hyper-masculinity is reinforced by fast editing and loud rap music that accompanies their manoeuvers.[13]

Based on a true story: realism in *Tropa de Elite I* and *II*

One of the strategies used by Padilha in the *Tropa de elite* films to claim authenticity and therefore a level of authority to voice an opinion on controversial issues is building a fictional narrative around a series of real-life events relating to public security. The security event around which the action of *Tropa I* is structured is Pope John Paul II's visit to Rio de Janeiro in 1997, during which time, against the advice of security experts, he stayed in the Archbishop's residence situated alongside Turano, then one of the most violent favelas in the city. Over the course of four months, BOPE killed 30 people and arrested 30 more as part of this so-called Operation Holiness. The operation is one of those featured in "Diários de Guerra" (War Diaries), the first part of the book *Elite da tropa*, upon which *Tropa I* is based.

The process of temporarily tightening security *pra inglês ver,*[14] as explored in *Tropa I*, would be familiar to residents of Rio de Janeiro. It is witnessed with every papal visit (1980; 1991; 1997; 2007 (São Paulo); 2013; 2016). It was seen at the time of the first post-dictatorship mega-event: the Earth Summit in 1992, in which the army occupied streets and favelas near the centre and tourist attractions and street kids were rounded up and temporarily relocated to care homes. Violence, and the street kids, soon returned. And many observers believe that the failed pacification process in Rio's favelas, dating from 2008 onwards, was always intended to be only a temporary measure in order to give a semblance of security in key areas on the run-up to and during the World Cup and Olympics. Padilha and his team reportedly spent two years researching the BOPE, interviewing officers, trainers and psychologists,

and amassing 1,700 pages of documents. The actors who play BOPE agents underwent training with security experts in how to both hold and handle weapons. A
number of military police officers were drafted in to play extras in scenes depicting
shoot-outs. And the authenticity of the language used among both the police and
criminals was ensured by the ex-BOPE captain Rodrigo Pimentel's indispensible
contributions to the script. Many of the aphorisms ascribed to Nascimento in the
films were taken from the pages of Pimentel's *Elite da tropa*,[15] along with the torture
and assassination methods used by both the police and drug dealers, such as the
microondas (literally microwave, but sometimes referred to as necklacing in English),
where victims are placed inside tyres and burnt, and attempted asphyxiation with a
plastic bag to elicit information.[16]

Thus, despite its flashy uniforms, logo, slogans, chants and almost robotic way of
moving when on the offensive which all appear to be modelled on a video-game
rather than real life, the BOPE as featured in the *Tropa* films is a relatively faithful
recreation of the real-life Rio special operations unit. Even the seemingly panto-
mimic excesses of BOPE's incursions into favelas as depicted in the films are not
perhaps as removed from reality as one might at first suspect. As discussed by Erika
Robb Larkins in her fascinating account of BOPE actions based on field work in
Rio's El Dorado favela, BOPE raids are "oddly non-confrontational" (2013: 554), in
what she describes as "choreographed performances of state and trafficker power"
(555). Larkins argues that BOPE uses spectacle to police the hyper-real favela
through three interrelated tactics: a discourse celebrating BOPE's efficiency, modernity, and "professional violence"; an institutional identity centred on "an occult
and magical triumph over death itself"; and actions in the favela that demonstrate
these qualities through "performative violence" (565).

> What emerges is a self-perpetuating feedback loop. BOPE requires the traffic,
> and the chaos it represents, to continue performances of power on the favela
> stage. The state can then be pictured coming into being, not as weak or inept,
> but as modern and efficient, performing its legitimacy for audiences beyond
> the favela – whose allegiances pay taxes and win elections.
>
> *(573)*

> Consequently, traffickers, police, and the very favela itself become hyper-real:
> they take on constructed, spectacular qualities that do not reflect reality in
> the favela.
>
> *(556)*

A notable exception in terms of realistic representation is the omission of the
caveirões or heavily armoured vehicles with which BOPE is closely associated. The
films thus give an impression of much greater use of stealth missions (and therefore bravery of the BOPE officers) than is the case in reality. Having the main
BOPE officers (Nascimento, Matias and Neto, for example) on foot in the favelas
enabled photographer Lula Carvalho to get in tight to his subjects, sacrificing

FIGURE 7.2 Getting in tight around subjects. A still from *Tropa de elite*

(*Elite Squad*, José Padilha, 2007)

light and rehearsed placement of actors for the sake of a sense of greater realism (Kleinpaul, 2007).

Tropa II, which takes some inspiration from the second part of Pimentel's *Elite da tropa*, inasmuch as it portrays BOPE as an unsuspecting pawn in a profoundly corrupt political game, retains the "ripped-from-the-headlines sensibility" (Koehler, 2011) of *Tropa I*: it is filled with references to real-life security related events. The most significant of these is the 2008 CPI das Milícias, or Public Inquiry investigating Rio's militias led by Marcelo Freixo, then a member of Rio's State legislature. Scriptwriter Bráulio Mantovani attended all the public inquiry sessions. Significantly, the character Diogo Fraga in *Tropa II* is based closely on Freixo. Like Freixo, Fraga is a history professor as well as human rights advocate and politician in *Tropa II* and in an early scene in which he explains prison history to a classroom full of students, Freixo makes a cameo appearance in the front row of the class.

According to Marcelo Freixo (in Carvalho, 2014), the call for a public inquiry into police involvement in organised crime had been shelved for 18 months, and the go-ahead was only granted as a result of the horrific kidnap and torture to which a female investigative journalist and male photographer from the *O dia* newspaper were subjected by *milicianos* in 2008. This catalyst for the inquiry is recreated in *Tropa II*, with a couple of journalists similarly taking up residence in a militia-run favela and being found out. However, the brutal torture of the *O dia* journalists appears to be conflated in the film with the notorious true-life 2002 torture and murder of *Globo* journalist Tim Lopes, the details of which are widely known in Brazil and almost unimaginably horrific. The journalists in *Tropa II* do

FIGURE 7.3 Marcelo Freixo's cameo. A still from *Tropa de Elite II*
(*Elite Squad II*, José Padilha, 2011)

not survive the torture ordeal. While viewers are spared images of their torture, rape and murder, we are shown the charred remains of their severed heads, as a *miliciano* removes their teeth in order to hide their identity while nonchalantly quoting Shakespeare ("Alas poor Yorick").

Like the *O dia* journalists, their fictional equivalents are tortured by police officers involved in organised crime. Two local politicians who were allegedly directly involved in the barbaric acts of torture and identified by one of the *O dia* journalists were never prosecuted. Collusion by politicians in the fictional torture and murder of the journalists in *Tropa II* is implied by the fact that the stronghold they discover in the favela contains both rifles stolen from a police station, and banners promoting candidates in the upcoming elections. The character Fortunato (André Mattos) in *Tropa II*, an overblown sensationalist presenter of true crime shows on TV and (corrupt) political hopeful, is modelled on local politician Wagner Monte, who has presented numerous crime shows. Fortunato in *Tropa II* serves to illustrate the unhelpful involvement of the sensationalist media in the fight against organised crime in Rio.[17]

Tropa II opens in spectacular fashion with a siege and hostage situation at Bangu I, Brazil's first maximum security prison, in a clear reference to the 2002 rebellion led by infamous organised crime boss Fernandinho Beira-Mar. In the film version drug lord Beirada, played by Brazilian pop singer Seu Jorge, demands that Fraga is brought in to assist with a resolution to the siege, provoking the disdain of Nascimento. When Marcelo Freixo worked for a human-rights NGO in prisons, he was regularly called upon to assist with rebellions and hostage situations. A notable difference, however, is that Freixo's services were called for by BOPE, and not the prisoners, and in the dozens of situations he was called upon to assist with, no prisoners or guards were ever shot (Escorel 2010).

Fascist, hero or both? The reception of Nascimento and the *Tropa de Elite* films

As discussed in Chapter 1 *Tropa I* highlights the extent to which film piracy is both widespread and lucrative in Brazil: a version of the film was stolen while still in post-production and quickly copied and sold via *camelôs* or street vendors. Bootleg versions of *Tropa I* were reportedly viewed by 11 million Brazilians (Heise, 2012: 122) with 2.5 million paying to view in film theatres. *Tropa II*, with its 11 million paying spectators,[18] held the record of the most successful Brazilian film at the box-office, until it was overtaken by the Universal Church of the Kingdom of God's two feature films discussed in Chapter 2.

Tropa I generated, and continues to generate, a very large volume of reviews, features and opinion pieces in online and traditional news media, making it the most talked about national film of the twenty-first century to date. While *Tropa II* garnered more favourable reviews than its predecessor, and while director Padilha joined forces in high-profile Q and As with Marcelo Freixo, the human rights advocate and politician on whom the character Diogo Fraga was based, the film failed to stimulate the same level of debate as *Tropa I*. From this one might extrapolate that it is the *Tropa I* incarnation of both BOPE and Nascimento, that is fixed in the critical and public imaginary. And it is that incarnation that has proved problematic, given the numerous claims that the representation of both BOPE and Nascimento in the film constitutes a glorification of fascism.

Both Padilha and actor Wagner Moura, both of whom were very active in promoting and debating *Tropa I*, maintained that the character Nascimento was to be read critically. Padilha asserted that the film offered a clear critique of violence and torture and that Nascimento was an "explicitly bad" character (*Roda Viva*, 2007). And that is certainly how the film was read by the six-member jury at the Berlin Film Festival, who voted unanimously to award the film the coveted Golden Bear in 2008. The fact that the jury Chair was none other than Costa-Gavras, a film-maker known for taking to task right-wing regimes in his films[19] and the fact that Padilha's previous film (*Bus 174*) had been Oscar-nominated and had offered a sympathetic portrait of hijacker Sandro do Nascimento that went against the grain of conservative reaction in the face of the real-life crime at home, appeared to point unequivocally to this reading. A number of reviewers and academics concurred. Sheila Johnston in *The Telegraph*, for example, refers to Nascimento as a "highly unreliable narrator" and cites the fact that BOPE tried to halt the release of the film as evidence of its critical stance (2008). Academic Tatiana Heise argues that "[b]y aligning us with Nascimento, the film is not necessarily asking us to 'identify' with him and interpret all his actions as morally acceptable […] by stressing his brutality and loss of moral reference, the film makes it difficult for the spectator to form an allegiance with the character" (2012: 124). Thus one way of engaging constructively with *Tropa I*, according to critics and academics such as Johnson and Heise, is to recognise the fascist tendencies of Nascimento, and understand the message of the film to be a critique of the character and his world-view.

Another form of defence against accusations of fascism in *Tropa I* is established by pointing to the multi-layered portrayal of Captain Nascimento. In the film he is suffering from stress: he has panic attacks, sweats profusely, self-medicates and barks orders at his pregnant wife, thus indicating strained marital relations. He confesses to beginning to feel remorse for his actions, which he interprets as a sign of weakness and a severe limitation on his ability to do the job. At one point he even becomes paralysed with fear, although notably this takes place when he is rock-climbing on a day off, rather than in the line of duty. The exhilarating police raid on a favela that opens the film is seemingly undermined when Nascimento remarks in voiceover: "I was starting to get tired of it all".[20]

Most film critics working in Brazilian broadsheets were unconvinced by either of these readings of *Tropa I*, however.[21] And the lack of impact of both *Tropa* films at the box-office in the US and the UK is likely to be related to the mostly scathing reviews *Tropa I* received there.[22] *Variety* correspondent Jay Weissberg's views on *Tropa I* were widely shared at the time and Weissberg himself commented further on the film in a number of online discussion boards. He dismissed it as a "one-note celebration of violence-for-good that plays like a recruitment film for fascist thugs" (2008). He criticised the film's "inescapable right-wing p.o.v." and stated that "charges of fascism by pic's critics aren't merely knee-jerk liberal reactions, but an unimpeachable statement of fact" (2008). Peter Bradshaw, a fan of *Cidade de Deus*, was every bit as scathing in his one-star review for the *Guardian*:

> Here is the biggest, fattest, dampest squib of the week: perhaps the most disappointing film ever to have won the Golden Bear at the Berlin film festival [...]There's an awful lot of very clichéd Brazilian slum–porn, gun–porn and poverty-porn, all knocked off from the influential favela masterpiece *City of God*. The movie's evasive cynicism, morphing gradually and insidiously into lipsmacking adoration of the macho lawmen in their SS-style black uniforms, is pathetic. The worst moment comes when the anti-hero Captain Nascimento (Wagner Moura) jeers at a feeble cop applying to join their ranks: "You belong with the whores, you belong with the pimps, you belong with the abortion clinics." Um, excuse me? Abortion clinics? Getting a reactionary sermon from a pumped-up man in uniform is the last thing we need.
>
> *(2008)*

The difficulty with accepting the argument put forward by, among others, left-wing actor Wagner Moura, for example, who tirelessly debated the film in Q and As upon its release, or by film critic Pablo Villaça, that it is critical of the police and public security policy,[23] is that it does not give due recognition to the distinction drawn in the film between the Military Police and the BOPE. "No BOPE, não entra polícia corrupta" (There are no corrupt police officers in BOPE), Nascimento informs us, and this vision of BOPE is sustained throughout both *Tropa* films. Nascimento is a troubled, politically incorrect but ultimately trustworthy character whose views are given precedence through his voiceover.[24] It is therefore with Nascimento, and the battalion he leads, that a public, tired of corruption and unlikely to sympathise with a positive portrayal of the Military Police force with such a poor reputation, can comfortably side.[25] One of the corrupt officers of the Polícia Militar in *Tropa I*, Russo (Sandro Rocha), reappears in *Tropa II* as a militia boss. He convinces the recently demoted Matias to join forces with him, and with one telephone call, Matias is back in BOPE. But the film refuses to countenance the possibility of BOPE containing a single corrupt officer: we later discover that Matias is fully aware of Russo and his outfit, and he works to his own agenda in recovering stolen weapons. Matias is subsequently shot in the back of the head by Russo.

Thus the *Tropa* films offer audiences a unique opportunity to take pride in Brazil's much-maligned security forces, not just through one lone character but an entire battalion. Nascimento's reaction to Matias's fatal shot in the prison siege at the beginning of *Tropa II* is typically ambiguous: his subordinate acted out of line and precipitated a media spectacle around the siege, but at the same time, as Nascimento informs us in freeze-frame of the shot being fired from his rifle,[26] Matias did precisely what he was trained to do. The shot could also be considered symbolic of a corrective to the past errors associated with BOPE: both the fatal error of the hijack depicted in *Bus 174*, where the BOPE marksman missed his target, and the numerous prison sieges gone wrong that gave rise to the creation of BOPE in the first place the late 1970s.

Tropa II, with its brilliantly executed set pieces (the prison siege was singled out for extended comment in the Making Of in the DVD extras, for example), and with its greater focus on political corruption and less emphasis on Nascimento as action hero, was a much more favourably reviewed film. But the old Nascimento of 14 years previously had not entirely disappeared. In *Tropa II* Nascimento launches a two-pronged attack on those responsible for the growth of militias in Rio. First, in a striking plot and character development, he combines forces with the human rights advocate Fraga and his testimony during the Public Inquiry, we are informed, results in numerous arrests and imprisonments. Not all of the guilty are convicted, however, and the film acknowledges that in some instances, politicians continued to get elected and wield power. The second prong of Nascimento's attack is therefore to wreak a vigilante-style vengeance on those who escaped punishment through legal means. Scenes of Nascimento punching and kicking his adversaries provided what is said to have been a particularly cathartic moment for spectators, with film theatre audiences cheering on the BOPE agent.[27] At the premiere of *Tropa II* at the Paulínia film festival, Nascimento's brutal physical assault of a politician was given a standing ovation.[28] It is therefore the continuation of this vigilante aspect of Nascimento's character that many viewers related most strongly to, rather than his gradual realisation of the futility of the war on drugs, or of the important role of human rights advocates such as Diogo Fraga and what they can contribute to the war on organise crime, or even of Nascimento's mic-dropping public declaration, when giving evidence, that the Military Police should be disbanded. As Sarah McDonald has argued, "[…] the identity of BOPE as "heroic protector", and the violence associated with this role becomes accepted as an intrinsic and necessary part of that identity" (2012: 75).

On the surface *Tropa II* presents an older and wiser Nascimento who is forced to confront many of the prejudices he expressed in *Tropa I*. However, the extent to which this represents an ideological repositioning, with regard to both Nascimento the character and the message of the film, is open to debate. An analysis of the character Diego Fraga offers an illustration of this ambiguity. In *Tropa II*, Nascimento informs viewers in voiceover that at first he refused to listen to Fraga's warnings about the existence of militias, implying that this was as a result of his prejudice against leftists and human rights activists. Importantly, Fraga's honesty, like BOPE's, is never questioned in the film, but what is constantly questioned is the impact that Fraga, and the ideology he represents, has on society more broadly. This concern is demonstrated on a micro level by Nascimento's relationship with his son Rafael, now living with Fraga. Father-son time revolves awkwardly around judo (shouting orders at him at a match, and then sparring with him at a dojo), suggesting that he considers his son's lifestyle (and by implication Fraga) to be a threat to his masculinity. On a macro level is it demonstrated in the portrayal of Fraga in his professional capacity as incorruptible but also ineffectual.

Consider, for example the scene where we are first introduced to Fraga, teaching in a classroom. In the scene the camera encircles Fraga but pauses longer than one might expect behind him, with the focus therefore falling not on the substance of his words (on prison numbers and lack of education) but on his performance (his

FIGURE 7.4 Captain Nascimento gives evidence at the inquiry into militias. A still from *Tropa de Elite II*

(*Elite Squad II*, José Padilha, 2011)

hand gestures in particular) and the environment in which he is performing: a class-room full of static students. While Fraga might well be making a strong case for his views on the need for prison reform, and while his words temporarily stand in for Nascimento's otherwise relentless voiceover as we watch the prison siege unfold, he is in a classroom (the "abstract world"), which reduces his views to theory. The scene is juxtaposed with one of a prison siege (the "real world", where practical decisions have to be made). Here viewers will likely recall a similar classroom scene in *Tropa I*, where BOPE new recruit and part-time law student Matias attends a class on the theories of Michel Foucault and ends up losing his temper with his (middle-class, white, dope-smoking) classmates whom he regards, along with Foucault, as out of touch with reality and too quick to criticise the security forces. Thus Nascimento's voiceover, which dismisses Fraga as an "intelectualzinho de esquerda" (crappy little leftist intellectual) and "Che Guevara", the references to the previous film and its critical take on middle-class university students, and the juxtaposition of scenes of Fraga in the classroom and being held at gunpoint by a notorious drug trafficker in a prison, all serve to undermine his approach to dealing with public security issues, or at best the lack of compatibility between the security forces and the kind of empathetic approaches to dealing with criminals Fraga espouses. Furthermore, the juxtaposition of Fraga's classroom defence of the poor and uneducated in prison with images of a carefully orchestrated and extremely violent prison revolt (i.e. the prisoners demonstrate agency and behave like barbarians) serves to question the validity of his ideological position.

In an analysis of the "message" of the *Tropa* films, questions can also be raised about the extent to which José Padilha himself is a "reliable narrator". And this is despite the fact that in the aftermath of the success of the *Tropa* films, he was regarded as enough of an authority on the subject to be called on by TV Globo to comment and advise on pubic security issues.[29] By way of example of his unreli-ability, in Q and As and interviews after the launch of *Tropa I*, Padilha vigorously advocated the legalisation of drugs in Brazil. "Whoever is buying drugs is funding the *favelas*. If you legalize drugs, you no longer have the problem", he told the *Huffington Post* (Badt 2008). Yet this point of view is refuted in *Tropa II*, which clearly demonstrates, based on the (real-life) facts of the Militia Public Inquiry, that removing drugs and traffickers from favelas can create a vacuum that is quickly filled by militias who run protection rackets and control the provision of illegal internet connections (the so-called *gato-nets*), gas supplies, and so on.[30] Already in 2008, the *Huffington Post*'s envoy to the Berlinale observed, in relation to Padilha's views: "It seemed a very limited perception of the "rules of the game" that make *favelas* and police brutality a reality in today's Brazil" (Badt 2008).[31] Robert Koehler in *Variety* (2011) described Padilha as "a filmmaker who remains hard to get a grip on in terms of ideas, content or style". Consider also Padilha's confused discussion of Game Theory in an introduction to *Tropa I* included in the English-language DVD version.

Padilha, who unusually for a Brazilian filmmaker has no social media presence, does occasionally give interviews with the release of his films and TV series (for example *Robocop* 2014 and *Narcos* 2015). His habit of insisting on talking politics, but limiting his comments to debates over ideology, where his arguments are frequently structured around dictionary definitions of socialism and capitalism, and his rejection of both, have not gone unnoticed by the predominantly left-leaning world of film criticism.[32] It would be naïve to suggest that Padilha's declared rejection of socialism and the Workers Party policies in the twenty-first century have not impacted on the reception of his work by critics. Furthermore, Padilha has struggled to articulate a clear defence against claims of fascism in *Tropa I* and has been equally reductive and literal in his assessment of the criticism.

Concluding remarks

The extent to which the two *Tropa de Elite* films have impacted on Brazilian culture cannot be overestimated. As well as the record-breaking viewing figures and wide ranging discussions they engendered, the film series spawned custom-made Nascimento dolls, BOPE t-shirts, a platinum-selling soundtrack and an endless number of memes on social media. Globo even approached Padilha to make a spin-off TV series, which never materialised due to creative differences. The film arguably strengthened sales of the *Max Payne 3* videogame, in development since 2009 and released 2011. The game is set in São Paulo and pitches special police units against favela gangsters. On its release Rockstar Games recommended that players watch *Tropa I* in order to prepare for playing the game. Some retailers sold the game together with the *Tropa* films.

Within audio-visual production the *Tropa* films have spawned parodies: *Totalmente inocentes* (Totally Innocents [*sic*] 2012); *Copa de elite* (Elite Cup, 2014), as well as the Parafernália YouTube series also called *Tropa de elite*).[33] A number of films have adopted the positive view of the Brazilian police which the *Tropa* films arguably instigated: these include *Polícia Federal: a lei é para todos* (2017) on the Operation Car Wash graft investigation, and *Operaçoes Especiais*, 2015, with its shift in focus to a female police officer as honest hero. And Rodrigo Pimentel has returned to filmmaking: he co-wrote the forthcoming *Intervenção* (Intervention, Caio Cobra), a fictional critique of the pacifying process in Rio's favelas.

Despite two attempts to take Padilha to court over *Tropa I*,[34] BOPE itself became a media phenomenon after the release of the film. Public figures, including celebrities, began to frequent the institution's headquarters.[35] The battalion was inundated with requests for information on how to join, mostly from young men who had seen the film. The BOPE *caveirões* or armoured cars that roamed the streets during the Confederations Cup of 2013 would be mobbed by members of the public keen to have their photograph taken alongside their controversial logo. Rodrigo Pimentel became a TV personality and security commentator for Globo. Ten years on and the fascination with BOPE continues: the latest craze is BOPE-themed parties, with children as young as four partying with balloons and cakes emblazoned with the BOPE logo, music from *Tropa* films, and the possibility of a BOPE-authorised appearance of a real-life officer (*O globo* 2017). While such engagement with *Tropa de Elite* might seem bizarre and offensive to many, it does not compare to the shocking reports of young people (mostly middle-class) uploading to YouTube images, whether fake or real, of the recreation of scenes of torture from *Tropa I* of asphyxiation using a plastic bag over the head of victims (*O globo* 2007).

Recognising the public enthusiasm for Captain Nascimento, images of Wagner Moura in character appeared on the cover of right-wing popular news magazine *Veja* on three separate occasions, as well as gracing the front page of *Epoca* news mazagine and even the left-leaning *Carta Capital*. On its 10 November 2010 cover, *Veja's* headline read "The first Brazilian super-hero. He is incorruptible, implacable with criminals and he beats up immoral police detectives". The by-line provocatively asks "What are the millions of Brazilians who watched and applauded the film telling us? (Saraiva 2013). *Veja* thus erroneously points to a single possible reading of the film: Nascimento as hero, with fans not only turning a blind eye to his methods, but approving of those methods, which according to the slogan of BOPE, are also the undisputed methods of the real-life battalion.[36]

After the release of *Tropa II* there were dissenting voices, however. While they may not have been directly inspired or influenced by the character Diogo Fraga, they were certainly sympathetic to an alternative approach to dealing with public security issues. Marcelo Freixo stood for Mayor of Rio twice and was narrowly defeated on both occasions, a considerable achievement for a left-wing candidate espousing Human Rights and from a small party (PSOL). But by 2016 the shift in public opinion towards the right was clearly manifested in the crashing defeat of university professor Fernando Haddad (PT) in the mayoral elections in São Paulo, and by the success of a bishop of the Universal Church of the Kingdom of God (Marcelo Crivella) in Rio de Janeiro. Despite the militias public inquiry (both in real-life and viewed by millions in *Tropa II*), the appetite to rid Rio of police-led organised crime appears to have abated, with Freixo lamenting the fact that the militias have returned to Rio's favelas in even greater number (Costa, 2018).[37] And in the most recent elections at time of writing (2018), the Rio state governorship has been won by a complete unknown, Wilson Witzel, a one-time Marine running on a ticket of arming the population, support for air strikes over favelas and a shoot-to-kill policy for police against any armed target. We can also, of course, allude here to the victory of Jair Bolsonaro in the 2018 presidential elections, in relation to whom the label fascist has been widely used. Tellingly, in January 2018 on the fortieth anniversary of the formation of BOPE, Bolsonaro, an ex-army Captain, was guest of honour at the battalion's celebrations. He also flaunted electoral laws by visiting the BOPE headquarters during his campaign. The extent to which Bolsonaro's supporters have at best condoned and at worst celebrated the offensive and threatening comments he has made publicly and on social media in relation to *favelados*, blacks, criminals and human rights activists is similar to a certain celebration of the so-called fascist Nascimento in the *Tropa* films.

Notes

1 The February 2018 policy is available at www.justica.gov.br/news/politica-nacional-de-seguranca-publica/minuta_pnasp.pdf

2 Only 5–8% of homicides are solved in Brazil, compared to 90% in the UK. See Brum (2018).

3 For a fascinating account of urban gang warfare in São Paulo, see Willis (2015).

4 Many observers interpreted intervention in Rio's security as having more to do with federal-level political manoeuvring than tackling crime. Some even feared that it was a rehearsal for the return of military dictatorship. See "Intervenção militar é assunto mais comentado no Twitter" (2018).

5 The deaths were perpetrated by ROTA, the "elite squad" of São Paulo's police force, which arguably led directly to the founding of the aforementioned criminal organisation Primeiro Comando da Capital (PCC). See "Facção criminosa foi fundada em 1993" (2006).

6 The three others are music, Globo-influenced soap and comedy productions, and faith-based material.

7 Funk balls, or *bailes funk*, are organised dances, often in favelas, which play Brazilian funk music (a hybrid musical form that emerged in the 1980s taking its inspiration in Miami Bass). Such dances are closely associated, at least by a generally disapproving media, with drug gangs. For more information, see Sneed (2008). *Tropa de Elite* opens with a police raid on such a Funk Ball.

8 As we have observed elsewhere in this book, *Cidade de Deus* is based on Paulo Lins' semi-autobiographical work and deploys a large number of non-professional actors from poor neighbourhoods who also contributed to the script; *Carandiru* (2003) is based on the true story of the prison massacre referred to above as recounted by prison doctor Dráuzio Varela in the book *Estação Carandiru*; *Quase dois irmãos* (*Almost Brothers*, Lúcia Murat, 2004) was co-scripted by Paulo Lins to ensure "authenticity" in scenes depicting gang culture in favelas, and as we will see, *Tropa de elite* I and II are based on the experiences of real-life police officers, captured in the book *Elite da tropa*.

9 *Pornomiseria* is a term used to describe a style of filmmaking that emerged in Colombia in the 1970s and held little back in terms of depicting the extreme conditions of poverty and suffering that many endured. The implicit criticism in the term is that such depictions were commercially motivated and served merely to titillate. A number of films produced in the 1990s, such as the festival favourite *La vendedora de rosas* (*The Rose Seller*, Victor Gaviria, 1998) have also been labelled *pornomiseria*.

10 Sandro's story was later recounted in Bruno Barreto's fictional film *Última parada 174* (*Last Stop 174*, 2008).

11 Padilha was keen to point out in interviews at the time that such a perspective was unique in Brazilian film history.

12 The so-called "faca na caveira" (knife in skull).

13 For a reading of hypermasculinity in the *Tropa* films, see McDonald (2012) and Whitfield (2017).

14 Literally "for the English to see", this is a well-worn expression in Brazil that denotes a token gesture to keep up appearances.

15 For example, "Missão dada é missão comprida" (A mission set is a mission completed).

16 The details contained in Pimentel's *Elite da tropa* of BOPE's actions are considerably more horrific and explicit (such as documenting the torture and killing of children and subsequent blaming of others), meaning that an identification with the Elite Squad is made much more difficult than in the film versions.

17 Despite being ridiculed in *Tropa II*, and despite the insinuation of involvement with militias, Monte's political career continues to progress in real life.

18 Spectators at the premiere of *Tropa II* were searched on entry to the cinema and the film was released only on 35mm.

19 Padilha acknowledges Costa-Gavras's support of *Tropa I* by including a scene in *Tropa II* of a film theatre screening a retrospective of his work.

20 The line is very similar to a view expressed by Pimentel in *Notícias de uma guerra particular*.

21 See, for example, Fraga (2007)

22 The high volume of subtitles, as a result of the continuous voiceover in both films, may well have been a cause of lack of engagement at the box-office: Koehler, 2011.

23 See Villaça's blog post on *Tropa* (n/d).

24 Padilha's Netflix series *O mecanismo* also privileges the point of view of a troubled police officer (in this case, a Federal Police officer) through use of voiceover, in its analysis of the Lava-Jato grafting scandal. The inclusion of Nascimento's voiceover in *Tropa I* was reportedly an afterthought on the part of the production team in the editing stage, whereby the shift in focus was moved away from Matias, originally conceived as a more central character and based loosely on Rodrigo Pimentel. Like Matias in *Tropa II*, Pimentel was imprisoned for 30 days for criticising government security policy while a BOPE officer.

25 See Roberta Gregoli's reception study of *Tropa de Elite* (2011). Shortly after *Tropa I* was released in Brazil, one of the country's biggest stars, TV Globo presenter Luciano Huck, in a letter to the *Folha de S. Paulo* newspaper complaining about crime levels, asked "Where is the Elite Squad? Send for Captain Nascimento! It's about time we had a serious discussion about public security" (2007). Hip-hop artist Marcelo D2's 2008 rap "Desabafo" also references Nascimento, but here the association is with indiscriminate violence, rather than a hero to be summoned in times of need.

26 A similar use of freeze-frame can be seen in the denouement of the opening sequence of *Tropa I*.

27 Audiences also applauded Nascimento's acts of violence, including the torture sequences, in *Tropa I* (Dieleke, 2009).

28 This is deeply ironic, given the sneering derision with which the character Nascimento treats the standing ovation he is given by members of the public in a restaurant after the prison siege in *Tropa II*.

29 For example, Padilha was interviewed on TV Globo in 2010 in the aftermath of the high-profile expulsion of drug dealers from the Vila Cruzeiro favela in Rio.

30 As Rodrigo Pimentel would later state: "I don't want to criticise *Tropa de elite*, but it was very naive of us to place the blame for criminality on university students who buy dope in the favelas": Bazarello 2018.

31 Badt continues: "I also could not quite put my finger on Padilha's specific political vision – if he had one".

32 Padilha's controversial 2018 Netflix series *O mecanismo*, based on the Lava-Jato grafting scandal (Operation Car wash) and screened on the run-up to presidential elections, reinforced the view held by many of the filmmaker as sworn enemy of the Left. The series was criticised for its lack of critical distance from the actions of the legal team behind the investigation, and for attributing to ex-president Lula a notorious phrase (estancar a sangria or stop the bloodletting, a reference to halting the investigation) spoken in fact by another politician from the right-wing MDB party.

33 Tatiana Heise (2012: 182) draws attention to two documentaries on elite police squads that were quickly released in the wake of *Tropa I*'s success: *PQD* (*PQD: Brazilian*

Paratroopers, Guilherme Coelho, 2007) and *Brigada Paraquedista* (*Parachute Troop*, Evaldo Mocarzel, 2007). The films "celebrate Brazilian nationhood with constant references to images, symbols, discourses and chants associated with nationalism" (Heise 2012: 182).

34 Police reportedly viewed a bootleg copy of *Tropa I* and unsuccessfully sued Padilha, demanding that the torture scenes be removed. Once the film was released, they launched a second law suit demanding he identify the 20 BOPE officers who assisted with the training in the film. The suit was quashed by the government after a public outcry.

35 For an interesting discourse analysis of BOPE's own promotional video, see Mayr (2015).

36 "Homem de preto, qual é sua função? Entrar pela favela e deixar corpo no chão" (Man in black, what is your role? To enter the favela and leave bodies on the ground).

37 The Polícia Civil in December 2018 announced that they had uncovered a plot to assassinate Freixo. He famously has an armed guard in Rio on the police's insistence.

References

Amâncio, T. 2017. "Policiais matam e morrem mais no Brasil, mostra balanço de 2016". *Folha de S. Paulo*. 30 October. www1.folha.uol.com.br/cotidiano/2017/10/1931445-policiais-matam-e-morrem-mais-no-brasil-mostra-balanco-de-2016.shtml.

Badt, K. 2008. "From the Berlinale: José Padilha's *Elite Squad*". *Huffington Post*. 28 March. www.huffingtonpost.com/karin-badt/from-the-berlinale-jose-p_b_87486.html.

Bazarello, P. 2018. "Intervenção": Visitamos os bastidores do filme policial brasileiro, do mesmo criador de "Tropa de Elite". *Cinepop*. 19 July. https://cinepop.com.br/intervencao-visitamos-os-bastidores-do-filme-policial-brasileiro-do-mesmo-criador-de-tropa-de-elite-181835.

Bellos, A. 2004 "He Will Kill Us All At Six". *Guardian*. 16 April. www.theguardian.com/film/2004/apr/16/1.

Bradshaw, P. 2008. "Elite Squad". *Guardian*. 8 August. www.theguardian.com/film/2008/aug/08/worldcinema.thriller.

Brum, M. 2018. Brasil não soluciona nem 10% dos seus homicídios". *Gazeta do povo*. 17 September. www.gazetadopovo.com.br/ideias/brasil-nao-soluciona-nem-10-dos-seus-homicidios-d726kw8ykpwh6xm41zakgzoue/.

Carvalho, J. 2014. "Seis anos após CPI, deputado diz que pouco foi feito no combate a milícias". *O globo*. 6 November. http://g1.globo.com/rio-de-janeiro/noticia/2014/11/seis-anos-apos-cpi-deputado-diz-que-pouco-foi-feito-no-combate-milicias.html.

Costa, F. 2018. "Omissão do Estado permitiu avanço das milícias nos últimos 10 anos, dizem Freixo e relator da CPI". *UOL*. 17 April. http://noticias.uol.com.br/cotidiano/ultimas-noticias/2018/04/17/em-dez-anos-governos-do-rio-permitiram-avanco-das-milicias-dizem-freixo-e-relator-da-cpi.htm.

Dalvi, B. 2017. "Termina a greve da PM no Espírito Santo após 21 dias de caos e insegurança". *O globo*. 25 February. https://oglobo.globo.com/brasil/termina-greve-da-pm-no-espirito-santo-apos-21-dias-de-caos-inseguranca-20982836.

Dieleke, E. 2009. "O Sertão Não Virou Mar : Images of Violence and the Position of the Spectator in Contemporary Brazilian Cinema". In Page, J. and Haddu, M. (eds) *Visual Synergies in Fiction and Documentary Film from Latin America*, New York: Palgrave Macmillan, pp. 67–86.

Escorel, E. 2010. "*Tropa de elite II*: realidade ou ficção?" *Revista Piauí*. 6 November. https://piaui.folha.uol.com.br/tropa-de-elite-2-realidade-ou-ficcao/.

Folha de S. Paulo. 2006. "Facção criminosa foi fundada em 1993". *Folha de S. Paulo*. 14 May. www1.folha.uol.com.br/folha/cotidiano/ult95u121460.shtml.

Fraga, P. 2007. "Não dá para aplaudir nem sob tortura". *Folha de S. Paulo*. 27 September. www1.folha.uol.com.br/fsp/ilustrad/fq2709200710.htm.

Globo. 2017. "BOPE vira tema de festas infantis no Rio". *O globo*. 16 May. https://oglobo. globo.com/rio/bope-vira-tema-de-festas-infantis-no-rio-21340618.

Globo Extra. 2007. "Jovens em cenas de tortura inspiradas em 'Tropa de elite' são condenados por especialistas que pedem alerta dos pais". *Globo Extra*.15 December. https://extra. globo.com/tv-e-lazer/jovens-em-cenas-de-tortura-inspiradas-em-tropa-de-elite-sao-condenados-por-especialistas-que-pedem-alerta-dos-pais-725984.html.

Gregoli, R. 2011. "Transnational Reception of City of God and Elite Squad". In *Participations: Journal of Audience and Reception Studies*. 8: 2. www.participations.org/Volume%208/ Issue%202/3d%20Gregoli.pdf.

Heise, T. 2012. *Remaking Brazil: Contested National Identities in Contemporary Brazilian Cinema*. Melksham: University of Wales Press.

Huck, L. 2007. "Pensamentos quase póstumos". *Folha de S. Paulo*. 1 October. www1.folha. uol.com.br/fsp/opiniao/fz0110200708.htm.

Jardim, L. 2018. "Ibope: 50% dos brasileiros acham que 'bandido bom é bandido morto'". *O globo*. 4 March. https://blogs.oglobo.globo.com/lauro-jardim/post/ibope-50-dos-brasileiros-acham-que-bandido-bom-e-bandido-morto.html.

Johnston, S. 2008. "Elite Squad: The Movie That Shook Brazil". *The Telegraph*. 18 July. www. telegraph.co.uk/culture/film/3556607/Elite-Squad-the-movie-that-shook-Brazil.html.

Kleinpaul, B. 2007. Lula Carvalho conta que adolescência no Rio foi referência para fotografia de "Tropa de elite". *O globo*. 9 October. https://oglobo.globo.com/cultura/ lula-carvalho-conta-que-adolescencia-no-rio-foi-referencia-para-fotografia-de-tropa-de-elite-4149708.

Koehler. R. 2011. "Elite Squad: The Enemy Within". *Variety*. 31 January. https://variety. com/2011/film/markets-festivals/elite-squad-the-enemy-within-1117944469/.

Larkins, E. R. 2013. "Performances of Police Legitimacy in Rio's Hyper Favela". *Law & Social Inquiry*, 38, pp. 553–575.

Mayr, A. 2015. "Spectacles of Military Urbanism in Online Representations of the Elite Squad of the Military Police of Rio de Janeiro: A Multimodal Approach". *Social Semiotics*, 25, pp. 533–557.

McDonald, S. 2012. "Favela Wars?: Masculinity and Legitimacy of Violent Conflict in *Tropa de elite* and *Tropa de elite: o inimigo agora é outro*". In González-Casanovas, R. J. (ed) *Reconfiguring Brazil: Interdisciplinary Essays*. Aukland Latin American Studies, pp. 71–85.

Ministério da Justiça e Segurança Pública. 2016. "Levantamento Nacional de Informações Penitenciárias".http://depen.gov.br/DEPEN/noticias-1/noticias/infopen-levantamento-nacional-de-informacoes-penitenciarias-2016/relatorio_2016_22111.pdf.

Pimentel, R., Batista, A. and Soares, L. E. 2006. *Elite da tropa*. Rio de Janeiro: Objetiva.

Revista forum. 2018. "Intervenção militar é assunto mais comentado no Twitter". *Revista forum*. 16 February. www.revistaforum.com.br/intervencao-militar-e-assunto-mais-comentado-no-twitter-veja-repercussao-nas-redes/.

Roda Viva. 2007. *Entrevista com José Padilha*. 8 Oct. Script available at www.rodaviva.fapesp. br/materia/327/entrevistados/jose_padilha_2007.htm.

Saraiva, C. A. 2013. "*Veja* transforma em 'super-herói nacional' assassinos de Amarildo". *Blog do Saraiva*. 11 October. http://saraiva13.blogspot.com/2013/10/veja-transforma-em-super-heroi-nacional.html.

Sneed, P. 2008. 'Favela Utopias: The Bailes Funk in Rio's Crisis of Social Exclusion and Violence'. In *Latin American Research Review*. 43, 2. http://lasa-4.univ.pitt.edu/LARR/prot/fulltext/Vol43no2/03_43.2sneed.pdf.

Villaça, P. n/d. "*Tropa de Elite*". *Cinema em Cena*. http://cinemaemcena.cartacapital.com.br/critica/filme/6191/tropa-de-elite.

Weissberg, J. 2008. "The Elite Squad". *Variety*. 11 Feb. https://variety.com/2008/film/markets-festivals/the-elite-squad-1200548140/.

Whitfield, J. 2017. "City of Control: José Padilha and the Policing of Rio de Janeiro in *Ónibus 174* (*Bus 174*), and *Tropa de Elite* (*Elite Squad*)". In Ring, A., Steiner, H. and Veel, K. (eds), *Architecture and Control*, BRILL, pp. 169–187.

Willis, G. D. 2015. *The Killing Consensus: Police, Organized Crime, and the Regulation of Life and Death in Urban Brazil*. University of California Press.

8

LÚCIA MURAT'S *OLHAR ESTRANGEIRO* (2005) AND THE REPRESENTATION OF BRAZIL ON FOREIGN SCREENS

Lúcia Murat's 2005 documentary *Olhar estrangeiro* is based on a book by academic Tunico Amâncio, *O Brasil dos gringos: imagens no cinema* (2000), an absorbing monograph that contains an exhaustive list of films made by foreign film directors that are set in, or include significant references to Brazil. While Amâncio's book attempts a wide coverage and provides an examination of a range of themes in relation to this representation, Murat's film concentrates on sex and sensuality ("a carne e o osso" [flesh and bones], as she states in voiceover in the documentary), the "clichés que nos perseguem" (clichés that follow us around), and the factual inaccuracies that filmmakers have been guilty of committing down the years. The film is made up of interviews with a number of directors, producers and actors involved in making films set in Brazil from the 1960s to the 1990s, including box-office hits such as *Blame it on Rio* (Stanley Donan, 1984), the Jean-Paul Belmondo vehicle *L'Homme de Rio* (Philippe de Broca, 1964) and the blockbuster *Anaconda* (Luis Llosa, 1997), as well as more "straight-to-video" fare such as *Last Stop Wonderland* (Brad Anderson, 1998) and *Lambada: The Forbidden Dance* (Greydon Clark, 1990). Murat informs us in voiceover that at the time of making her documentary 220 films featuring Brazil had been made outside the country, so if sheer volume is anything to go by, a feature-length documentary on the representation of Brazil on foreign screens is amply justified. It is surprising that so few critical works exist, whether film or essay, that engage substantively with this broad and fascinating subject.[1]

This chapter presents an analysis of *Olhar estrangeiro*, considering both the extent to which Murat successfully "turns the tables" on foreign filmmakers, as she claims to do in the opening section of her film, and what is omitted from the film, along with the significance of such omissions. It then seeks to continue the discussion begun by Amâncio's text and Murat's film, incorporating reflections on more recent audio-visual representations of Brazil produced outside of the country.

The bulk of Murat's documentary is made up of illustrative clips from a select number of films, coupled with carefully edited "talking head" interviews (with very little interruption from Murat) by those linked to the films in question. Both occasional commentary by Murat and intertitles provide production details of the films, along with the odd factual curiosity (such as the fact that more than 40 films involve criminals fleeing to Brazil). Murat also includes footage of interviews with members of the "foreign" public in unspecified places (although one such place appears to be a beach in Rio, as well as, we assume, the places in the United States and Europe that she visits to interview filmmakers). The documentary shows Murat setting up a makeshift booth in which to conduct these public interviews on the beach: its shape and bright materials remind one of Hélio Oiticica's famous and very influential Tropicália art installation, itself a tongue-in-cheek reference to the excessive exoticisation with which Brazil is visually associated.[2] And sure enough, some (but interestingly not all) of the members of the public who take part in the interviews come up with clichés when asked to describe Brazil and Brazilian people, thus demonstrating the extent to which they chime with filmic portrayals of Brazil on foreign screens.

While Murat rarely intervenes during the interviews with filmmakers, she does take her interviewees to task on three occasions, in a seemingly uncontrollable sense of frustration, to comment (off camera) during the interviews in order to correct three erroneous notions about Brazil: that topless bathing is common, or even permitted, that monkeys roam the coast in Rio de Janeiro, and that the city of São Paulo has a beach. Other recurring errors that are commented on in the documentary include the juxtaposition of the city of Rio de Janeiro and the Amazonian rainforest, voodoo weddings and use of the Spanish language, or mispronunciation of key terms and names in Portuguese. Some of Murat's interviewees play down the significance of the errors, while others attempt to explain them away by claiming

FIGURE 8.1 Mimicking Hélio Oiticica's Tropicália installation, Lúcia Murat sets the scene for the foreign view of Brazil. A still from *Olhar estrangeiro*

(*Foreign View*, Lúcia Murat, 2005)

that filmmakers have licence to present fantasy spaces on screen. Murat makes the very salient observation that the level of fantasy that has been used in representations of Rio would not be possible, say, in relation to the city of New York. New York cannot be represented in realist mode as, for example, having a jungle within its confines, because the audience knows for a fact that no such jungle exists. It is thus the lack of knowledge to start with, or perhaps lack of historical interest in looking beyond clichés, of places such as Rio de Janeiro or Brazil more broadly, that make such creative licence problematic.

Rewatching the documentary in 2018 in the context of the #metoo movement and the large number of cases of sexism and historical sexual abuse within Hollywood that have recently come to light, it is difficult not to be offended by the laddish, dismissive and frankly clueless humour of most of the interviewees. By way of a solution to the constant representation of Brazil as a site of sensuality, and in order for Brazil to be taken seriously, British actor Michael Caine suggests that Brazilian women should stop dancing and become uglier. French popular comedy director Philippe Clair makes lewd comments about fifteen-year-old Brazilian teens in tight shorts. And Gerard Lanzier, a French filmmaker based in Brazil, says of his own behaviour "I'm responsible but I'm not to blame". In other words, Rio, and Brazil more broadly, are inherently sinful places that give visitors and film-makers alike a licence to misbehave. The default mode of reacting to these reflections of foreign film-makers and actors is, I imagine, one of disdain, as their own choice of words and descriptions of Brazil reveal them to be prejudiced and/or ignorant. In this very important sense Murat successfully "turns the tables" on her interviewees.

In relation to this idea of shirking responsibility, it is interesting to note that the emblematic *Blame it on Rio*, discussed at length in Murat's film, was a remake of the French film *Un moment d'égarement* (1977 and remade in 2015) which was set on

FIGURE 8.2 Michael Caine instructs Brazilians to dance less and become uglier. A still from *Olhar estrangeiro*

(*Foreign View*, Lúcia Murat, 2005)

the (topless) beaches of the Côte D'Azur. Seemingly, in the US imaginary, somewhere was needed *outside* the borders of the US (and south of the equator, where Hollywood has taught us there is no such thing as sin) to signal what the Côte D'Azur represented in the French version of the film (licentiousness, sexual expression, contrast from the stuffy working world of the metropolis). The very title of the film *Blame it on Rio*, particularly given the film's focus on inter-generational relationships (middle-aged men with teenage girls), reinforces this sense of licence to misbehave, and in that sense, in the context of Murat's documentary, it is by far the most portentous with regard to the promotion of harmful myths about a country and its people.

The impact of the film *Blame it on Rio* on the international imagination in relation to Brazil can be seen in the borrowing of the title for what is now one of the most notorious episodes of the cartoon TV series *The Simpsons*, "Blame it on Lisa" (2002): so notorious that it elicited a widely reported-on letter of complaint from Rio's Tourist Board for the allegedly negative image of the city that it portrayed, with its rat-infested streets, thieving street children on every corner, kidnappings and Murat's bug-bears: a tropical rainforest in the middle of Rio de Janeiro and exotic, predatory animals roaming city spaces. Even the then president, Fernando Henrique Cardoso, was quoted at the time as describing the episode as giving a "distorted vision of Brazilian reality" (Bellos, 2002). Producer James L Brooks then publicly apologised for the episode, although this did not prevent *The Simpsons* from revisiting many of the problematic clichés and stereotypes in a follow-up episode in 2014 at the time of Brazil's hosting of the World Cup.

The omission of any reference to "Blame it on Lisa" in Murat's film had to do with budget constraints and access to filmmakers as much as anything else,[3] but the omission is perhaps convenient, given that the use of tongue-in-cheek humour, deliberately extreme comic scenarios that cartoons can get away with, and a healthy dose of social critique typical of *The Simpsons*, problematise the issue of representation and make it more difficult to dismiss it as entirely negative or unjust. Consider, for example, the exotic representation of Brazil in the more recent feature-length cartoons *Rio* (2011) and *Rio 2* (2014). In their article on *Rio 2*, Figueiredo Lopes et al. (2017) reference Nogueira (2010), who argues that "this genre exists pacifically alongside the unreal, since it occupies a space in the world of dreams, of fantasy, of fables and of abstraction". Cartoons can "suspend, manipulate, subvert or challenge the laws of physics, cultural norms, ethical premises, and so on" (p. 59). *Blame it on Rio* is a much easier target, then, than "Blame it on Lisa" or *Rio* in terms of a discussion of misrepresentation of Brazilian culture. And with regard to the (admittedly scant) references to sex and sexuality, which after all is the focus of Murat's film, those images are perhaps not as exaggerated and removed from reality as other aspects of Brazilian culture depicted in the *Simpsons* episode.[4] Here I am referring in particular to the appearance of Xoxchitla as viewed on TV in Brazil by Bart Simpson: the nipple-tassle-clad Xoxchitla is a parody of children's TV and film superstar Xuxa, who would have been known to some viewers in the US from a short-lived attempt to break into the Latino TV market and was renowned in the

1980s and 1990s for her overtly sensual costumes while heading up kids'TV shows in her native Brazil.[5]

Notwithstanding the strength of feeling at the time of the release of "Blame it on Lisa" and its potential impact on tourism in Rio de Janeiro in particular,[6] the episode pales into insignificance when we consider it alongside the violent horror film *Turistas* (John Stockwell, 2006), released after Murat's documentary. The titular *turistas* are American backpackers whose dream holiday turns into a nightmare when they are duped, drugged and murdered for their organs by evil locals. Another missive was quickly dispatched, this time by the National Tourist Board Embratur, to the film's producers, and not just as a result of portrayal of the country in the film itself, but more specifically the fake tourist website used to promote the film. Thus there is a keen awareness in Brazil, both at the level of the State and within the culture industry itself, of the extent to which the nation has been a victim of negative stereotyping, which perhaps needs to be borne in mind when evaluating both academic works and acts of government that criticise how Brazil has been portrayed on screen.

A further "omission" in Murat's film can be traced in part to the scholarly text on which the documentary is based. The title of Amâncio's text, *O Brasil dos Gringos*, is deliberately playful, but the use of the term *gringo* does suggest that we are limiting ourselves to a similar kind of stereotype, when it comes to talking about other cultures, that we see being critiqued in Murat's documentary. The term *gringo*, like many culturally specific terms, is a loaded one. While it problematically lumps all foreigners together, it also tends to be used exclusively to refer to (white) Europeans and Americans who are usually cast as feeling or acting somehow "superior" (more often than not this expresses itself as having an economic advantage) in relation to Brazilians. Thus the term pre-emptively locates Brazilians at a disadvantage to non-Brazilians, in a place of inferiority,

FIGURE 8.3 Foreign backpackers in Brazil get more than they bargained for in a still from *Turistas*

(John Stockwell, 2006)

seemingly reinforcing the simplistic cliché of the so-called Brazilian mongrel complex.[7] Murat may have wisely avoided the term *gringo* in her filmic adaptation of Amâncio's book, but it is interesting to note that the *olhar estrangeiro* or foreign view that she investigates in her film is almost exclusively represented by white, middle-aged men from the United States, France and Northern Europe, such as the British actor Michael Caine and US scriptwriters Larry Gelbert and Charlie Peters (*Blame it on Rio*); French director Philippe de Broca (*L'Homme de Rio*) and American director Zalman King (*Wild Orchid*).

Olhar estrangeiro arguably reinforces the notion that only certain foreign views matter. So what the documentary does not capture, for example, are works by Latin American directors that portray Brazil as a land of plenty, and Brazilians as hardworking and enterprising, such as the critically acclaimed Uruguayan film *Whisky* (2004).[8] No mention is made, for example, of the earlier hit German film *Stefanie in Rio* (Curtis Bernhardt, 1960) which despite its name does spend some time on location in the then brand new capital, Brasília. Brazil is portrayed positively as a forward-looking, modern space, very much within the *país do futuro* or country of the future mode.[9] And it is worth recalling that the two lead males in *Blame it on Rio* are in fact based initially in São Paulo, but take a vacation in Rio as a result of overwork.[10] The cult hit *The Girl From Rio* (aka *Rio70*) (1969) makes excellent use of the futuristic architecture of Rio's Modern Art Museum and Santos Dumont airport. The women in the film may be sexually irresistible and dangerous, thus adhering on one level to a particular stereotype of Brazilian womanhood, but the Amazons of lore are transformed in the film into an exclusive, strong group of women occupying a materialistic, modern, style-driven space set up within Brazil. Arguably our reading of the film as genre/exploitation/science fiction offers another way of appreciating the images on screen: it was, after all, directed by cult Spanish filmmaker Jesús (Jess) Franco.

Within the pantheon of foreign films that trouble critics for their inaccurate representation of Brazil, it is interesting to note that critically acclaimed, award-winning films will often escape the full brunt of criticism. This is the case with the 1959 French-Brazilian co-production *Orfeu negro (Black Orpheus*, based on the play *Orfeu da Conceição* by Vinícius de Moraes and directed by French filmmaker Marcel Camus). The film won both the Palme D'Or at the Cannes film festival in 1959 and the Oscar for best foreign film in 1960. No mention is made of *Orfeu negro* in Murat's documentary, despite a certain revisionism on the part of critics with regard to the film's highly exotic representation of Brazilian culture.[11] According to Tiago Mata Machado (2001), "no other foreign film has reinforced the clichéd image of an exotic Brazil as much as Camus's film. *Orfeu negro* is a classic of 'voodoo for tourists' (macumba para turista)".

A similar absence of criticism of the portrayal of Brazil and its people can be found in relation to a more recent film by a critically acclaimed director: Pedro Almodóvar's *La piel que habito (The Skin I Live In*, 2011). In the film Antonio Banderas plays Robert Ledgard, a morally challenged plastic surgeon[12] who is Spanish and based in Spain, but has some kind of ill-defined family connection to Brazil. In relation to the problematic family that he heads and its Brazilian connection, *Isto é* magazine reported the following:

> Already expecting a negative reaction over here, the director declared at the time of the film's release in Spain: "I didn't want them [the family] to bear the weight of a Judeo-Christian upbringing. I hope the Brazilians understand: I love their country.
>
> *(Claudio 2011)*

While the Brazilian connection to Ledgard might be tenuous and unclear, Brazil is represented in the film in extreme caricature in the guise of Zeca, Ledgard's half brother. Zeca, a one-time drug dealer brought up in the poverty of Brazil's favelas, a violent thief and rapist with seemingly no moral compass whatsoever, is introduced in the film at Carnival time, dressed in an inexplicably ultra-camp tiger costume. Zeca is played by Spanish actor Roberto Álamo, who fails to pronounce convincingly the Portuguese lines he is given to mark his nationality and provenance.

It is perhaps unwise to conduct superficial readings of Almodóvar's work, given that we are dealing with an auteur who regularly makes creative, critical use of stereotypes. After all, if we did, we would likely arrive at the conclusion that the objectification of women was the driving force behind all of his films. What is necessary, however, in the context of this present study, is to at least acknowledge that there has been almost no questioning of, or even engagement with, the potentially problematic Brazilian thematic present in *La piel que habito*. It is striking that the implications of choosing a Brazilian connection to *lighten* the weight of a Judeo-Christian education on the Ledgard family has not been the source of discussion in Brazil, or elsewhere for that matter, and nor has the character Zeca. The negative reaction that Almodóvar awaited simply never materialised.

This kind of deeply disturbing portrayal of Brazil and Brazilians is of the kind that we see so frequently in the contemporary period in relation to foreign films (and exportable domestic productions[13]) portraying, for example, the violence of Brazil's cities, a subject not covered in Murat's documentary but arguably much more dangerous in terms of the negative marking of a nation. Such portrayals seem far removed from the low-impact Brazilian love story movies that make up a sizeable portion of the film production that Murat refers to in her film. As Ivana Bentes (2002) argued on the release of *Cidade de Deus*:

> We are no longer fighting against the foreign exotic gaze on our dire poverty which, according to Glauber Rocha in 1965 transformed everything "into a strange tropical surrealism". We are now capable of producing and circulating our own clichés in which healthy, glistening black men with a gun in their hand can think of nothing better to do than perform mutual extermination.

When it comes to love stories there is a quite typical filmic way of portraying Brazil. For a start, good love stories start and end in the city of Rio de Janeiro, whose representation on screen in such films has changed little since the days of Hollywood's technicolor *That Night in Rio*-style musicals. Let us consider, for example, the British film *Girl from Rio* (2001), a film that is not commented on in Murat's documentary, perhaps because it was released after Amâncio's monograph was published. It features in the lead role Hugh Laurie, who was at the time of the release of the film already a big comedy star in the UK (but before his international success in the hit US TV series *House*).

Girl From Rio opens with banker Raymond, played by Laurie, running his weekly samba percussion class at a local community centre. The stiff Brits have no rhythm and seem more interested in refreshments (the obligatory cup of tea) than improving their performance. With his personal and professional life in tatters, he steals a large sum of money from the bank and heads to Rio de Janeiro. The idea of starting over in Brazil on ill-gotten gains is typical of so many of these films: lack of extradition treaties is a common plot device to get characters to Brazil[14] and it was made all the more pertinent to the British context thanks to the infamous train robber Ronnie Biggs, whom Laurie references in the DVD extras. According to Vanessa Barbara (2015),

> Perhaps the first film to reference the peculiar attraction that Brazil holds for international runaways was *The Lavender Hill Mob*, a 1951 British comedy starring Alec Guinness. His character steals one million pounds in gold from the Bank of England, melts the bars into miniature Eiffel Towers and comes "straight on to Rio de Janeiro. Gay, sprightly, land of mirth and social ease".

In *Girl from Rio*, Raymond acquires a shady local sidekick (played by Spanish actor Santiago Segura, who is best known for his recurring role as politically incorrect cop Torrente on the Spanish big screen).[15] Such films inevitably involve images of the erstwhile stiff lead man both relishing the heat, sun and feel-good vibe of Brazil in contrast to a grey, dull, boring Britain, inevitably forcing him to spontaneously burst into dance (this occurs both on Copacabana beach and at the Salgueiro samba school in *Girl From Rio*), and falling for the impossible charms of a beautiful, rhythmic local woman. The idea of fleeing the cold, grey, dull North for the warmth of the tropical, colourful South was fixed in the 1940s with the raft of very influential Technicolor musicals produced during the Good Neighbour era. Such films have been used by Ana López (1993: 68) to argue the case for Hollywood as Ethnographer, by which she means "to think of Hollywood not as a simple reproducer of fixed and homogenous cultures or ideologies, but as a *producer* (my emphasis) of some of the multiple discourses that intervene in, affirm and contest the socio-ideological struggles of a given moment". López demonstrates her argument by focusing on Latino stars in Hollywood, including the Brazilian Carmen Miranda, who despite her importance for discussions on the celluloid image of Brazil, and especially in relation to exoticism, sex and sensuality, is barely mentioned in Murat's film.

FIGURE 8.4 A tropical Carmen Miranda in a still from Hollywood musical *The Gang's All Here*

(Busby Berkeley, 1943)

The presence of foreign film crews on Brazilian soil has arguably increased with greater incentives being made available to make films in the country,[16] and more active and organised regional film commissions and production services companies. As well as a great many TV commercials screened in the UK, which are often recognisable as filmed in Brazil only to those who are familiar with, for example, the Arcos da Lapa in Rio or the Minhocão in São Paulo, a number of films and TV adverts take advantage of the favourable incentives and film their movies in Brazil without explicitly referencing the country. A notable recent example is *The Twilight Saga: Breaking Dawn Part Two* (2012) which was filmed in and around Paraty. And images of the remote planet Vormir in *Avengers Infinity War* (2018) were filmed in the stunning Lençóis Maranhenses National Park in Brazil's Northeast.

Some might regard this increase in the pursuit of production services as a positive step in terms of the viability of the film production market in Brazil, and comparably harmless in terms of representation. Not everyone is happy with this development, however. The pressure group Rio: Mais Cinema, Menos Cenário (Rio: More Films, Less Background), made up of film producers and academics, has challenged what it sees as the Commissions' permissive approach to the use of Brazilian locations. Set up in 2014, arguably as a reaction to the presence of neoliberal Sérgio Sá Leitão in the presidency of Riofilme, Rio: Mais Cinema, Menos Cenário sought to draw attention to the number of films (both foreign and local) that make use of the city's production services without engaging meaningfully or authentically on-screen with the social and political issues affecting Rio. The context for some of the frustrations expressed by this pressure group, which was launched at the Rio Film Festival in 2014, is the sense that Brazil has long been systematically misrepresented on foreign screens.

Concluding remarks

It is important to acknowledge, when describing "omissions" in *Olhar estrangeiro*, that we are ultimately talking about a low-budget production and director Lúcia Murat did well to access so many key filmmakers and actors, and to include so many clips from relevant films in her documentary. Murat's documentary, and Amâncio's book, ably demonstrate that, notwithstanding the examples cited in this chapter to the contrary, along with one or two exceptions to the rule highlighted in Murat's film[17], foreign filmmakers who descend on Brazil have down the years shown scant regard for the consequences of erroneous representations of the country, its culture and its people. Consequently, we would do well to remember, when discussing cultural diplomacy, branding and soft power, for example, that the issues and tensions facing emerging nations such as Brazil in relation to their image abroad and the motivating factors for wanting to promote, challenge, or increase the presence of that image abroad, will not be the same as the issues facing, say, the United Kingdom or Spain. Hence reputation management is quite a large part of the soft power story in Brazil where it might not be in the United Kingdom, for example.

Brazil has undoubtedly been a victim of negative stereotyping on foreign screens but the story is much more complex than *Olhar estrangeiro* suggests, with its focus on sex and sensuality. Drugs culture and its attendant violence are arguably a bigger issue for Brazil to deal with in terms of its international image (hence the outcry over a film like *Turistas* in 2006). The film also fails to acknowledge at any point the contribution made by organs of the Brazilian State which interact with international communities (such as Embratur) to sustain this harmful myth of sexy, available women being Brazil's main attraction. The focus of Murat's film is very much Rio de Janeiro rather than Brazil as a whole, but the subtitle of the documentary is "um personagem chamado Brasil" (a character named Brazil), with an accompanying image of a sexualised indigenous woman. With this we are taken back to times of first contact, as discussed in Chapter 6, and to Brazil's first national foundational text: Pero Vaz de Caminha's letter to the Portuguese court sent in 1500 which demonstrates that ever since "gringos" discovered Brazil, sex and sexuality, particularly in relation to women, has been the focus of attention. The extent to which such myths have been appropriated into Brazilian culture through the centuries, and particularly in relation to some regional groups more than others, complicates the perhaps too simplistic binary of "foreign" and "national" in such discussions.

Notes

1 As well as Amâncio's book, worthy of mention here is Silvio Back's film mentioned in Chapter 6, *Yndio do Brasil* (1995), a poetic exploration of the (mis)representation of

Brazil's indigenous peoples at the hands of both foreign and Brazilian filmmakers (and inclusion of both foreign and national attempts to portray indigenous peoples on screen tellingly problematises the notion of "foreign" in relation to such peoples in Brazil). An important essay by Sérgio Augusto, "Hollywood Looks At Brazil: From Carmen Miranda to Moonraker", first published in 1982, appears in Randal Johnson and Robert Stam's *Brazilian Cinema* (1995). Bianca de Freire Medeiros has explored a similar theme: see, for example, "Hollywood Musicals and the Representation of Rio de Janeiro 1933–1953" (2002). See also Lisa Shaw and Maite Conde's book chapter "Brazil through Hollywood's Gaze" (2005) and the short film *Brazil on Foreign Screens* (Dennison, 2019).

2 Originally shown in Rio in 1967, the immersive art installation was on display at the Tate gallery in London 2017–2019.

3 As reported by Murat in conversation with the author, April 2018.

4 The follow-up episode amusingly predicted both Brazil's crashing defeat at home in the 2014 World Cup, and the appalling reputation acquired by Brazilian player Neymar for falling and claiming injury in the 2018 World Cup finals in Russia.

5 For a reading of the star text of Xuxa, see Simpson (1993; 1998) and Dennison (2013).

6 The episode was viewed by more than 11 million Americans on its release: Bellos 2002.

7 The expression *complexo de vira-lata* to denote a national inferiority complex was coined in 1958 by writer Nelson Rodrigues. It is discussed further in Chapter 9.

8 Likewise in a later Uruguayan/Brazilian/French film, the film festival hit *El bano del papa* (*The Pope's Toilet* 2007), Brazil is portrayed as the economically stronger neighbour and Brazilians as wealthy saviours of a small town hoping to make money from an imminent visit by the Pope. And another "festival film" and co-production, *Plastic City* (2008), cites São Paulo as an optimal place for Chinese immigrants to do business, even if that business is shady.

9 The Brazil-based German author Stefan Zweig showered praise on his adopted land in a 1941 book *Brasilien ein land der zukunft* (Brazil, Country of the Future), the title of which has been widely adapted into popular use, often to indicate ironically that the country consistently fails to live up to its potential.

10 It is worth noting the difference between Rio and São Paulo in terms of how foreign travellers engage with the two cities: travel to São Paulo is almost exclusively for the purposes of doing business.

11 Barack Obama famously dismissed the film as objectifying black people: See Bradshaw (2009).

12 Almodóvar's fascination with plastic surgery was purportedly piqued by the work of world-renowned Brazilian surgeons such as the late Ivo Pitanguy.

13 Let us consider the impact of well-travelled home-grown films such as *City of God* and *Elite Squad* on a younger generation's understanding of Brazil.

14 At the time of researching this chapter (February 2018) it cropped up once again in the storyline of 1960s period drama *Endeavour* on primetime British television.

15 This casting is perhaps explained by the fact that the film is a co-production with Spain.

16 While no formal mechanism exists to offer financial incentives to film in Brazil, other incentives such as a range of production services and the support of a number of regional film commissions make filming in Brazil attractive, particularly for bigger-budget productions.

17 Orson Welles's ill-fated film-making journey in Brazil and the unfinished masterpiece he produced (*It's All True*, 1943) is praised in Murat's film, as is *Hung Up* – a French film from 1973 which has seemingly been lost.

References

Amâncio, T. 2000. *O Brasil dos gringos: imagens no cinema*. Rio: Intertexto.

Augusto, S. 1995. "Hollywood Looks At Brazil: From Carmen Miranda to Moonraker". In Johnson, R and Stam, R (eds). *Brazilian Cinema*. New York: University of Columbia Press, pp. 351–411.

Barbara, V. 2015. "Brazil: The Outlaw's Paradise". *New York Times*. 5 February. https://www.nytimes.com/2015/02/06/opinion/vanessa-barbara-brazil-the-outlaws-paradise.html

Bentes, I. 2002. "*Cidade de Deus* promove turismo no inferno". *Estado de São Paulo*. 31 August.

Bellos, A. 2002. "Doh! Rio Blames it on The Simpsons". *The Guardian*. 9 April. https://www.theguardian.com/media/2002/apr/09/broadcasting.internationalnews.

Bradshaw, P. 2009. "Why Obama is Wrong About Black Orpheus". *Guardian*. 2 February. https://www.theguardian.com/film/filmblog/2009/feb/02/barack-obama-black-orpheus

Claudio, I. 2011. "Os brasileiros de Almodovar". *Isto É Online*. 2 November. https://istoe.com.br/172011_OS+BRASILEIROS+DE+ALMODOVAR/.

Dennison, S. (2013). "Blonde Bombshell: Xuxa and Notions of Whiteness in Brazil". *Journal of Latin American Cultural Studies*. 22: 3, pp. 287–304.

Freire Medeiros, B. 2002. "Hollywood Musicals and the Representation of Rio de Janeiro 1933–1953". *Cinema Journal* 41: 4. pp. 52–67.

Figueiredo Lopes, R, Souza Nogueira, W and, Cardinale Baptista, M. L. 2017. "Imaginário, cinema e turismo: uma viagem por clichês culturais associados ao Brasil, no filme Rio 2". In *Revista Rosa dos Ventos – Turismo e Hospitalidade*, 9 (III), pp. 377–388.

Lopez, A. 1993. "Are All Latins From Manhattan? Hollywood, Ethnography and Cultural Colonialism". In King, J., Lopez, A. and Alvarado, M. (eds). *Mediating Two Worlds: Cinematic Encounters in the Americas*. London: BFI Publishing. pp. 67–80.

Mata Machado, T. 2011. "'Orfeu Negro', clássico da 'macumba para turista', chega em DVD". *Folha Ilustrada Online*. 12 September. www1.folha.uol.com.br/folha/ilustrada/critica/ult569u318.shtml.

Nogueira, L. 2010. *Manuais de cinema II: gêneros cinematográficos*. Covilhã: LabCom Books.

Shaw, L. and Conde, M. (2005). "Brazil through Hollywood's Gaze: From the Silent Screen to the Good Neighbor Policy Era". In Shaw, L. and Dennison, S. (eds), *Latin American Cinema: Essays on Modernity, Gender and National Identity*. Jefferson NC: McFarland Press, pp. 180–208.

Simpson, A. 1993. *Xuxa: The Mega-Marketing of Gender, Race and Modernity*. Philadelphia: Temple University Press.

Simpson, A. 1998. "Representing Racial Diffference: Brazil's Xuxa at the Televisual Border". In *Studies in Latin American Popular Culture* 17, pp. 197–212.

Zweig, Stefan. 1941. *Brasilien ein land der zukunft*.

9

HOPE SPRINGS FROM RUBBISH

Trash (2014) and the garbage aesthetic

Brazil's rubbish

Brazil is the world's fifth largest producer of waste. It produces over 80 million tonnes of rubbish per year and only 3% of it is recycled (Agência Brasil 2018).While producing large quantities of waste on one level reflects the ability of a society to spend and consume, and therefore to lay a tentative claim to an elevated "first-world" economy and standard of living, the flipside to this in Brazil is the army of economically disenfranchised who in order to survive are forced to go through that rubbish in search of something that can be reused, recycled, refashioned, or in some cases, consumed. As we will see, the idea of a large underclass of Brazilians reduced to picking through the leftovers of consumer society both literally and metaphorically, has haunted the national psyche and tends to dominate global images of consumerism in relation to the country. By way of example, in 2014, 294,200 tonnes of aluminium cans were produced in Brazil and 289,500 of those were recycled, making the country the most successful recycler of aluminium in the world (Linnenkoper 2015). But it is the *catadores*, the rubbish pickers working in the most unsavoury conditions, who are mostly responsible for separating the rubbish for recycling. It is estimated that there are between 400,000 and 600,000 rubbish pickers in Brazil, with 70% being black or mixed-race women (Mori 2017). They have notoriously few rights and extremely low incomes: only just over 30,000 are members of labour associations or co-operatives. The poorest of these are those who separate plastic and paper, living in or around the very dangerous and highly polluted rubbish tips.

According to Brazilian sociologist Roberto DaMatta (2014), the existence of *catadores* and others who work informally with rubbish in Brazil, are a modern manifestation of master-slave relations, whereby the privileged few are completely unaware of the implications of the rubbish produced by their lifestyle. DaMatta posits that the idea of cleaning up after oneself is alien to most Brazilians and constitutes a major character flaw. A recent example of this negative take on the Brazilian character was witnessed in the enthusiastic coverage in the press and social media, during both the 2014 World Cup and the 2016 Olympic Games, of Japanese supporters bringing refuse bags to stadia in Brazil and, in sharp contrast to host nationals, clearing away their own and others' rubbish. Or of the images of Rio de Janeiro's beaches covered in litter as a result of the *garis* or street cleaners' strike in 2014: beaches such as Copacabana are usually pristine, given that they are meticulously cleaned every day by *garis*. The strike revealed the shocking extent to which sunbathers littered the beaches, happy in the knowledge that (normally) someone else would clean up after them. The inability of the State to deal with the volume of waste produced in Brazil and its potential to pollute was also captured by the global news media in relation to failed promises to depollute Rio's Guanabara Bay and Lagoa regions in the run-up to hosting the Olympics. Much was made of the instruction given to Olympic rowers in Lagoa to "not swallow the water", should their boats capsize.[1]

In the context of waste management, it is open dumps, as opposed to covered landfill sites, that are most cited as indicators of underdevelopment. Often emerging unchecked on the outskirts of large cities in the developing world, they are disease-ridden eyesores that offer a visual shorthand for poverty, global pollution and extreme contrast between the haves and the have-nots. To put it callously, as one *Guardian* commentator did, they are "an urban planner's nightmare and a filmmaker's dream" (Watts 2015).

Jardim Gramacho, the inspiration for the setting of the film *Trash: a esperança vem do lixo* (*Trash*, Stephen Daldry and Christian Duurvoort, 2014), was one of the world's largest open-air rubbish dumps. It was closed in 2012, in the run-up to the Rio+20 Global Sustainability Conference, the first of three "mega-events" hosted in the city between 2012 and 2016 (the World Cup football final and the Summer Olympics being the other two). The dump was initially filled in, covered with trees and its gas emissions were trapped and tapped for electricity generation. The closure of Jardim Gramacho was, then, held up as a symbol of progress, yet its closure has resulted in an increase in fly tipping elsewhere, given the cost of more automated recycling practices. In 2018 the site itself continues to be used for rubbish tipping: the illicit practice, to which the city council turns a blind eye, is now managed by drug gangs (Diniz 2018). The promises of compensation and retraining made to the 5000 *catadores* who worked at the Jardim Gramacho landfill site were also barely fulfilled (Watts 2015), and the region, in Duque de Caxias just outside Rio de Janeiro continues to be one of the poorest in the state.

Garbage as cultural conceit

The concept of *lixo* (rubbish, garbage, trash, discarded goods, detritus and leftovers) is one that has "contaminated" much Brazilian culture, serving both to negatively label some more popular cultural production, and at the same time heralding sites of intense creativity. A well-known example of the latter phenomenon is the national dish, *feijoada* (black bean stew), whose tradition of incorporating cheaper cuts of meat, like US soul food, stems from its origins as a meal prepared by slaves and made from meat that was discarded from the Casa Grande or slave-owners' home. As Robert Stam (1997: 56) reminds us, the black diaspora has always transformed detritus, and eye-catching examples abound of this in Brazilian culture. Take for instance, the literal illustration offered by Gabriel Joaquim dos Santos (1892–1985), the son of a slave who transformed his lowly dwelling in the fishing village of São Pedro d'Aldeia in the state of Rio de Janeiro into a palace and now popular tourist attraction by lovingly decorating it over the course of 60 years with carefully selected pieces of garbage.[2] And much was made in the impressive opening ceremony of the Rio Summer Olympics in August 2016 of the spirit of *gambiarra*, the idea of making do with and strategically refashioning the scant resources one has at one's disposal to create something culturally stimulating.[3] As João Luiz Vieira (2003: 92–93) has argued,

> Garbage is hybrid, it is the site of the promiscuous mingling of rich and poor, centre and periphery, the industrial and the handicraft, the domestic and the public, the durable and the transient, the organic and the inorganic, the national and the international. The ideal post-modern and post-colonial metaphor, garbage is mixed, syncretic, a radically decentred social text.

But not all sectors of Brazilian society view the nation's relationship with *lixo* as culturally transformative. In 1958 the reactionary and highly influential playwright and journalist Nelson Rodrigues coined the still frequently used expression *complexo de vira-lata* (mongrel complex) in relation to his fellow Brazilians.

> By mongrel complex, I mean the position of inferiority in which Brazilians voluntarily place themselves in relation to the rest of the world. Brazilians are inverted narcissists who spit at their own reflection. This is the thing: we cannot find any personal or historical pretext for self-esteem
>
> *(Rodrigues 1993: 52)*.

The term *vira-lata*, a term used mostly to describe a mongrel or stray dog, literally refers to the act of turning over rubbish bins. Thus, interestingly, the national inferiority complex as defined by Nelson Rodrigues, has at its heart the idea of picking through garbage. This inferiority complex, which can be read literally as a failure to reproduce (or copy) genes, arguably influenced the back-handed compliment paid to his fellow Brazilians by the equally influential critic Paulo Emílio Salles Gomes when he claimed that they had a "creative incapacity for copying" (Conde and Dennison 2018: 194). In other words Brazilian creativity stems from a lack, a failed attempt to copy consecrated cultural models.

As seen in Chapter 1 the popular film comedies of the 1930s-50s, the *chanchadas*, were dismissed as disposable anti-modern embarrassments, to be swept from view. Although the origin of the term is unclear, the etymology stems from the word swine, suggesting something that is not fit even for pigs. The domestic film industry's historical inability to compete with the budgets and quality of "first-world" cinema was for decades construed as a source of shame. It was arguably not until the Cinema Novo, with its "sad, ugly […] desperate films" (Rocha 1995: 70) that turned scarcity into a signifier, that Brazil's lack was understood as a potential aesthetic strength. Later, the *chanchadas* and their offshoots the *pornochanchadas* would be recuperated by scholars (such as Paulo Emílio Salles Gomes) and fans, and in particular the parodic films, in so much as they would send up the big-budget and arguably wasteful pretensions of Hollywood's first-world filmmaking.[4] The cheap, sleazy quality of the *pornochanchadas* would eventually be seen as a celebration of a garbage aesthetic: a refusal to be subjected to the fake order and progress being promoted by the dictatorship of the 1970s.

Ella Shoat and Robert Stam (2014: 310) celebrate the creativity of the film movement that emerged in the wake of the early Cinema Novo period (1962–1966) by referring to it as "tropical detritus".

> Its favoured technique was an aggressive collage of discourses, an anthropophagic devouring of varied cultural stimuli in all their heterogeneity. Tropicalist filmmakers framed a resistant strategy premised on a low-cost "aesthetic of garbage". Where the earlier [Cinema Novo] metaphor of an "aesthetics of hunger" had evoked famished victims redeeming themselves through violence, the garbage metaphor proposed an aggressive sense of marginality, of surviving within scarcity, of being condemned to recycle the materials of dominant culture. A garbage style was seen as appropriate to a Third World country picking through the leavings of an international system dominated by First World capitalism.

Shoat and Stam take inspiration in their terminology from the film production region of the centre of São Paulo known as the Boca do Lixo (Mouth of garbage). While it is frequently associated with the quota-quickie soft and later hard-core films of the 1970s ad 1980s, garbage cinema here refers to films associated with the underground movement of the early 1970s known as *cinema marginal*.[5]

The influence of this garbage aesthetic can be seen in two more recent "postmodern" films (Vieira 2001: 91), in which waste is used as both a literal and metaphorical motif. In Jorge Furtado's award-winning short film *Ilha das Flores* (*Isle of Flowers*, 1992), we follow the journey of a tomato, from being planted to ending up in the "Isle of Flowers" municipal dump in the south of Brazil. The critique hangs on the faux didactic style of the voiceover, frequently mismatched with images of hunger and suffering. In *Cronicamente inviável* (*Chronically Unfeasible*, 2000), Sérgio Bianchi's scathing critique of modern life in Brazil, and in particular of the inability of successive generations of intellectuals and lawmakers to bridge the economic divide between rich and poor, we see sunbathers on a polluted beach in the northeastern city of Salvador, beggars helping themselves to food from restaurant bins

FIGURE 9.1 The poor pick through society's leftovers in a still from *Ilha das Flores* (*Isle of Flowers*, Jorge Furtado, 1989)

(and worse, being shooed away in favour of a stray dog), and there is even a reference in the film to Brazil being God's toilet. Both films set out to tackle, in a deeply ironic way, precisely the lack of visibility that Roberto DaMatta (2014) refers to in relation to what happens to the rubbish produced by Brazil's elites, and the extent to which it belies social injustice. *Ilha das Flores* in particular portrays the link between those who consume and those who dispose of the leftovers of this consumption, via the journey of the tomato. This link, as per DaMatta's previously mentioned observation, is very rarely exposed.

Catadores on screen

A number of documentaries, some of which have circulated widely both within Brazil and abroad, have chronicled the lives of those who survive by working on rubbish dumps. In a seemingly remarkable coincidence, it is another UK-Brazil co-production, the Oscar-nominated *Waste Land* (Lucy Walker, João Jardim and Karen Harley, 2010), that is the best known of these films.[6] The film follows the acclaimed artist and philanthropist Vik Muniz as he works with a group of litter pickers at Jardim Gramacho to reproduce classic works of art made from rubbish, in what clearly is not only an artistic endeavour, but also one that is both consciousness-raising and life-affirming for the participants: for good reason the Portuguese title of the film translates as "extraordinary rubbish". Marcos Prado's lyrical portrait of Estamira, in the 2004 film of the same name, likewise reveals treasure (the remarkably insightful, if troubled, 63-year-old, a 20-year veteran of the Gramacho dump). What these films have in common with *Trash* is that they challenge the idea of the worthlessness of the lives of those who survive on landfill site, revealing something of value amidst the waste, rather than the more prevalent view of them belonging on society's scrapheap.

In *Boca de lixo* (*The Scavengers*, 1993) acclaimed documentary filmmaker Eduardo Coutinho encouraged his "subjects" (the litter pickers) to emerge from a position of deep suspicion and shame at being caught on camera, to sharing their life stories. So while Coutinho admitted to being initially struck by the poverty of the Itaoca landfill site in São Gonçalo near Rio de Janeiro, where humans "fry eggs and play football" amongst the detritus (Mesquita 1999), humanising stories are gradually revealed and allowed to stand out and replace the images of extreme poverty that open the film. Boca de Lixo, and to a lesser extent *Estamira* and *Waste Land*, eschew the sweeping overhead shots of the monstrous eyesores of landfill sites, the "film-maker's dream" (Watts 2015) to which the *Guardian* correspondent had referred above, for close-ups of the people themselves.

Trash: synopsis

Trash is a UK–Brazil co-production, shot almost entirely in Portuguese with a mostly Brazilian cast and crew and filmed on location in Rio de Janeiro. The film is a faithful adaptation of English children's fiction writer Andy Mulligan's novel of the same name which was first published in 2010. Despite being dropped from the *Blue Peter* shortlist for best fiction award for containing one violent scene and the word "shit" (Pauli 2010), the book is a firm favourite on UK school reading lists. Mulligan's book is a fast-paced adventure story aimed at 12 year olds and set in an unnamed developing country (but the inspiration was a rubbish dump Mulligan visited in The Philippines, where he was working as an English teacher) with three child protagonists, Rafael, Gardo and Rat, who take it in turns to tell the tale of how they found a wallet in the rubbish dump where they worked, how the key inside it eventually led them to a fortune stolen by a political dissident from a corrupt politician, and how they were able to trick fate and gain access to a better life as a result. In Mulligan's words, the book "asks children to engage with brave, fierce street kids who dare to take on a dangerous world. They win, and in the process grow" (in Pauli 2010).

The film version is set in Rio de Janeiro and the shared narration is partly resolved in the film by an increase in dialogue, and partly by the introduction of a new element into the drama: the kids are filmed by their English teacher Olivia telling their story straight to camera, in a mixture of broken English (these sections were used for the eye-catching film trailer) and Portuguese. The film opens in true *pornomiseria* style, with a kid (Rafael, played by Rickson Tevez) pointing a gun at a man's head and being encouraged to kill him by another kid (Gardo, played by Eduardo Luis). It then pulls back both literally and metaphorically from this cliché. In the subsequent shot Rafael, looking straight to camera, informs viewers that if we are watching this, that he is probably dead: the police are after him because he has something belonging to an important politician. Then in a series of flashbacks and flash forwards, the story is very effectively set up. We then pick the story up and

Kill him - let's go!

FIGURE 9.2 Rafael (Rickson Tevez) being encouraged to shoot a detective. A still from *Trash: a esperança vem do lixo*

(*Trash*, Stephen Daldry and Christian Duurvoort, 2014)

follow it chronologically from the moment Rafael finds a wallet on the rubbish dump where he works.

Rafael's friend Gardo is introduced, as are the two English-speaking cast members: Father Juilliard, played by Martin Sheen, and charity worker and English teacher Olivia (Rooney Mara). Before night falls the police have already arrived at the dump in search of the wallet. Rafael's silence and awkward body language rouse the suspicions of a detective, Frederico. He will later return for Rafael, but not before the two boys have taken the wallet to an acquaintance, Rat (Gabriel Weinstein), an illiterate boy of a similar age who lives in the sewers, smells and is covered in sores. Rat recognises a key inside the wallet as belonging to lockers at the train station. A mini adventure ensues with upbeat chases as they dodge fellow street kids and security guards to open the locker and find, to their disappointment, nothing but a letter.

The letter leads the kids to a prison, yet more corrupt guards, a bible full of secret codes, the home of a corrupt politician, Santos, a cemetery with a coffin full of money and a ledger, another brush with the detective, and the kids' final escape to the coast. The ledger, which contains details of the payments received from a variety of businesses, is left with Father Juilliard and Olivia, who use the internet to expose Santos' corruption. The result of this is captured on a TV screen, which blends real-life footage of the June 2013 street protests with fictional street demonstrations in support of the missing kids and demanding that the corrupt Santos be brought to justice. We are in 2013, of course, and so the relationship between social media and political protest had not yet taken the very dark turn we witnessed on the run-up to the 2018 elections.

There are a number of references to iconic Brazilian films in *Trash*. The locker key leads the boys to the Central do Brasil, Rio's Central Station and the subject of the classic *retomada* film of the same name by Walter Salles (1998). In Salles's film the Central Station is the setting for a bag snatch of the kind staged by Gardo in *Trash* to create a diversion. However, in *Central do Brasil*, the young thief is dealt summary justice off-screen by the guard. Both films feature aerial shots of the famous serpentine Pedregulho social housing complex in Rio's São Cristóvão neighbourhood.[7] Like *Trash* and its three excellent young leads, and *City of God* before it, *Central Station* made use of an endearing non-professional actor from a deprived background, in this case Vinicius de Oliveira in the role of the young Josué. A now adult Leandro Firmino da Hora, Zé Pequeno (L'il Zé) in *City of God*, makes an appearance in *Trash*. In *Trash* the photography and mise-en-scene of the prison sequence are very reminiscent of Hector Babenco's blockbuster prison film *Carandiru* (2003). The original music, released on CD and digital download in 2015, was scored by Antonio Pinto who worked on *City of God* and *City of Men* (as well as Asif Kapadia's critically acclaimed documentaries *Senna* [2010] and *Amy* [2015]). The soundtrack includes the now iconic funk anthem Rap da Felicidade (Happiness Rap) by Cidinho e Doca, made famous by its inclusion in the dramatic opening sequence of *Tropa de Elite*.

There are two scenes of the kids swimming in the polluted lake by the rubbish dump: one during the day where the filth and health risks are made manifest, and another, at night time, with the surrounding favela lit up and a couple of shiny green plastic bottles as the only evidence of pollution in the water. There is something magical about the image, a favela seemingly at peace after the working day is over, which is reminiscent of both the original and the remake of *Black Orpheus* (*Orfée Negre* [Marcel Camus, 1959] and *Orfeu* [Carlos Diegues, 1999]) (see Chapter 8) and illustrates clearly the film's attempt to blend both realist and fantastical elements into both storytelling and style. A further example of this is the contrast between the entertaining mini-adventure referred to above, as the kids dribble round the law at Central Station, and the torture sequence which ensues when the corrupt

FIGURE 9.3 A battered and bruised Rafael (Rickson Tevez). A still from *Trash: a esperança vem do lixo*

(*Trash*, Stephen Daldry and Christian Duurvoort, 2014)

detective Francisco, played one-dimensionally by a woefully miscast Selton Mello, snatches Rafael from the dump, covers his head with a sack and drives him around at top speed in a car in an attempt to batter information out of him. As Rafael comments: "a polícia trata a gente que é pobre que nem lixo" (the police treat we poor people like rubbish).

Production

The adaptation was the brainchild of Kris Thykier of UK-based Peapie Films, a production company which, according to its website, has the ambition to a) make UK films with international appeal and b) to position itself. "as an able producer in local language in foreign territories". Thykier joined forces with the hugely successful UK production company Working Title, who brought on board two of the biggest and most successful directors and writers in film: the multi-Oscar nominated Stephen Daldry as director and Richard Curtis as scriptwriter. Daldry had previously worked with Working Title on *Billy Elliot* and Curtis on *Four Weddings and a Funeral*. Andy Mulligan was reportedly delighted with both the choice of production team, and the finished film: "As far as I'm concerned this is the dream-team, and what has really impressed me is their desire to tell the story as it is, without coating it in sugar. They 'get' the book, and you can't ask for more than that." (in Dawtrey 2011).

With Universal set to distribute worldwide, Fernando Meirelles' Brazil-based O2 Filmes were approached with a view to setting the film adaptation in Rio de Janeiro, and assisting with casting: both Brazilian megastars (Selton Mello; Wagner Moura) and new talent (Tevez, Luis and Weinstein). O2 brought on board Christian Duurvoort, an experienced acting coach, to both locate and train the new talent. Rickson Tevez and Gabriel Weinstein were spotted at initial workshops held in the Rocinha and Cidade de Deus favelas respectively, while Eduardo Luis hails from Inhauma, in the working-class north zone of Rio. Duurvoort worked with the kids for months prior to shooting: their dialogues were reportedly improvised, lending their performances a more authentic quality. Duurvoot's contribution, like that of Kátia Lund's in *City of God*, is acknowledged with a co-director credit.

Tulé Peake, who worked on *Tropa de Elite* and was Fernando Meirelles's production designer on *Domésticas* (2001), *City of God* and *Blindness* (2008), explained how he had to build from scratch a rubbish dump, a community on stilts, and a lake. The idea of the lake was to convey a sense of contamination: "an impactful image we tried to recreate was of a photograph in which poor kids are cheerfully swimming among the rubbish" (Ristow 2014). The likely reference here is a widely circulated photograph that first appeared in the *Jornal do Comércio* in 2009 of a small child swimming in what appears to be a lake made up entirely of filth and detritus.

In terms of the generation of an appropriate paracinematic narrative pre-and post-film release in order to garner attention and boost sales, producers and director played their parts accordingly. Reports described director Stephen Daldry's determination to live in Brazil on the run-up and throughout filming (for seven

FIGURE 9.4 Gardo (Gabriel Weinstein) takes a dip at the rubbish dump. A still from *Trash: a esperança vem do lixo*

(*Trash*, Stephen Daldry and Christian Duurvoort, 2014)

months in 2013, according to one report, and 18 months according to another), during which time he witnessed the June protests and what he interpreted to be a positive moment of hope for the country. Other reports focused on the meticulous selection process of the child actors (either 200 or 10,000 were screen-tested, depending on the news source: three were chosen), and on the landfill site built especially for filming to the west of Rio, with its use of (clean) recyclable plastic and paper.[8] Journalists were invited to visit the site, in the Complexo da Covanca in Jacarepaguá, during the 2013 Rio Film Festival. Co-producers discussed the film as a special case study feature at the same Festival's Film Market. Daldry attended a screening of *Billy Elliot* 2000 with disadvantaged children in the Complexo do Alemão favela as part of the British Council Transform cultural activities. He made much in interviews of the fact that Rooney Mara has worked in a children's charity in Kenya, and that Martin Sheen was involved with an NGO based in a landfill site in the Philippines over a 10-year period.[9] The film returned to the Rio Film Festival for its premiere in 2014, where it was the closing film. The cast, crew and production team were there en masse, as were a number of foreign film critics flown in by Universal, in what was one of the most glitzy premieres in the history of the Rio festival.

John Hopewell (2014) writing in *Variety* points to the "pioneering strategy" used by the producers of *Trash*, whereby the film started off on paper in the UK, and was then produced and launched in a different "home market" (Brazil). Hopewell thus reminds us of the many different ways that co-productions are made and the implications for the production companies involved and for the nations that they are frequently seen to represent. The film predates the UK-Brazil co-production treaty, signed in 2012 as part of a series of Olympic handover activities but only ratified in 2017. Given the complexity of making bilateral co-productions in Brazil without the support of a formal treaty, a

German producer was recruited to get round any bureaucratic constraints. The Germany-Brazil co-production treaty was signed in 2004 and has yielded critically acclaimed films, including a number by Berlin-based director Karim Ainouz, such as *Praia do Futuro* (*Future Beach*, 2014), discussed in Chapter Four, and *Central Airport THF* (2018).

With a keen eye on the potential that the Brazilian domestic market presents (which, as we saw in Chapter Two, generates audiences of upwards of five million for the most successful domestic products), the film was shot almost entirely in Portuguese. As producer Thykier put it: "Language is not the issue it once was. There's an audience willing to accept that people speak in different languages" (*Chicago Tribune* 2013). According to Daldry, a test screening was held in Los Angeles and the audience did not appear concerned that the dialogue was predominantly in Portuguese. It is worth recalling that the Portuguese-language *City of God* grossed $30 million in worldwide sales (and three times as much abroad as at home), while the English/Hindi *Slumdog Millionaire* (Danny Boyle 2008) made just under $378 million worldwide. In contrast, the last film made by Oscar-nominated Brazilian director Hector Babenco, *Meu amigo hindu* (*My Hindu Friend*, 2016): is set in São Paulo, stars Willem Dafoe, and is spoken entirely in English. It was poorly received by critics and the public, with the choice of language being highlighted as a particular weakness.

Reception and impact

Trash opened in Brazil on 300 screens within days of its star-studded premiere at the Rio film festival in October 2014. It sold 250,000 cinema tickets, a solid, but certainly not remarkable performance. By way of comparison, a similar number of tickets were sold to see *Jean-Charles* (Henrique Goldman, 2009), a film based on the last months of the life of Jean-Charles de Menezes, the Brazilian who was mistaken for a terror suspect and shot dead in Stockwell tube station in London in 2005. *Jean-Charles* is also a UK-Brazil co-production, and a film that has never been released commercially in the UK. *Trash* certainly outsold *Hoje eu quero voltar sozinho* (*The Way He Looks*, Daniel Ribeiro), the surprise "arthouse" hit of 2014 and Brazil's (unsuccessful) submission to the Oscars in 2015. But *The Way He Looks* cost under one million dollars to make, while *Trash* cost 12 million.

So why did a big-budget, mainstream, Portuguese-language film distributed by Universal, directed by three-times-Oscar-nominated Stephen Daldry and scripted by the hugely popular Richard Curtis not make a bigger dent at the Brazilian box-office? For a start, our analysis in this volume suggests that the backing of Globo Filmes, the film production arm of the mighty Globo media group, and the attendant TV advertising that comes with such backing, is more often than not essential in ensuring box-office success for domestic productions. The kind of popular appeal needed to get more than one million ticket sales at cinemas is not usually generated either in film festival launches, saturation advertising at art-house film theatres, or with token roles for American stars (Sheen and Mara).

That the film received a lukewarm reaction from Brazilian film critics will not have helped either, and a number of criticisms levelled at the film are difficult to challenge. There are flaws in the script which risk making the story incredulous beyond the point where the audience can play along and suspend disbelief: the ease with which the corrupt detective Frederico identifies the kids who had found the wallet on the dump site; the complete lack of repercussions from the blowing up of an entire community living alongside the dump; the fact that the political dissident's young daughter had been living in a graveyard and instantly helps and then runs away with the trio from the dump; and the scene (not in the book) where the three boys are rescued from a favela by older lads on motorbikes whom they had never met before. The awkward link between the final scenes, where the boys throw the money they find up in the air at the dumpsite to share with others, and popular revolt (in reference to the street protests of June 2013), and the previously mentioned torture scene, sit uncomfortably with the humorous, upbeat tone of what is otherwise an immensely enjoyable heist movie. While director Daldry may have liked the tonal complexity of the film which made it difficult to pigeon-hole (Wiseman 2015), this clearly was an issue for critics in Brazil.

In the UK, the promotion of *Trash* as a Working Title/Stephen Daldry/Richard Curtis/BAFTA-nominated vehicle ultimately amounted to nothing, with the film making a negligible impact at the box-office. It seems fair to suspect that the release date (squeezed into the busy pre-Oscar schedule) together with UK audiences' traditional aversion to (mainstream) subtitled films, and a reported lack of enthusiasm for the film on the part of Universal, resulted in *Trash* flopping in one of its two "home" markets. Producers may well have been banking on the film's superficial similarities to two of the most successful subtitled films in the UK market, *City of God* and *Slumdog Millionaire*, to attract large audiences, and there were certainly plenty of critics who made the connection both in the UK and Brazil, but both of these films could rely on a sophisticated and large-scale promotional strategy supported by multi-festival awards en route to their release in the UK. *Trash* won the Rome Film festival and played well in Italian cinemas,[10] and it was nominated for a British BAFTA for best film not in English, but it is hard to decipher a marketing strategy in place on the run-up to its release in the UK. Furthermore, no concession was made to cater for the readership that made the source text into a best-seller in the UK: the book's target age group (12-year-olds) were too young to legally view the film in theatres, and the text they had read, while being set in an unnamed developing country, was written in English.[11]

Through Focus World, a label launched by Focus Features (owned by Universal) in 2011 which concentrates on the video on demand (VOD) market, *Trash* gained a limited theatrical release and simultaneous VOD release in the US one year after its initial release in Brazil. Once again, the film failed to make an impact at the box-office, despite a number of optimistic features in the specialist film press and rumours of a never-realised Broadway musical adaptation. *Trash* thus failed to recoup even half of its cost in worldwide cinema ticket sales.

Concluding remarks

The optimism of which director Daldry had enthused when he witnessed the street protests of June 2013, with demonstrators dressed in Brazilian colours and singing the national anthem, had taken on arguably sinister connotations by 2014 and the time *Trash* was released. What had started as a bottom-up social-media-fuelled protest about the cost of public transport in São Paulo, particularly in the context of the massive public spending involved in hosting the Confederations Cup and later the World Cup football competitions, was rapidly transformed from the Movimento Passe Livre (Free Fare Movement) into the Movimento Brasil Livre (Free Brazil Movement), a libertarian-inspired movement which would later be instrumental both in drumming up the largest protests ever witnessed in Brazil in support for the legally dubious ousting of President Dilma Rousseff in 2016, and in the spreading of fake news and a pro-gun, anti-socialist sentiment on the run-up to presidential elections in 2018. As early as 2014 the closely fought presidential elections had already pointed to a deeply divided society and a noted shift by traditional centre-ground parties towards the right. Thus the link the film forges between the euphoria of the erstwhile disenfranchised street kids overcoming forces of evil in the guise of corrupt politicians, and the street protests, is confusing to say the least, and belies a lack of appreciation of Brazilian culture and history of the kind that "gringo" filmmakers are regularly accused of, as discussed in Chapter 8.[12]

One of the main good-news stories being promoted at the time of Brazil's hosting of the Rio +20 Global Sustainability Conference in 2012 was one of cutting down on waste: a law introduced in 2010 provided for the closure of all open landfill sites by 2014.[13] At the same time critical eyes were firmly placed on the organisers of both the World Cup and the Olympic Games with regard to needless spending at a time of economic crisis. The construction in 2013, from scratch, of a fictional open-air landfill site, less than one year after Jardim Gramacho was erased from domestic and international view, at a cost of millions of dollars and which would be burnt to the ground shortly after its construction for the purposes of making a two-hour British-backed movie, appeared to go against the direction of national socio-political and cultural travel in Brazil. This included efforts to clean up the environment, to provide evidence of the eradication of extreme poverty and to celebrate the spirit of *gambiarra*. One could also argue that the fable-like quality of the film, with its blending of realism and fantasy, was at odds with the narrative trajectory of Brazilian cinema at the time. And perhaps the action-packed, fast-paced dirt-poor street kids story had been told often enough. As critic Jean-Claude Bernardet has argued, "once it is aestheticised, poverty becomes depoliticised" (in Marcolin 2014).

Trash, directed by a white, middle-aged, well established British director, does not offer the worthy narrative of inclusion, widening participation and agency of those from deprived areas that is offered, for example, by *5x favela, agora por nós mesmos* (2010), the episodic film discussed in Chapter 5 made by graduates of the Cinema Nosso film programme.[14] Nor does it offer the testosterone-charged favela violence that proved popular with cinema-goers in relation to *Tropa de Elite I* and *II* discussed in Chapter 7, with their uniformed and armed crusader (police captain Nascimento). As Jean Montezuma (2015) observes, "the message delivered by the closing sequences [of *Trash*] is that change can only be achieved via collective action, and not by an individual project or by the heroic saviour typical of Hollywood films". The collective action in *Trash* relates to combatting high-level corruption of the kind witnessed in the Operation Car Wash grafting scandal, already in the news at the time of the film's development. What makes *Trash* unique is that it places three destitute but determined kids with a strong moral compass at the centre of the collective action against corruption. As Daldry stated:

> I wasn't going to impose some western idea [...] that everybody in these communities is immoral. It was challenging for some Brazilians to handle the idea the kids could have a strong moral compass. Many just want to build walls around those communities.
>
> *(Wiseman 2015)*

The kids do not serve as an exotic gun-touting or drug-dealing adornment, or as a lost cause in the crime-ridden context of favela life in Brazil. It is they who are committed to doing what is right (a phrase repeated in the dialogue), rather than the ineffectual potential (foreign) white saviours in the guise of Father Juilliard and Olivia.

> Rafael, Gardo and Gabriel in the real Brazil, according to the racist status quo, would be criminalised because of their race and class, animalised, and considered the personification of the enemy to be defeated. Through the story narrated in *Trash* they are given a voice, sentiments, identity: in short, they rediscover their humanity.
>
> *(Montezuma 2015)*

Notes

1 The idea of Rio as a fearful place of disease and contamination, which has plagued the city ever since it was founded in 1565 and became prone to outbreaks of yellow fever during the summer months, was exacerbated during the Rio Olympics by an untimely outbreak throughout the country of the Zika virus.
2 Dos Santos is the subject of a 1991 documentary by Eduardo Coutinho, *O fio da memória* (The Thread of Memory).
3 Three filmmakers: Fernando Meirelles, Daniela Thomas and Andrucha Waddington, were responsible for the artistic direction of the opening ceremony.
4 A good example of this phenomenon is *Bacalhau* (*Codfish*, Adriano Stuart, 1976), a "parody" of *Jaws* (Steven Spielberg, 1975) in which the mammoth and realistic shark is replaced with a cheap metal codfish. For more information see Dennison and Shaw (2004: 159–160).

5 Shoat and Stam's illustrative film of choice is the iconic *Bandido da luz vermelha* (*Red Light Bandit*, Rogério Sganzerla, 1968).

6 I have found no interviews with the cast and crew of *Trash* that refer to this film, released to great acclaim as *Trash* went into development.

7 Pedregulho also appears in *Fast Five* (Justin Lin 2011)

8 Seventy lorries were needed to transport the material to the set, where litter pickers, who also served as extras in the film, were paid to separate out any sharp objects. Everything was then washed with bleach: Ristow 2014.

9 What is surprising is that none of this fascinating paracinematic material is captured in a "Making Of", which would surely have enhanced DVD sales.

10 This success might be partly explained by the features *Trash* shares with Italian film traditions and in particular post-WWII neorealist films such as (*Rome, Open City*, Roberto Rossellini 1945) and *Ladri de biciclette* (*Bicycle Thieves,* Vittorio de Sica, 1948), with their underdog kids in crime-ridden cities filled with adventure, and the denunciation of corruption.

11 The DVD is used in classrooms in secondary schools in the UK as supporting material for the study of Mulligan's novel, and it occasionally finds its way onto viewing lists in Brazilian schools for its sociological value.

12 Jay Weissberg in *Variety* (2014) aptly describes Daldry's approach here as a desire to "work all angles".

13 "That the deadline was missed will surprise few Brazilians. More unsettling is that the law made virtually no difference at all. In 2010 42.4% of rubbish was dumped unsafely, according to ABRELPE, a group that represents the sanitation industry. By last year that had fallen – to 41.6%. In absolute terms the amount of misdirected garbage rose, from 23m to 32m tonnes": *Economist* 2015.

14 As far as I am aware, unlike *City of God, Slumdog Millionaire* and *Waste Land,* there was no legacy work conducted in relation to the poor communities and actors involved in *Trash.*

References

Agência Brasil. 2018. "Brasília hosts int'l conference on solid waste management". *Agência Brasil.* 4 June. http://agenciabrasil.ebc.com.br/en/internacional/noticia/2018-05/brasilia-hosts-intl-conference-solid-waste-management.

Conde M. and Dennison, S. (eds). 2018. *Paulo Emílio Salles Gomes: On Brazil and Global Cinema.* Cardiff: University of Wales Press.

DaMatta, R. 2014. "O que se faz sem pensar?". *O globo.* 12 March. https://oglobo.globo.com/opiniao/o-que-se-faz-sem-pensar-11853058.

Dawtrey, A. 2011. "Working Title, Thykier Nab *Trash*". *Variety.* 5 April https://variety.com/2011/film/markets-festivals/working-title-thykier-nab-trash-1118034983/.

Diniz, E. 2018. "A realidade de Gramacho seis anos depois". *Jornal da PUC.* 25 May. http://jornaldapuc.vrc.puc-rio.br/cgi/cgilua.exe/sys/start.htm?infoid=7532&sid=29.

Hopewell, J. 2014. "Stephen Daldry's *Trash* to Close Rio Festival". *Variety.* 6 September https://variety.com/2014/film/festivals/stephen-daldrys-trash-to-close-rio-festival-1201299709/

Economist. 2015. "Legislative Landfill". *Economist.* 13 August https://www.economist.com/the-americas/2015/08/13/legislative-landfill.

Linnenkoper, K. 2015. "Brazil Sets New Can Recycling World Record". *Recycling International*, 16 December. https://recyclinginternational.com/non-ferrous-metals/brazil-sets-new-can-recycling-world-record/.

Mesquita, C. 1999. "Eduardo Coutinho e o rito da palavra". *Revista Palavra.* September.

Montezuma, J. 2015. "'A polícia trata a gente que é pobre que nem lixo': Reflexões sobre o filme *Trash*". *Esquerda Online*. 7 September. https://blog.esquerdaonline.com/?p=5354.

Mori, L. 2017. "'Acham que a gente é lixo': a rede invisível de catadores que processa tudo o que é reciclado em SP". *BBC Brasil Online*. 20 July. https://www.bbc.com/portuguese/brasil-40664406.

Marcolin N. 2014. "Jean-Claude Bernardet: um critico contra a estética da miséria". *Revista pesquisa.* October. http://revistapesquisa.fapesp.br/2014/10/09/jean-claude-bernardet-um-critico-contra-estetica-da-miseria/.

Pauli, M. 2010. "Andy Mulligan Talks Trash". *Guardian.* 20 December. https://www.theguardian.com/books/2010/dec/20/andy-mulligan-trash-blue-peter.

Ristow, F. 2014. "Equipe de *Trash* conta como foi feito o lixo cenográfico do filme". *Globo.* 9 October. https://oglobo.globo.com/cultura/filmes/equipe-de-trash-conta- como-foi-feito-lixao-cenografico-do-filme-14109991.

Rocha, G. 1995. "An Esthetic of Hunger". In Johnson, R. and Stam. R (eds). *Brazilian Cinema.* New York: Columbia University Press, pp. 68–71.

Rodrigues, N. 1993. *À sombra das chuteiras imortais.* São Paulo: Companhia das Letras.

Shoat, E. and Stam, R. 2014. *Unthinking Eurocentrism: Multiculturalism and the Media* 2nd Edn London and New York: Routledge.

Stam, R. 1997. *Tropical Multiculturalism: A Comparative History of Race in Cinema and Culture.* Durham and London: Duke University Press.

Chicago Tribune. 2013. "*Trash*: A pioneering UK-Brazil Co-production". *Chicago Tribune.*

Watts, J. 2015. "Life Amid the Trash of a Rio Dump". *Guardian*. 19 January. https://www.theguardian.com/world/2015/jan/19/trash-rio-de-janeiro-waste-tip-film.

Vieira, J. L. 2003. "*Chronically Unfeasible*: The Political Film in a Depoliticised in with World". In Nagib, L. (ed) *The New Brazilian Cinema.* London and New York: IB Tauris, pp. 85–94.

Weissberg, J. 2014. "Film Review: *Trash*". *Variety*. 7 October. https://variety.com/2014/film/festivals/film-review-trash-1201323827/.

Wiseman, A. 2015. "Stephen Daldry, *Trash*". *Screen Daily*. 23 January. https://www.screendaily.com/awards/stephen-daldry-trash/5082125.article.

10

A CORDIAL VIEW FROM BRAZIL'S NORTH-EAST

Kleber Mendonça Filho's *Aquarius* (2016)

Aquarius is the second feature film by Kleber Mendonça Filho, film critic-turned director from the northeastern city of Recife whose feature debut *O som ao redor* (*Neighbouring Sounds*) was received with huge critical acclaim in 2012. With five-star reviews in Brazil's main broadsheets, *Aquarius* was described in the foreign press as "tremendous" (Collin 2017), "marvellous (Scott 2016), "remarkable" (Kermode 2017) in what was a consensually positive reaction when compared to the other high-profile critical hits of the twenty-first century, *Cidade de Deus* (*City of God*, Fernando Meirelles and Kátia Lund, 2002) and *Tropa de elite* (*Elite Squad*, José Padilha, 2007). With an impressive trajectory through the international film festival circuit (Cannes official competition and prizes in Sydney, Mar del Plata, Havana and Cartagena), *Aquarius* also marked the return to form (and a strong role) for veteran film and TV actress Sônia Braga, a fact equally celebrated in most reviews of the film. *Aquarius* also proved its commercial worth by being snapped up by Netflix (worldwide except Brazil) shortly after its appearance at Cannes.

The purpose of this chapter is twofold. First, it examines the film itself, and in particular the tropes of intimacy and cordiality as manifested in the relationship between the two principal female characters. In this it builds in part on ideas explored in Chapter 3 in relation to *Que horas ela volta?* (*The Second Mother*, Anna Muylaert, 2015) and the representation in the shift in relations between maids and mistresses in the twenty-first century. Secondly, it reads *Aquarius* within the broader cultural context as illustrative of the complex relationship films can have with public diplomacy goals, particularly in times of political reorganisation and a re-consideration of national narratives.

Intimacy in Brazilian culture and the roots of the "cordial man"

There is a growing interest, on the part of scholars, social media users and increasingly of filmmakers, in the shift in perceptions of the role of maids and nannies in

Brazil. The archaic presence of a live-in and frequently uniformed maid in an ultra-modern home has become increasingly viewed as anachronistic in contemporary Brazilian society, particularly after the passing of the so-called *PEC das domésticas* (the constitutional amendment that regulates the working conditions of domestic workers). A frequent discussion point on social media is that, as a result of greater access to higher education for women and improvements in female workers' rights, including those of domestic workers, middle-class families can no longer afford to keep a maid. Suddenly the erstwhile invisible maids and nannies have shifted to centre stage on social media when an opportunity for ironic photography presents itself, particularly when it is set up to mock white privilege. By way of example, during the pro-impeachment street protests of 2015 and 2016 a series of images went viral of families protesting on a Sunday, accompanied by their uniformed maids.[1]

More nuanced discussions of the relationship between maids and their mistresses (*empregadas* and *patroas*) have been explored by contemporary filmmakers, and these discussions are clearly inspired by the work of two of the "foundational fathers" of Brazilian national identity: Sérgio Buarque de Holanda and Gilberto Freyre, explored briefly here. A number of public intellectuals have made recent reference to the idea of the "Homem Cordial" (the cordial man), first coined by poet Ribeiro Couto (Bezerra, 2004) but more commonly attributed to Sérgio Buarque de Holanda and his foundational text *Raízes do Brasil* or Roots of Brazil, first published in 1936. The most cited section from Buarque de Holanda's book is Chapter 5, entitled "O homem cordial". And some of those intellectuals (Maria Rita Kehl [in Vianna, 2014], Lilia Schwarcz [2008] and Jessé Souza [2017], for example) have been at pains to point out that Buarque de Holanda's "Cordial Man" as he conceived him has nothing to do with being cordial in the sense of friendly and hospitable, or any such definition that is often used to define the supposedly infinitely likeable Brazilians. The blame for this misappropriation of Buarque de Holanda's theorising is laid firmly at the feet of poet Cassiano Ricardo (1959), charged with simplifying the term to mean something positive: *bondade* or goodness/kindness. Rather, according to those at pains to redress this misunderstanding of Buarque de Holanda's concept, the "Homem Cordial" is someone who is driven by emotions (etymologically, cordial derives from *cordis*, from the heart), which are not, necessarily, exclusively positive. According to Buarque de Holanda, one of the results of this emotional drive is an inability to distinguish between the private and the public (Buarque de Holanda 2004: 145).

This reading of Buarque de Holanda's work is not strictly accurate, however. One implication of Brazilians being driven by emotions and being incapable of distinguishing between the private and the public sphere, is a particular way of interacting socially whereby the default is a kind of familiarity that one might describe as intimate (Buarque de Holanda 2004: 148). Buarque de Holanda himself describes the "Cordial Man" as characterised by gentleness in personal encounters, hospitality and generosity (146). And this is certainly how the idea of the "Homem cordial" has been interpreted over the years. When Buarque de Holanda argues that it would be wrong to suppose that these virtues would translate as good manners and civility (148), what he is pointing to is *not* how these social interactions are played out, but to their real meaning. In other words, they serve as a kind of façade or mask (147).

Another important reference with regard to questions of intimacy and present-day maid/mistress relations is Gilberto Freyre's seminal *Casa-grande & senzala* (*The Masters and the Slaves*), first published in 1933. In it Freyre argues that sugarcane plantation society of the Northeast of Brazil (and in particular the state of Pernambuco, where *Aquarius* is set) provided the blueprint for social interaction in Brazil thereafter. Freyre's most significant contribution to debates about Brazilian national identity was to argue for a positive interpretation of *mestiçagem* or race mixing. Within this interpretation he made the claim that the slave system was softer than in other slave cultures such as the United States and Spanish America. It is a claim that still has currency in many circles to this day. The set-up of the sugar mills led to an intimacy between the races, whereby whites and blacks lived together (the slave quarters or *senzalas* were in close proximity to the *casa-grande* or the big house) and domestic slaves, we are told, enjoyed access to the private spaces of the *casa-grande* as well as private family moments. Thus, for example, much is made of the employ of black wet nurses. In fact the wet nurse is used by Freyre to illustrate the extent to which even white Brazilians can claim *mestiçagem*, and it is worth noting that this exchange of bodily fluids is mentioned in the same sentence as the exchange of bodily fluids of the first sexual encounters of young masters with supposedly lascivious female slaves (Freyre, ND, 279).

I am simplifying Freyre's arguments considerably here, for it is certainly not the case that Freyre was incapable of being critical of slavery and of the treatment of slaves at the hands of their masters and mistresses. But in this chapter I am seeking merely to tease out the origins of this idea of intimacy between masters and domestic servants that is so important for appreciating the message, or at least one of the very many messages, of *Aquarius*, and of Kleber Mendonça Filho's work more broadly. It also speaks to a host of other films released in the second decade of the twenty-first century that tackle these thorny issues.

A number of recent films have taken as their main focus a questioning of what would otherwise be deemed outmoded social relations between maids and mistresses: as well as *Que horas ela volta?* there is Consuelo Lins's *Babás* (*Nannies*, 2010) and Gabriel Mascaro's *Doméstica* (*Housemaids*, 2012) and others that deal more generally with social "throwbacks" to the alleged cordiality and intimacy of plantation times, as witnessed in the very titles of films such as *Casa Grande* (2014), *As boas maneiras* (*Good Manners*, 2017) and *O animal cordial* (*Friendly Beasts* in English, but literally *The Cordial Animal*, 2017). Mendonça Filho's concern to reflect on contemporary north-eastern Brazilian culture and society within the paradigm of plantation society as defined by the likes of Gilberto Freyre and Sérgio Buarque de Holanda in the 1930s was already made explicit in two of his films that predate *Aquarius*: the short film *Recife frio* (*Cold Tropics*, 2009) and his first feature film *O Som ao redor*. Looking first at *Cold Tropics*, the film portrays in tongue-in-cheek style the impact on a range of people of an inexplicable freezing cold front that hits Recife, a city where daily temperatures rarely fall below 30 degrees centigrade. Some inhabitants make a better job of attempting to adapt than others, such as the handicraft seller who quickly introduces characters in scarves and bobble hats into his repertoire of souvenir figurines for sale. One wealthy family in particular struggles to cope with the new realities the cold front brings: having deliberately chosen an apartment that is designed to take advantage architecturally of whatever little breeze there was in the built-up and poorly planned city, the family cannot get warm at home. But in traditional large middle-class apartments with space tucked away from the airy family and social areas to the back of the kitchen designed for use by domestic staff, there will always be an impossibly warm room: the one originally designated for a live-in maid. In *Cold Tropics* a teenage boy swaps bedroom, without thinking twice about it in what is played out as a perfectly natural course of action to take, with the maid, who is clearly unhappy with the situation, and freezing cold, but whose behaviour also suggests that the swap is an acceptable course of action, just one of the "taken-for-granted asymmetries of daily life" (Pinho 2015: 104).

It is this cordial normalisation of otherwise peculiar and unequal power relations between social groups that seem to hark back to plantation times (the physical proximity but extreme difference in conditions between those that occupied the *casa-grande* and the *senzala*, for example) that Mendonça Filho is clearly interested in. *O som ao redor* opens with a scene that is set up to demonstrate the extent to which modern middle-class life in Recife continues with plantation traditions, with its juxtaposition of old black and white photographs of plantation buildings and moving images of middle-class kids playing in the social space of a modern apartment block, with a static line of maids and nannies lined up in the background. In fact, the interactions of middle-class families in a traditional wealthy neigh-bourhood in Recife with those they employ in a domestic setting (maids, nannies, security guards, porters, and so on), and the tensions and subsequent breaks in cor-diality that ensue from challenges to ingrained social conventions that dictate these interactions, lie at the heart of much of the narrative of *O som ao redor*. Mendonça Filho also demonstrates in this film his fascination with the subject of the modern maid. For example, a shot of the interior of an apartment in which the screen is split in two by a pillar, with the uniformed maid one side working, and the neigh-bourhood "patriarch" on the other at leisure, visually spells out the hierarchical divisions that continue to exist. Mendonça Filho goes on to problematise this static vision of social hierarchies, and hint at a change, by granting the maid some agency: she is seen getting changed out of her uniform and meeting up with a lover for an impromptu sexual encounter while out on an errand for her boss.

But my focus here is Mendonça Filho's second feature film *Aquarius*, and while there is a great deal else to say about the broad issues of intimacy and cordiality in relation to the film,[2] I will for the purposes of this chapter concentrate on the relationship between the protagonist, Clara, played by Sônia Braga, and her maid Ladjane, played by Zoraide Coleto.

FIGURE 10.1 Spatial separation in the modern-day *casa-grande*. A still from *O som ao redor*

(*Neighbouring Sounds*, Kleber Mendonça Filho, 2013)

"Almost family": Clara and Ladjane

When we meet Clara as played by Sônia Braga[3] the maid Ladjane has been with her for nineteen years. Clara is a widow and retired music critic in her sixties who desperately wants to stay in her Recife beach-front apartment in the Aquarius block, the apartment where she has lived for most of her life, and where she brought up her three children. But she is under pressure from a property development company, and in particular the young and ambitious Diego to sell up and move on: she is the only remaining occupant in the building. Our sympathies very much lie with Clara, not just because of her playing David to the property developers' Goliath, but also because she is smart, sassy, seemingly liberal and progressive in her thinking, and refreshingly sexually liberated.

This is the main focus of the film and Clara's relationship with Ladjane is at first glance presented as background detail. Ladjane appears to be part of a network of "friends" and extended family members (along with her favourite nephew Tomás, her sister-in-law Fátima, her lawyer friend and confidant Cleide, the lifeguard Roberval who keeps her from danger as she takes her daily swim in the sea, and so on) who support her in one form or another and enable her to live the independent lifestyle she has come to enjoy. A kind of extended family as it were, that compliments her immediate family comprising her three grown-up children, but without the tensions that can come from such blood ties. Such tension is demonstrated, for example, in the film by her daughter Ana Paula who confronts her mother over her decision to stay on in the apartment.

Ladjane is portrayed as Clara's first line of defence against the "evil" property developers, so much so that in one of our first encounters with her, she is gently scolded by Clara for not answering the door to Diego and his grandfather, in order to spare her employer the ordeal of an awkward conversation on her doorstep[4] about her future in the building. As mentioned previously, Mendonça Filho had already reflected on the occupation of different spaces within the home of maids and the middle-class families they serve in his previous work. But unlike *O som ao redor*, in which one of the (much younger) maids depicted is shown to have an adventurous private life beyond the home in which she works, Ladjane is mostly filmed working in a good-humoured fashion, in the kitchen. In fact, Ladjane is only filmed beyond Clara's apartment and its grounds when she appears in one scene in her own home, thus binding her exclusively to the domestic sphere. It is interesting to note that, in one of Clara's displays of intimacy in the form of physical affection towards Ladjane on the occasion of her birthday, she sings the first couple of bars of an alternative Happy Birthday song (more on this later) that references happiness within the home. But as we shall see, there is a time and place for such displays of intimacy and for them to be socially acceptable, they must be initiated by Clara.

The positioning of Ladjane at work in the kitchen warrants further comment here. As Patricia Pinho reminds us in her excellent study of maid/mistress relations in Brazilian "common sense", the commonplace image of maids constantly busy in the kitchen enables them to be understood as an "endless source of labour" (Pinho, 2015, 116).[5] We witness this in a scene in *Aquarius* in which Clara is spending time with her three grown-up children (one assumes at the weekend and on the maid's day off). In what turns into a tense conversation about the disadvantages of staying in the otherwise empty apartment block, Clara suddenly interrupts to remind them to wash up their wine glasses, "porque hoje não tem Ladjane" (literally "because there's no Ladjane today"), offering a kind of X ray of how otherwise liberal middle classes live and the extent to which they depend on a maid for the most basic of activities. Had she been present, Ladjane would have been expected to wash the glasses, regardless of what other tasks she had scheduled to carry out.

Subaltern hauntings

There is one scene in *Aquarius* that problematises the relationship between maids and their mistresses and moves us away from what could otherwise be understood, as it most often is in Brazil, as a cordial and therefore both a natural and special relationship between employer and employee. In the scene some family members (Clara's brother, sister-in-law and nephews, plus their girlfriends) are in Clara's apartment. One of the nephews is getting married and wants to look through old family photos to incorporate some into their wedding video. While looking through the photos Clara comes across images of a one-time family maid whose name initially escapes her. That is, until something jogs her memory: Juvenita the maid, or some kind of vision of the maid, fleetingly appears in the corridor. Clara is initially indignant about the fact that the maid had stolen from the family, but later agrees with her sister-in-law who contextualises this within a culture of exploitation:

> **Fátima:** Mas é inevitável, né? A gente explora elas. Elas roubam a gente de vez em quando. E assim vai, né?
> **Clara:** Tá certo.

(**Fátima:** Yeah, well, it's inevitable, isn't it? We exploit them. They steal from us here and there. And so it goes, huh?

Clara: You're right.)

In this sequence Mendonça Filho also reflects on the "normalisation" of this practice of truncating or erasing, in the selection of photos of the mysterious, thieving maid Juvenita, whose name they now barely recall. She first appears truncated in a photograph, then in full frame but the features of her face cannot be seen. She is thus transformed into an embodiment of blackness and that blackness is perceived as threatening and dangerous, upsetting an otherwise joyful journey back in time via the family photos. It is telling that the nephew, who is capturing images of the old photos on his mobile phone, performs a gesture designed to distance himself from the threat, and from a whole social group, one might argue, by literally whitening himself: he uses an app on his phone to "brighten" his face and arms in an image he has captured of himself as a young child.[6]

For most of the photo-sharing scene in the film, the camera mimics a curious gaze, panning across and upwards on the photos, zooming in and out, honing in, for example, on the word *Bacharéis* (or graduates), in what has to be an ironic gesture to supposedly socially situate the middle-class people in the photo. I say most, but not the whole scene, for the camera remains static, indifferent, perhaps, when photos of Juvenita are produced, as if suggesting for viewers that there is nothing interesting to be seen here. The photos of Juvenita interrupt the otherwise natural flow of the conversation and the movement of the camera. This indifference continues when Ladjane interrupts the family photo-viewing session, ostensibly to offer the guests a top-up of wine. She then produces a photo of her dead son (we learn earlier that he was killed in a road accident and the police had done nothing to find his killer). We are not shown this photo (it is the discomfort on the faces of the family members for the untimely interruption that we focus on). And in this shot Ladjane is also tellingly truncated, both at the level of the narrative (as the awkward, mostly silent response to her interjection demonstrates), but also in the shot itself.[7] Ladjane, by interrupting the social time of her *patroa* in a non-work-related gesture, demonstrates a failure to "know her place" (Pinho, 2015, 107). Pinho draws on the work of Brazilian philosopher Marilena Chauí and argues that there is "a binary contrast between those who produce 'competent discourse' and are consequently entitled to give orders, and those who are deemed 'socially incompetent' and are therefore expected to obey" (Chauí 1981). The central rule that governs competent discourse is that "it is not anybody that can say anything to anybody else in any occasion in any place" (Pinho 2015: 117). In the scene under discussion everyone, Clara and her sister-in-law included, are complicit in pointing this out to Ladjane and thus prolonging this practice.

In *Aquarius* a seeming levelling takes place in a dream sequence, which appears shortly after the sequence under discussion. The sequence makes canny use of a split optic to show both Juvenita, foregrounded (and thus in close up and, unusually, her dark skin is very effectively lit), and Clara in the background. Both are in focus,

FIGURE 10.2 The maid Ladjane's truncated body. A still from *Aquarius* (Kleber Mendonça Filho, 2016)

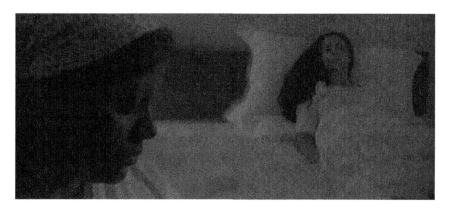

FIGURE 10.3 The maid Juvenita appears to Clara in a dream. A still from *Aquarius* (Kleber Mendonça Filho, 2016)

thus arguably levelling the two women and their life stories. Juvenita is noticeably sitting on Clara's bed, thus breaking one of the unwritten rules of etiquette within mistress/maid relations.[8] But of course this levelling does not take place in the real world: Clara is both dreaming and arguably disadvantaged through illness, since a reference is made by Juvenita to Clara's bleeding breast.

At home with Ladjane

Returning to Clara's relationship with Ladjane: as a "mistress" Clara may well come across as progressive in the sense that she is happy to visit Ladjane's home in the poorer end of town on the occasion of her birthday. This certainly would not be a common practice in traditional Brazilian *patroa/empregada* relations. In the scene

Clara walks along the middle-class Pina beach with her nephew and his girlfriend who has just arrived from Rio de Janeiro. Clara points out the sewer that literally and figuratively separates rich and poor on this part of Recife's coast (another demonstration of the physical proximity yet huge disparity in quality of life between rich and poor in the city). They are now in the favela of Brasília Teimosa. But one might also read the visit to Ladjane's less as a selfless and generous gesture and more as an opportunity to demonstrate to her visitor from Rio, whom she seems keen to impress, how progressive she is by offering her an alternative sightseeing opportunity, not that far removed from the *favela tours* that have become popular in Rio de Janeiro even among liberal-minded tourists. And when Clara gets to Ladjane's house, she is more interested in gossiping with her best friend Letícia[9] about her night of passion with a male escort.

While in her own milieu Ladjane is allowed to show the photo of her son: a poster-sized image is on display and notably not commented on by Clara in the scene. The next day Clara and Ladjane share a tender moment, as they chat intimately about the party and Clara compliments Ladjane on how lovely she looked. But the conversation notably takes place in Clara's kitchen (and Ladjane's "space"), and not in the lounge, thus fusing demonstrations of kindness with paternalism. As Pinho argues, "although perceived as benevolent gestures, these practices serve to keep the class boundaries and the structure of domination very much in place" (109).

Singing songs of cordiality

Recalling the sister-in-law's aforementioned observation about the condition of domestic servants in Brazil, Ladjane is seen in *Aquarius* to be exploited, in as much as she serves as a substitute nanny for Clara's grandson when her daughter Ana Paula sacks her own nanny. This takes place in the film in the most natural and

FIGURE 10.4 Ladjane's humble abode in Brasília Teimosa, overshadowed by middle-class high-rises in Recife. A still from *Aquarius*

(Kleber Mendonça Filho, 2016)

matter-of-fact way: Ana Paula arrives at Clara's apartment looking anguished, asks her mother to look after the child, but hands him to Ladjane. And it is interesting to note the language of exchange used by Ana Paula in describing sacking her nanny and seeking a replacement, pointing to an objectification of nannies and maids whereby domestic help continues to be treated as chattel. We here recall the juxtaposition in the photo-sharing scene described above of images of maids and images of cars, and their implied equivalence in relation to the status of middle-class families.

This same grandchild, who gains a nanny who is not contracted to work for him, but who assumes the role through social convention, is played a tune by grandma Clara from the Canções de Cordialidade. The "Songs of Cordiality" were written by nationalist composer Heitor Villa Lobos, with words by the modernist poet from Recife Manuel Bandeira in the mid-1940s as "cordial" songs that could be sung in domestic settings to encourage friendliness and hospitality. The Brazilian Happy Birthday song, for example, which is one of the five Canções de Cordialidade, is played as an alternative in both *O som ao redor* and *Aquarius*. And the book that notably took Clara away from her children for a few years to conduct research (a sore point in particular for Clara's daughter Ana Paula in the film), was a biography of Villa Lobos. This reference to cordiality makes explicit Mendonça Filho's concern to weave into the very fabric of the film the kind of discussion of what remains of sugar plantation culture in social relations in Recife, and hints at a perpetuation of such social relations. Thus, in *Aquarius* the past flows into the present in terms of social practices, just as it does in the film through music, photographs, furniture, apartments, and so on.

Clara might well strive to be progressive in many aspects of her life but she is trapped within a very culturally specific set of social conventions as demonstrated by her relationship with Ladjane and her inability to not play the "sinhazinha" or plantation mistress, and here I am borrowing a term used by actress Sônia Braga in the DVD commentary to describe Clara's relationship with Ladjane. As Pinho argues, within this very specific Brazilian dynamic "intimacy and emotion soothe inequality" (113), and, we might argue, the cordiality of these relations prolongs the existence of the unequal power relationship between *patroa e empregada* or mistress and maid.[10] This in turn helps to maintain a lingering sense that the work and status of a live-in maid are somehow "special" and should thus not be subject to the same scrutiny to which we subject other forms of labour relations in Brazil. It is worth observing that Clara resorts to the same vices of personalism, patronage and nepotism to resolve her "issue" in the film (that is, how to get the property developers off her case).[11]

On the surface the plot of *Aquarius* focuses on the rampant, unplanned and ethically suspect real-estate speculation and its impact on the lives of those who live in the city of Recife, Mendonça Filho's home town. In comparison the critique of maid/mistress relations is subtly embedded in the narrative. Like the photographs of truncated, blurred and hidden maids mentioned earlier, we have to work hard as viewers to spot them, and particularly given that we are dealing with a lead character that is otherwise portrayed as a liberal-minded heroine.

The impact of *Aquarius* at home and abroad

In Chapter 1 I made reference to the protest staged by Mendonça Filho and members of his cast and crew at the Cannes film festival. The director and other representatives of the film held aloft A4 sheets of paper written in English and French stating "A coup took place in Brazil", "The world cannot accept this illegitimate government" and "54, 501, 118 votes set on fire". The backlash at home on social media was initially aimed at Sônia Braga, who as a Hollywood player in her heyday in the 1970s and 80s served as a Brazilian soft-power asset through her promotion of Brazilian film culture.[12] Sônia had no business bringing shame upon the nation, critics at home insisted (this was a widely used phrase on social media at the time), and she had no business commenting on politics, because she is based in New York. Criticisms were also voiced by the new Minister of Culture Marcelo Calero, who described the protest as "childish". "It's wrong", he said in interview on national television, in a reference to the director Mendonça Filho, "in the name of a personal political position, to cause damage to the reputation and image of Brazil" (*Globo* 2016). Mendonça Filho did not hesitate to respond directly to Calero via his personal Facebook page, reminding him that *The New York Times* had listed his debut feature as one of the top films of 2012, while in the same post drawing attention to a report by the newspaper into corruption in Brazil's interim government. Mendonça Filho wrote: "Perhaps this will make you rethink the notion of bringing shame onto Brazil" (ZH Entretenimento, 2016).

Calero abruptly resigned from his post as Culture Minister in November 2016, claiming to have been placed under pressure by a fellow government minister to take advantage of his position and interfere with a national heritage decision. The irony here is that the case in question involved a real estate issue that is uncannily similar to the one at the heart of the plot of *Aquarius*. Calero's subsequent TV interview, in which he claimed to have been taken by surprise at the corruption within government, was greeted with derision on social media by Mendonça Filho.

Suspicion that the overtly political gesture in Cannes had ruled *Aquarius* out of consideration to represent Brazil at the Oscars (for best film not in English) was raised when Marcos Petruccelli, a vociferous critic of Mendonça Filho and his political views, was appointed to the local selection committee. The film was then granted an 18 certificate of release in Brazil, a veritable box-office "kiss of death".[13] Suspecting foul play, three filmmakers, Anna Muylaert, Gabriel Mascaro and Aly Muritiba withdrew their films (*Mãe só há uma* [*Don't Call Me Son*, 2016] discussed in Chapter 3, *Boi Neon* [*Neon Bull*, 2016] and *Para minha amada morta* [*For My Beloved*, 2016] respectively) from the selection in protest. Under pressure, two of the committee members then resigned. The depleted committee selected *O pequeno segredo* (*Little Secret*, David Shurmann, 2016), something of a mystery to most, given that it had not been released at the time of selection.

Even if we were to dismiss the convincing claims that the selection process was fixed,[14] this decision appears to demonstrate a complete lack of awareness on the part of audio-visual and government personnel who make up these selection panels of what constitutes a likely Oscar winner, and as a corollary to this, of what film can do for a nation's public diplomacy. Oscar-winning best foreign films tend to be those that have, or will have played on the festival circuit and have garnered prizes along the way, thus increasing their chances of playing as widely as possible in the US. They often have their own provocative back story. They usually have achieved both critical and public support. And crucially, they are more likely to challenge than endorse the socio-political status quo. As soft-power theorist Joseph Nye (2013) has highlighted, there is little international audience for "brittle propaganda". The rejection of *Aquarius* is symptomatic of the kind of government intervention that potentially compromises the investment and energy put into raising the visibility of Brazilian cinema abroad, from a soft power or public diplomacy perspective.

Worthy of consideration in relation to *Aquarius* is the fact that in reviews of the film in the international press, we see no real focus on any negative features of the nation that the socially conscious story throws up: uncontrolled real-estate speculation,[15] corruption, outmoded social practices, and so on. Instead, as captured in Robbie Collins's giddy review of the film in *The Telegraph* (2017), the country portrayed in *Aquarius* is cordial in the sense of supremely likeable: Collins declares that watching the film will make us want to move to Brazil.

In May 2018 Mendonça Filho published an open letter addressed to the Brazilian Ministry of Culture, in which he made public that he had received a demand for the return of funding awarded to his first feature film, *O som ao redor*, based on the assertion that his production company Cinemascópio had also secured funding from Funcultura, the state cultural funder in Pernambuco. In his open reply, which was reproduced by the national broadsheets, Mendonça Filho stated that Cinemascópio had indeed secured funding beyond the low-budget film award they received, but that they had followed regulations by consulting with the Ministry of Culture's Audio-visual Secretariat first, all of which is documented. Mendonça Filho also drew attention to the fact that *O som ao redor* cost less than 500,000 dollars to make. "The Ministry of Culture should reward producers who achieve so much with a film budget that is so modest" (Mendonça Filho 2018).

What is striking in this case is that demands for the return of funding are usually made in the case of film projects that have not come to fruition, or where there is an issue relating to how accounts have been presented (see Chapter 1). The impression that many observers were left with, therefore, was that the Ministry of Culture, and specifically the Minister, Sérgio Sá Leitão, took advantage of the cumbersome bureaucracy of film funding mechanisms to falsely accuse a politically dissenting filmmaker of corruption.

In relation to the controversy surrounding *Aquarius* in Brazil film critic Luiz Zanin made an observation in relation to politics and film culture that, in the light of Mendonça Filho's ongoing battles with the State, may prove to be prophetic:

Brazilian democracy is in danger. Part of Brazilian culture, almost alone as a focus of resistance, is beginning to suffer systematic persecution. Another part, as far as one can tell, has already adhered. This part takes no risks and will flatter any regime. They settled for the military dictatorship, so why wouldn't they settle now?

(Zanin Oricchio 2016)

Notes

1 See, for example, the widely commented controversy surrounding the participation of a middle-class white family accompanied by their black nanny in an anti-government demonstration: Felix 2016.

2 Consider for example the gradual increase in tension in the interactions between the film's protagonist Clara and her nemesis, the young estate agent Diego. The relationship is dramatically undone towards the end of the film, when Clara sets aside any pretence at social nicety and tells Diego what she really thinks of him.

3 The first section of the film is set in 1980 and a younger Clara is played by Barbara Colen.

4 This doorstep encounter will prove important later in the film, when Diego's grandfather (and Head of the property development company) chastises Clara for not following the rules of Brazilian cordiality and inviting her social equals into her home and offering them refreshments.

5 Pinho (2015: 107) suggests that part of the reason for this common-sense notion of the *empregada* as being constantly available to work dates from the omission of domestic work from the otherwise radical and far-reaching 1943 Brazilian labour laws: the duties of the *empregada* were regarded as "non-economic labour". "By excluding domestic workers from its benefits, Brazilian legislators maintained the status quo of millions of poor (and mainly black) women, thus contributing to further naturalizing their position as 'less than' laborers".

6 *The Wall Street Journal* published an article in 2018 reporting that there has been a 3000% rise in demand for semen from US sperm banks by Brazilians in the last five years, and that the demand is explicitly for light-skinned, blue-eyed donors. See Pearson 2018.

7 In this context it is interesting to reflect on the fact that, given the very shallow focus which Mendonça Filho uses to capture Clara's reactions to the property developers on her doorstep, in our first glimpse of Ladjane, who appears in the background of the shot, the features of her face are entirely out of focus. With regard to these blurry images of maids, one cannot help recalling the lines of perhaps the best-known poem of Recife first published in 1955, João Cabral de Melo Neto's *Morte e vida severina* (2006): "Somos todos severinos, iguais em tudo e na vida" (50) (We are all Severinos, equal in everything and in life), in which the poor migrant worker's ability to represent the collective both depersonalises him and makes him expendable.

8 "Because the body of the maid is imagined as inherently polluted, she is expected never to sit on beds or sofas": Pinho: 2015: 108.

9 Leticia is at the party because her own maid is Ladjane's sister.

10 A brief aside: surprisingly, there was little media discussion in Brazil at the time of its release of the complex relationship between mistress and maid in Afonso Cuaron's *Roma* (2018), despite the nuanced explorations we see in Brazilian films such as *Aquarius* and *Que horas ela volta?* Film critic Ignacio Araujo (2018) reads the maid Cleo as being unproblematically treated as a member of the family in *Roma*.

11 For more on this, see Juliana Cunha's blog entry "Mostra que tu é intenso" (2017). Similarly, Ismail Xavier describes *O Som ao Redor* as being evocative of Gilberto Freyre and Sérgio Buarque de Holanda: "Everything is resolved by personal relations, by power, by command, by subservience, unconnected to the abstract notion of citizenship and to democratic institutional order. It denotes the survival of certain traditions that modernisation hasn't undone"; quoted in Mena, 2013.

12 Sonia Braga rose to stardom outside of Brazil with the international success of *Dona Flor e seus dois maridos* (*Dona Flor and Her Two Husbands*, Bruno Barreto 1976), followed up with *Eu te amo* (*I Love You*, Arnaldo Jabor 1981). She went on to work in a number of US film and TV productions and received Golden Globe nominations for *Kiss of the Spiderwoman* (Babenco 1985) and *Moon over Parador* (Mazursky 1988). For a reading of Sônia's "star text", see Dennison and Shaw (2007).

13 Film critic Luiz Zanin Oricchio (2016) posted an image of the Cannes protest in his blog in the *Estado de Sao Paulo* and asked in the headline "Is this the scene that is inappropriate for under-18s?".

14 A claim vehemently denied by the Head of the selection panel, filmmaker Bruno Barreto. See Maria 2016.

15 The issue of real estate speculation foregrounded in *Aquarius* instantly brings to mind the Concórcio Novo Recife, a consortium of real estate companies accused of corruption in their dealings with local government in order to get permission to reconfigure the José Estelita Quay in the centre of Recife. Their actions and plans for the city, which were interpreted as elitist in the extreme, produced a high-profile and ultimately successful protest movement entitled Ocupe Estelita. Among other headline grabbing actions the movement made the short film *Recife cidade roubada* (Recife: Stolen City, 2014) which features *Aquarius* star Arandir Santos. No foreign and relatively few Brazilian critics interpreted *Aquarius* as a critique of the Concórcio Novo Recife: see, for example, Domingos de Lima (2016).

References

Alves de Souza, M. 2013. "Contribuições de Gilberto Freyre e Sérgio Buarque de Holanda ao pensamento social brasileiro". *Revista EnFil*, 1, pp. 1–4. http://en-fil.net/ed2/conteudo/archives/ed002_Mirian.pdf.

Araújo, I. 2018. "Filme *Roma* é uma demonstração da sensibilidade e do caráter de Cuarón". *Folha de S. Paulo*. 30 October. www1.folha.uol.com.br/ilustrada/2018/10/filme-roma-e-uma-demonstracao-da-sensibilidade-e-do-carater-de-cuaron.shtml.

Bezerra, E. 2004. "Ribeiro Couto e o Homem Cordial". Academia Brasileira de Letras. www.academia.org.br/abl/media/prosa44c.pdf.

Buarque de Holanda, S. 2004. *Raizes do Brasil*. São Paulo: Editora Schwartz.

Collin, R. 2017. "*Aquarius* Review: Sonia Braga's Role of a Lifetime Turns Struggle Into Pure Pleasure". *Telegraph*. 23 March. www.telegraph.co.uk/films/2016/05/17/aquarius-will-make-you-want-to-move-to-brazil---review/.

Cunha, J. 2017. "Mostra que tu é intenso". *Já matei por menos*. 2 May. http://julianacunha.com/blog/.

Domingos de Lima, J. 2016. "O que o filme *Aquarius* diz sobre a realidade urbana do Recife". *Nexo*. 10 September. www.nexojornal.com.br/expresso/2016/09/10/O-que-o-filme-%E2%80%98Aquarius%E2%80%99-diz-sobre-a-realidade-urbana-do-Recife.

Felix, R. 2016. "Babá negra cuidando de bebês em protesto causa polêmica". *Gazeta do Povo*. 13 March. www.gazetadopovo.com.br/vida-publica/baba-negra-cuidando-de-bebes-em-protesto-causa-polemica-2h74sdosebc8evn8jknfjraqr.

Freyre, G. ND. *Casa-Grande & Senzala*. Lisbon: Livros do Brasil.

JC Online. 2018. "Kleber Mendonça Filho lança carta aberta ao Ministro da Cultura". *JC Online*. 29 May. https://jconline.ne10.uol.com.br/canal/cultura/cinema/noticia/2018/ 05/29/kleber-mendonca-filho-lanca-carta-aberta-ao-ministro-da-cultura-341199.php.

Kermode, M. 2017. "*Aquarius* Review: She Shall Not Be Moved". *Guardian*. 26 March. www. theguardian.com/film/2017/mar/26/aquarius-review-kleber-mendonca-filho-sonia-braga-brazil.

Melo Neto, J. C. 2006. *Morte e Vida Severina*. Rio de Janeiro: Nova Fronteira.

Mena, F. 2013. "No Quintal de Kleber Mendonça Filho". *Folha Ilustríssima*. 17 Feb. www1. folha.uol.com.br/ilustrissima/2013/02/1231445-no-quintal-de-kleber-mendonca-filho.shtml.

Mota Rocha, M. E. 2015. "O Estelita é mais do que o Estelita" *El país Brasil*. 30 November. https://brasil.elpais.com/brasil/2015/11/30/opinion/1448840154_656256.html.

Nye, J. S. 2013. "What China and Russia Don't Get About Soft Power". *Foreign Policy*. 29 April. https://foreignpolicy.com/2013/04/29/what-china-and-russia-dont-get-about-soft-power/.

Pearson, S. 2018. "Demand for American Sperm is Skyrocketing in Brazil". *The Wall Street Journal*. 22 March. www.wsj.com/articles/in-mixed-race-brazil-sperm-imports-from-u-s-whites-are-booming-1521711000.

Pinho, P. S. 2015. "The Dirty Body that Cleans: Representations of Domestic Workers in Brazilian Common Sense". *Meridiens. Feminisms, Race, Transnationalism* 13: 1, pp. 103–128.

Ricardo, C. 1959. *O Homem Cordial e Outros Pequenos Estudos Brasileiros*. São Paulo: Instituto Nacional do Livro.

Sakamoto, L. 2016. *O que aprendi sendo xingado na internet*. Sao Paulo: Leya.

Schwarcz, L. M. 2008. "Sérgio Buarque de Holanda e essa tal de 'cordialidade'". *Revista de psicanálise e cultura*. 31: 46, June, pp. 83–89.

Scott, A. O. 2016. "In *Aquarius*, a Widow Fights to Keep her Home". *New York Times*. 13 October. www.nytimes.com/2016/10/14/movies/aquarius-review.html.

Souza, J. 2017. *A Elite do Atraso: Da Escravidão à Lava-Jato*. São Paulo: Leya.

Vianna, L. F. 2014. "Violência autorizada: quatro perguntas para Maria Rita Kehl". *Blog IMS*. 9 September. https://blogdoims.com.br/a-violencia-autorizada-quatro-perguntas-para-maria-rita-kehl/.

Zanin Oricchio, L. 2016. Esta é a cena proibida para menores de 18 anos? 23 August. https:// cultura.estadao.com.br/blogs/luiz-zanin/esta-e-a-cena-proibida-para-menores-de-18-anos/.

EPILOGUE

On 1st January 2019 the successful far-right candidate in the Brazilian presidential elections, Jair Bolsonaro, was sworn into the presidency.[1] The impact of this dramatic political shift, from 2003 and the victory of the Workers Party (PT), to the seeming collapse of the PT project (impeachment of Dilma Rousseff, imprisonment of Lula, electoral rejection of the PT presidential candidate Fernando Haddad), is a state of fear and uncertainty on the part of those who arguably benefitted from successive PT governments, given that, like Michel Temer before him, Bolsonaro seems intent on erasing all evidence of inclusion, diversity and creativity initiatives associated with the PT. A number of chapters in this volume have referenced Bolsonaro's prejudices in relation to women, LGBTQ, Afro-Brazilians and indigenous peoples, expressed both during his campaign and while a congressman. The make-up of his initial cabinet, then, will have come as little surprise. It includes Damares Alves, head of the newly formed Ministry of Human Rights, Family and Women. Alves, an evangelical church minister who claims to have seen a vision of God in a guava tree, and who is under investigation for allegedly illegally removing her adoptive daughter from an indigenous reservation, provoked considerable reaction in the news and on social media by declaring at the time of her appointment that from now on young men would once again be princes, women would be princesses, boys will wear blue and girls will wear pink. Her words were clearly designed to undermine feminist and LGBTQ causes and echo Bolsonaro's relentless attack on so-called gender ideology during his presidential campaign (and political career as a whole). While Bolsonaro dismissed the importance of Alves and her Ministry (Lara 2019), he did make another very controversial appointment to the key post of *Chanceler* (Foreign Minister): the career diplomat Ernesto Araújo. For the US-based left-wing *Jacobin* magazine Araújo is "the worst diplomat in the world" (Pagliarini 2019) and even the centre-right Brazilian broadsheet *O estado de Sao Paulo* (2019) described him as having "weird personal beliefs" and as delivering an inaugural speech which was "deranged". This speech included references to global warming and "globalism" as a Marxist conspiracy. Araújo was recommended to Bolsonaro by Olavo de Carvalho, the "philosopher" of the Bolsonaro government (see Chapter 1), whose own extensive conspiracy theories include the belief that Pepsi uses the cells of unborn foetuses to sweeten soft drinks.

For a number of observers, recent declarations that Nazism was a socialist movement (Ernesto Araújo), that Dutch nursery school teachers routinely masturbate young children in their care (Damares Alves) and tweets asking what is a golden shower (Jair Bolsonaro) are nothing more than Trump-inspired "firehosing", carried out in order to deflect attention away from draconian pension reform legislation, and from speculation over the Bolsonaro family's involvement with militias and the death of politician and human rights activist Marielle Franco in 2018. For his supporters, Bolsonaro's choice of Sérgio Moro, the judge behind the Operation Car Wash graft investigation, as Minister of Justice, his perceived tough stance on public security, and his witch-hunt of "leftists" are causes for continued support and celebration. In March 2019 Bolsonaro, with encouragement from his government filled with ex-army generals, sanctioned national commemorations of the 55th anniversary of the military coup of 1964, now rebranded a "revolution".

Film culture under Bolsonaro

Before Bolsonaro took office two film-policy-related incidents occurred that arguably contributed to setting the future direction of travel of film culture in Brazil, in what seems to be a move away from support for the local film industry. The first involved the revamping of the Conselho Superior de Cinema (the Higher Film Council), a consultative body that makes recommendations on film policy, which now controversially includes representatives of Netflix, Google, Facebook and the US Majors (Ikeda 2019). Secondly, the screen quota, declared annually by presidential decree, was not confirmed by the end of the year (2018). While this meant in practice that the previous year's quota was maintained, the move was believed to have been carried out deliberately to create a sense of unease among the filmmaking community.

In an essay published in early February 2019 on the future of the audio-visual industry, Marcelo Ikeda, an academic and one-time Ancine employee, describes a sense of general fear of a return to an early 1990s Collor-style era of darkness as marking the start of the Bolsonaro administration. Ikeda (2019) reminds his readers that Ancine is a regulating body and not an organ of the State, and that directors are appointed for a period of four years, all of which gives the body some kind of autonomy (and, one assumes, protection from the whims of the current government). However, Ikeda predicts tension between Ancine and its new "home", the Ministry of Citizenship, within which the downgraded Special Secretariat for Culture now sits, given that the President of Ancine, Christian de Castro, was appointed by the previous government of Michel Temer. As we go to press, Ancine has frozen all film investments, including funding already in train, reportedly as a temporary measure while its processes are revised.

In early 2019 the cultural investment arm of Petrobras (Petrobras Cultural) announced that it was to radically rethink its sponsorship programme. Film initiatives affected by this include Adhemar Oliveira's Cinearte arthouse cinema chain (See Chapter 1) and the Sessão Vitrine film distribution initiative, as well as a number of annual film festivals that rely on Petrobras funding. There has already been a steady growth throughout the century thus far in the production of films and other audio-visual products aimed at children and teenagers, and this growth looks set to continue, with a shift in sponsorship by entities such as Petrobras to "ideologically safe" cultural activities that focus on young people, and audio-visual funding focused on videogame development. Film production also stands to be affected by a shift in funding focus away from popular culture to more erudite forms, such as classical music.

In the short term, given the run-in time needed to get most films from idea to screen, the film scene in Brazil appears buoyant from the outside, with a mix of commercial and international festival hits either released or eagerly anticipated. 2019 looks set to produce at least two mega-blockbusters: the *globochanchada Minha vida em Marte* (My Life in Mars, Susana Garcia) starring Paulo Gustavo had already been viewed by 5,000,000 people in cinemas by March, and the sequel to the record-breaking *Nada a perder* (*Nothing to Lose*), the biopic of Universal Church of the Kingdom of God founder Edir Macedo, is expected shortly. By February Brazilian cinema already had its controversial talking point grabbing international headlines (at least within the specialist film press) with *Marighella*. Directed by Wagner Moura (Captain Nascimento in the *Elite Squad* films – see Chapter 7) and based on the life of the communist subversive who was killed during the dictatorship and starring singer/actor Seu Jorge in the title role, *Marighella* premiered at the Berlin Film Festival (along with 11 other Brazilian films on a broad range of topics by both established and new directors). Moura in press conferences did not miss the opportunity to both criticise Bolsonaro and draw parallels between his government's first few weeks and the run-up to the military takeover of Brazil in 1964. The Brazilian Embassy in Berlin notably cancelled its annual reception for Brazilian filmmakers attending the festival, foreshadowing a worrying crisis in the relationship between Itamaraty (the Brazilian foreign office) and filmmakers in relation to promotion of Brazilian films abroad. There was also a conspicuous absence of commemoration on the part of Ancine, the Foreign Ministry and the Culture Secretariat of the news that Kleber Mendonca Filho's *Bacurau* had been selected for official competition in Cannes 2019.

While both commercial and art-house films continue to be released, thus lending on the surface a sense of continuity to Brazilian film culture, the bleak reality is that as a result of "restructuring" of mechanisms of support for cultural production, Brazilian cinema risks grinding to a halt: "Funding calls are being held on standby, productions are being put on the back burner, the market is in a state of suspension, and the production chain is stagnating" (Nunomora and Medeiros 2019). As each new day seems to bring a fresh jaw-dropping news story relating to the current government, the "Bolsonaro project" will likely provide ample narrative inspiration for Brazilian film culture for years to come, assuming, that is, that filmmakers are able to make films with a modicum of State financial support and free from censorship.

Note

1 For a summary of Bolsonaro's rise to power and early months in office, see Anderson, J. A, 2019 and Anderson, P. 2019.

References

Anderson, J. L. 2019. "Jair Bolsonaro's Southern Strategy". *The New Yorker.* 1 April. www.newyorker.com/magazine/2019/04/01/jair-bolsonaros-southern-strategy.

Anderson, P. 2019. "Bolsonaro's Brazil". *London Review of Books.* 7 February. www.lrb.co.uk/v41/n03/perry-anderson/bolsonaros-brazil.

Ikeda, M. 2019. "Quais são os riscos para a política audiovisual brasileira?" *Nexo jornal.* 5 February. www.nexojornal.com.br/ensaio/2019/Quais-s%C3%A3o-os-riscos-para-a-pol%C3%ADtica-audiovisual-brasileira.

Lara, M. 2019. "Bolsonaro diz que não toma decisões sozinho:'Ouço qualquer ministro. Até a Damares'". *O estado de São Paulo.* 22 March. https://politica.estadao.com.br/noticias/geral,bolsonaro-diz-que-nao-toma-decisoes-sozinho-ouco-qualquer-ministro-ate-a-damares,70002764574.

Nunumora. E. and Medeiros, J. 2019. "Com retaliações e esvaziamentos, Bolsonaro asfixia produção cultural". *Carta capital.* 26 March. www.cartacapital.com.br/cultura/com-retaliacoes-e-esvaziamentos-bolsonaro-asfixia-producao-cultural/.

O estado de São Paulo. 2019. "Obscurantismo". *O estado de São Paulo.* 7 January https://opiniao.estadao.com.br/noticias/notas-e-informacoes,obscurantismo,70002669366.

Pagliarini, A. 2019. "The Worst Diplomat in the World". *Jacobin.* 26 February. https://jacobinmag.com/2019/02/ernesto-araujo-jair-bolsonaro-brazil?fbclid=IwAR1R1j-w_PVEBkt4ES8xRLjbdJC6V_cga93g2UeZGWf2nlnKY_MciOE17Ho.

INDEX

Printed in Great Britain
by Amazon

19046026R20127